A Step by Step Guide to Analyze Price Volume

An Essential Book to Read the Market

Who this book is for

If you are struggling to succeed and find your trading stressful and emotional, then this book is for you. By the end of it, you will have discovered how to banish these emotions FOREVER. You will become a confident and emotionless traders, as all your decisions will be based on simple logic and common sense. You will be able to forecast the market's next move, quickly, easily and with confidence. From confidence comes success, and from success comes wealth. Trade without emotion and you will succeed whether as a speculator or investor, in **ANY** market. Yes, **INCLUDING forex!** It has been written by someone with over 16 years trading experience who uses this approach every day, so you will be learning from someone 'who does'.

There are only two leading indicators in trading. One is price, the other is volume. In isolation, they are weak and reveal little, but put them together, and just like gunpowder, they become an explosive combination. In discovering the power of Volume Price Analysis for yourself, you will be shocked and wonder why you never used this before.

Suddenly you will be able to read the market, **BEFORE** it moves. When this happens for the first time, you will be shocked, surprised, even stunned. Then the truth will dawn on you. Using two simple indicators, you now have the power and knowledge to anticipate the market's next move.

In short, Volume Price Analysis reveals the DNA of the market, and places this awesome power in the palm of your hand. You will become a confident and assured trader. Emotional trading and stress will be banished forever. You will start to enjoy your trading, for one simple reason. You KNOW where the market is going next based on simple logic and the power of volume and price.

What this book covers

A Complete Guide To Volume Price Analysis explains everything you need to know to apply VPA in your own trading. Each chapter builds on the next, working from first principles on both price and volume before bringing them together, using simple and clear examples. Suddenly as you delve deeper in the book you will begin to understand the insights that Volume Price Analysis can deliver for you, in all markets and in all timeframes.

Table of Contents

An introduction to Volume Price Analysis and how it all began for me. I was one of the lucky traders who began my own journey in trading based on volume. It has been the cornerstone of my success and I want it to be yours as well. This is why I wrote the book. To help you, achieve your own personal ambitions through trading. Volume Price Analysis is the ONLY way to reveal the secrets of the market and in doing so, follow the 'smart money'.

If you thought that Volume Price Analysis was a new concept. Think again. This was the approach used by the iconic traders of the past, such as Charles Dow, Jesse Livermore, and Richard Wyckoff. These traders built huge fortunes using this technique, using nothing more than the ticker tape, pencil and paper. Here I explain how they achieved their success, and how little the concepts have changed in over a 100 years.

Not an unreasonable question. In this chapter I explain why volume is the ONLY leading indicator, which when combined with price, truly reveals the future direction of the market. In addition, volume reveals something EQUALLY important. Whether the price action is valid or false.

The second component which then creates the explosive combination, of VPA. Price on its own simply reveals the buying and the selling. What it never reveals is the extent of any future price move, and more importantly whether that price move is a fake move.

Here I introduce the basic building blocks of Volume Price Analysis. In simple terms we are really only looking for one of two things in our analysis. Either a confirmation that volume and price are in agreement, or an anomaly, where volume and price do NOT agree. This is then our first warning signal of a possible change.

Chapter Five : Volume Price Analysis - Building The Picture

In this chapter I explain the concepts of accumulation and distribution which underpin Volume Price Analysis. These occur in all time frames and in all markets and are rounded off with the firework display, which is the selling or buying climax. This marks the end of the campaign and the start of a new trend. All we have to do, is follow the insiders, and buy and sell, when they are buying and selling. In this chapter you will discover how to see this for yourself in any market.

Chapter Six : Volume Price Analysis - The Next Level

Here we start to build on the concepts from the previous chapter and begin to look at VPA in action using the three most powerful candles. In addition I explain stopping volume and topping out volume, as we start to build our VPA knowledge into a complete approach to market analysis.

Chapter Seven : Support And Resistance Explained

Support and resistance is one of the cornerstones of technical trading. Yet when combined with volume, this essential technique becomes even more powerful. Few traders ever discover how to identify when the markets are moving into a congestion phase, or equally important to validate when they are breaking out. In this chapter you will discover both!

Chapter Eight : Dynamic Trends And Trend Lines

Forget traditional trend and trend lines. By the time these are developed you are just getting in when the smart money is getting out! In this chapter you will learn how to create dynamic trend lines, which when coupled with VPA get you in at the start of the trend, and NOT at the end. If you have ever struggled with the concept of traditional trend theory, this is for you and will revolutionize your trading.

Chapter Nine : Volume At Price (VAP)

Volume Price Analysis or VPA is one thing. Volume at price of VAP is something entirely different, and which gives you a visual and instant picture of the density of volumes at price levels on the chart. This is so powerful, it's amazing more traders don't use this approach. After all, a breakout from one of these regions means one thing - a new trend! And when confirmed with

VPA - money!

Chapter Ten : Volume Price Analysis Examples

Here we examine some 'worked' examples across various markets in detail. See VPA applied to stocks in the cash markets, currencies in the spot FX market, indices in the futures markets and commodities using tick charts. In fact virtually every market and type of chart from tick to time based charts, all detailed and annotated for you. If you still need to be convinced, I hope this chapter will do it for you!

Chapter Eleven : Putting It All Together

Now it's time to pull all the elements together. In addition I explain some of the most powerful congestion patterns which have worked consistently over 16 years of trading, and when combined with volume, give us simple and clear trading opportunities - provided you can be patient!

Chapter Twelve : Volume And Price - The Next Generation

In the final chapter I introduce some of the latest developments in Volume Price Analysis, and where this methodology may go in the future. Charles Dow and the other iconic traders of the past would love these extensions of their original work.

Acknowledgments & Trader Resources

List of the chart providers used in this book along with details of free resources for traders.

Hi,

Made up my mind.. I want to learn "forex trading" – after many months searching online you're the only authentic person I come across!! Can you help me??

Regards,

Ali

Hello,

Just found your site and am starting to dig in – seems like an endless source of knowledge – thank you for your effort to put it up. I am new to forex – still study the bits. My tendency is for buff trading-price action. Question is: how do you identify the psychology of the market?

Hello!

I am very much impressed with your articles and your success story in the FX world. I am a beginner...You may also call me a newbie..as I only know the operation of the MT4 - platform...none of others...Since, it is my beginning...I will try all my best to learn, as much as I can, from anywhere in the world...Kind regards, - MBZ

Hi

That was really a nice and wonderful update of the market. I really enjoy it and wish the best in your trading. But I still continue to ask to be shown how to get the USD index install in my system. And are you still trading the forex fixed odd. Which broker do you use for that.

Thanks for your time.

Kevin

Hi,

Love your Covered Call website. Lucid and wise. I'm now a believer.................

Regards

Gordon

Hi,

Your site(s are absolutely brilliant! Really informative and well written..........

Kind regards.

Rich

Hello

I am enjoying your many websites and wish that I had found you a long time ago. I appreciate your writing style and content. Please include me on the list for your book. How often do you publish your newsletter?

Best wishes

James

Hi

you are a daisy amongst weeds !!

thank you for your reply – I think I will stick to initial path for a while yet since travelled so far down this route......thanks again

Anna

Hi,

your site is excellent – I wish I had found you sooner!! thank you for sharing such valuable

information – it really is priceless, well written and comprehensive – I too am interested in your

book. Ann

Hi

Very useful thoughts as usual, thank you – I presume the hammer candle is a "reversal" indicator – i.e. you could have the reverse situation after a period of increasing prices?

Regards

Alex

How I use the CFTC cot data - I've been a follower of Anna Coulling for a while now. I suggest you check out this video. She's worth bookmarking in my opinion. [...]

One of my favourite analysts whom I frequently check for her across the Pond perspective is Anna Coulling and her thoughts today are worth reading: Gold Forming Strong Pennant on Daily Chart.

Hi,

Great to meet you at the traders expo . I will keep an eye on your web site.

Hi,

I have followed your website and Facebook page for a while now and I find your work really helpful – thanks!

I see gold has now broken through the triple top resistance of $1,425 – so I've bought GLD LEAPS and Gold June 2011 futures today – but now I see your comment about buying on strength – have I jumped the gun and bought too early do you think?

Regards

Alex

*This is the best of times for those willing to study, learn quickly, work hard …
learn from the past to succeed in the future.*
Robert Kiyosaki (1947-)

This is a very personal book for me, and one I have been planning to write for many years.

Finally I have found the time to write it!

I hope, that once you have read it, the single analytical trading technique I am going to share with you, will have as profound an effect on your trading, as it has had on mine. I stumbled on this methodology many years ago, in an almost surreal way, when I first became interested in trading. And I am eternally grateful that I did, even though, as you will see, it cost me a great deal of money at the time. Learning this method, was a defining moment in my life and trading career. I hope that this book will be equally life changing for you too.

So what is this trading technique and what makes it so special? Well, it's been around for over 100 years, and was used by all the iconic traders of the past. Despite this heritage, many traders today, ignore (or are unaware) of this immensely effective analytical method. Why this is, I have no idea. It has been the cornerstone of my own trading and investing for over 16 years, and remains so today. It is immensely powerful, and in many ways 'just makes sense'. My purpose in writing this book is to convince you to embrace this for yourself.

All I ask is that you open your mind, and accept the simple logic and power of what I refer to as Volume Price Analysis, or VPA for short.

Volume Price Analysis is my own terminology. You will not find this description anywhere else. The reason I use it, is that it precisely describes the methodology in three simple words. After all, as traders, there is only one question we want answered with some degree of certainty, every time we trade. The question is 'where is the price going next.'

Volume Price Analysis will answer this question for you.

It can be applied to all markets in all time frames, and can be used to trade all instruments. Using volume to validate and forecast future price action, has been at the heart of my trading success, and I hope that in reading this book, it will change your approach to trading forever. As I said earlier, please just open your mind to the simple logic that is VPA, and once you have read this book, you will be able to interpret charts, and forecast price action, instantly.

The first time this happens will be a life changing moment for you, as you suddenly realise that you have the most powerful trading technique at your finger tips.

As a trader you will become confident and calm, as your trading decisions will be based on logic, and on your own analysis of the price volume relationship. However, as I said earlier, there is nothing new or mystical here.

The methodology you will discover is grounded in the approach used by the iconic traders of the past. For them, there were no computers or the internet. Everything was done manually, with hand drawn charts, and price reading from a paper tape. We are lucky. All this is now done for us, on an electronic chart. All we have to do is interpret the price volume relationship, and to do that you need a good teacher.

I hope to be that teacher, and deliver the lessons in this book.

However, how did I stumble on volume, and its symbiotic and interdependent relationship price? Well, it is a rather odd story, and in relating it, I hope it will become apparent, that even though it was hugely expensive, in hindsight I know I have been lucky, because I started my trading journey with volume. Many traders spend years trying different trading approaches, becoming increasingly disillusioned as each one fails to live up to the expectations of the marketing hype, before arriving at the same conclusion.

It is only in hindsight I can appreciate how extremely fortunate I have been, and now I want to share this knowledge with you. So, if you are reading this book as a novice trader, then you too are lucky. You have avoided the pain and expense of a long, fruitless journey. If you are a seasoned trader, welcome to this book and I hope that it fulfils your expectations, and that you have enough enthusiasm left for reading just one more book about trading!

In telling my story here, I have not changed any of the names, and many of these people are still involved in the trading world.

How It All Started

In the late 1990's I couldn't understand why my pension and investments did not reflect what was happening in the stock market, which was extremely bullish. In these dark days before the internet I could only rely on newspapers, and it was in January 1998 that I read an article in the Sunday Times about a trader who had made significant sums from trading, and was now looking for recruits to train in his methods. That trader's name was Albert Labos.

Two weeks later, on an early Sunday morning, I joined hundreds of other hopefuls in a packed room, on the HMS President. The President is a famous anti-submarine Q-ship completed in 1918 moored on the River Thames close to Blackfriars Bridge. I arrived, cheque book in hand, ready to sign up to whatever was on offer.

The event was shrouded in mystery from the start. First, Albert exhorted the 'spies' in the room to leave. He knew who they were and why they were there, and as he told us later, these were spies from the major banks, come to learn his secret trading techniques. These were trading techniques which could take on the cartel, currently enjoyed by these market makers.

We were then introduced to a Tom Williams. We were told that Tom was partially sighted, and I can't quite remember if he had a white cane. We were also told that Tom was an ex 'syndicate trader'. However, to this day I am not entirely certain what a 'syndicate trader' is or does. But at the time it sounded very impressive. Various charts were presented during the pitch and all the while Albert explained he was searching for an elite group of traders. However, spaces were limited and only a select few would be taken and trained.

Like many others there I wanted to join, and happily paid my £5,000 for a two week course, grateful to have been accepted for this 'once in a lifetime opportunity'.

If all the above sounds slightly bizarre, it was, but I felt confident because Albert had been endorsed by a very reputable newspaper, and I was anxious to learn.

During the two week course we had to write an essay and we were encouraged to read Reminiscences of a Stock Operator by Edwin Lefevre, which is a thinly disguised biography of Jesse Livermore. A book all traders and investors should read.

Throughout the two weeks, the over-riding message was that all financial markets are manipulated in one way or another. And the only way to know whether a price move was genuine or false was by using volume. Volume cannot be hidden. It is there for everyone to see.

I was so convinced by the volume story that I also persuaded my husband, David to take Albert's course.

With hindsight the costs were outrageous as the course could have been condensed into a couple of days. However, David and I took the basic principles of price and volume and since then, have integrated them into our own trading and investing methodology. In the intervening years, we have successfully traded virtually every market, and for the past five years have shared our knowledge and experience across our network of 70 websites.

This book now gives us the opportunity to pass on this knowledge in more detail to the next generation of traders and investors, of which I hope you will be one.

Chapter One

There's Nothing New in Trading

Nihil sub sole (there is nothing new under the sun)
Ecclesiastes 1:9

Let me start if I may with a book I have read, many, many times, and was the 'course book' recommended to us by Albert as we sat, innocent and expectant on that first morning, clutching this book in our hands.

The book in question was Reminiscences of a Stock Operator, written by Edwin Lefevre and published in 1923. It is an autobiography of one of the iconic traders of the past, Jesse Livermore, and is as relevant today, as it was then. But one quote in particular stands out for me, and it is this:

"there is nothing new in Wall Street. There can't be because speculation is as old as the hills. Whatever happens in the stock market today has happened before and will happen again"

This in essence sums up volume, and Volume Price Analysis. If you are expecting some new and exciting approach to trading, you will be disappointed. The foundations of Volume Price Analysis are so deeply rooted in the financial markets, that it is extraordinary to me how few traders accept the logic of what we see every day.

It is a technique which has been around for over 100 years. It was the foundation stone on which huge personal fortunes were created, and iconic institutions built.

Now at this point you may be asking yourself three questions:

1. Is volume still relevant today?

2. Is it relevant to the market I trade?

3. Can it be applied to all trading and investing strategies?

Let me try to answer the first if I can with an extract from Stocks and Commodities magazine. The following quote was by David Penn, a staff writer at the time for the magazine, who wrote the following about Wykcoff in an article in 2002:

"Many of Wyckoff's basic tenets have become de facto standards of technical analysis: The concepts of accumulation/distribution and the supremacy of price and volume in determining stock price movement are examples."

The second question, I can only answer from a personal perspective.

I began my own trading career in the futures market trading indices. From there I moved into the cash markets for investing, commodities for speculating, and finally into the currency markets in both futures and spot. In all of these, I have used volume and price as my primary analytical approach to each of these markets, even spot forex. And yes, there is volume in forex as well! Volume Price Analysis can be applied to each and every market. The approach is universal. Once learnt you will be able to apply this methodology to any time frame and to every instrument.

Finally, the best way to answer the third question of whether Volume Price Analysis can be applied to all trading and investing strategies, is with a quotation from Richard Wyckoff who, as you will find out shortly, is the founding father of Volume Price Analysis. He wrote the following in his book 'Studies in Tape Reading'

"In judging the market by its own actions, it is unimportant whether you are endeavouring to forecast the next small half hourly swing, or the trend for the next two or three weeks. The same indications as to price, volume, activity, support, and pressure are exhibited in the preparation for both. The same elements will be found in a drop of water as in the ocean, and vice versa"

So the simple truth is this. Regardless of whether you are scalping as a speculator in stocks, bonds, currencies and equities, or you are trend, swing, or position trader in these markets, or even investing for the longer term, the techniques you will discover here are as valid today as they were almost 100 years ago. The only proviso is that we have price and volume on the same chart.

For this powerful technique we have to thank the great traders of the last century, who laid the foundations of what we call technical analysis today. Iconic names such as Charles Dow, founder of the Dow Jones, Dow Theory and the Wall Street Journal, and generally referred to as the grandfather of technical analysis.

One of Dow's principle beliefs was that volume confirmed trends in price. He maintained that if a price was moving on low volume, then there could be many different reasons. However, when a price move was associated with high or rising volume, then he believed this was a valid move. If the price continued moving in one direction, and with associated supporting volume, then this was the signal of the start of a trend.

From this basic principle, Charles Dow then extended and developed this idea to the three principle stages of a trend. He defined the first stage of a bullish trend as, 'the accumulation phase', the starting point for any trend higher. He called the second stage 'the public participation phase' which could be considered the technical trend following stage. This was usually the longest of the three phases. Finally, he identified the third stage, which he called 'the distribution phase'. This would typically see investors rushing into the market, terrified that they were missing out on a golden opportunity.

Whilst the public were happily buying, what Charles Dow called 'the smart money', were doing the exact opposite, and selling. The smart money was taking its profits and selling to an increasingly eager public. And all of this buying and selling activity could all be seen through the prism of volume.

Charles Dow himself, never published any formal works on his approach to trading and investing, preferring to publish his thoughts and ideas in the embryonic Wall Street Journal. It was only after his death in 1902, that his work was collated and published, first by close friend and colleague Sam Nelson, and later by William Hamilton. The book published in 1903, entitled The ABC of Stock Speculation was the first to use the term 'Dow Theory', a hook on which to hang the great man's ideas.

Whilst volume was one of the central tenets of his approach to the market, and consequent validation of the associated price action, it was the development of the idea of trends, which was one of the driving principle for Charles Dow. The other was the concept of indices to give investors an alternative view of the fundamentals of market behaviour with which to validate price. This was the reason he developed the various indices such as the Dow Jones Transportation Index, to provide a benchmark against which 'related industrial sectors' could provide a view of the broader economy.

After all, if the economy were strong, then this would be reflected in the performance of companies in different sectors of the market. An early exponent of cross market analysis if you like!

If Charles Dow was the founding father of technical analysis, it was a contemporary of his, Richard Wyckoff, who could be considered to be the founding father of volume and price analysis, and who created the building blocks of the methodology that we use today.

Wyckoff was a contemporary of Dow, and started work on Wall Street as a stock runner at the age of 15 in 1888, at much the same time as Dow was launching his first edition of the Wall Street Journal. By the time he was 25 he had made enough money from his trading to open his own brokerage office. Unusually, not with the primary goal of making more money for himself (which he did), but as an educator and source of unbiased information for the small investor. This was a tenet throughout this life, and unlike Charles Dow, Wyckoff was a prolific writer and publisher.

His seminal work, The Richard Wyckoff Method of Trading and Investing in Stocks, first published in the early 1930's, as a correspondence course, remains the blueprint which all Wall Street investment banks still use today. It is essentially a course of instruction, and although hard to find, is still available in a hard copy version from vintage booksellers.

Throughout his life, Wyckoff was always keen to ensure that the self directed investor was given an insight into how the markets actually worked, and in 1907 launched a hugely successful monthly magazine called The Ticker, later merged into The Magazine of Wall Street, which became even more popular. One of the many reasons for this was his view of the market and market behaviour. First, he firmly believed that to be successful you needed to do you own technical analysis, and ignore the views of the 'so called' experts and the financial media. Second, he believed that this approach was an art, and not a science.

The message that Wyckoff relayed to his readers, and to those who attended his courses and seminars was a simple one. Through his years of studying the markets and in working on Wall Street he believed that prices moved on the basic economic principle of supply and demand, and that by observing the price volume relationship, it was possible to forecast future market direction.

Like Charles Dow and Jesse Livermore, who Wyckoff interviewed many times and subsequently published in the Magazine of Wall Street, all these greats from the past, had one thing in common. They all used the the ticker tape, as the source of their inspiration, revealing as it did, the basic laws of supply and demand with price, volume, time and trend at its heart.

From his work, Wyckoff detailed three basic laws.

1.The Law of Supply and Demand

This was his first and basic law, borne out of his experience as a broker with a detailed inside knowledge of how the markets react to the ongoing battle of price action, minute by minute and bar by bar. When demand is greater than supply, then prices will rise to meet this demand, and conversely when supply is greater then demand then prices will fall, with the over supply being absorbed as a result.

Consider the winter sales! Prices fall and the buyers come in to absorb over supply.

2.The Law of Cause and Effect

The second law states that in order to have an effect, you must first have a cause, and furthermore, the effect will be in direct proportion to the cause. In other words, a small amount of volume activity will only result in a small amount of price action. This law is applied to a number of price bars and will dictate the extent of any subsequent trend. If the cause is large, then the effect will be large as well. If the cause is small, then the effect will also be small.

The simplest analogy here is of a wave at sea. A large wave hitting a vessel will see the ship roll violently, whereas a small wave would have little or no effect.

3.The Law of Effort vs Result

This is Wyckoff's third law which is similar to Newton's third law of physics. Every action must have an equal and opposite reaction. In other words, the price action on the chart must reflect the volume action below. The two should always be in harmony with one another, with the effort (which is the volume) seen as the result (which is the consequent price action). This is where, as Wyckoff taught, we start to analyse each price bar, using a 'forensic approach', to discover whether this law has been maintained. If it has, then the market is behaving as it should, and we can continue our analysis on the following bar. If not, and there is an anomaly, then we need to discover why, and just like a crime scene investigator, establish the reasons.

The Ticker described Wycoff's approach perfectly. Throughout his twenty years of studying the markets, and talking to other great traders such as Jesse Livermore and J P Morgan, he had become one of the leading exponents of tape reading, and which subsequently formed the basis of his methodology and analysis. In 1910, he wrote what is still considered to be the most authoritative book on tape reading entitled, Studies in Tape Reading, not published under his own name, but using the pseudonym Rollo Tape!

Livermore too was an arch exponent of tape reading, and is another of the all time legends of Wall Street. He began his trading career when he was 15, working as a quotation board boy, calling out the latest prices from the ticker tape. These were then posted on the boards in the brokerage office of Paine and Webber where he worked. Whilst the job itself was boring, the young Jesse soon began to realise that the constant stream of prices, coupled with buy and sell orders was actually revealing a story. The tape was talking to him, and revealing the inner most secrets of the market.

He began to notice that when a stock price behaved in a certain way with the buying and selling, then a significant price move was on the way. Armed with this knowledge, Livermore left the brokerage office and began to trade full time, using his intimate knowledge of the ticker tape. Within 2 years he had turned $1000 into $20,000, a huge sum in those days, and by the time he was 21, this had become, $200,000, earning him the nickname of the 'Boy Plunger'

From stocks he moved into commodities, where even larger sums followed, and despite a roller coaster ride, where he made and lost several million dollars, his fame was cemented in history with his short selling in two major market crashes. The first was in 1907, where he made over $3 million dollars. However, this gain was dwarfed in the Wall Street crash of 1929, where conservative estimates suggest he made around $100 million dollars. Whilst others suffered and lost everything, Jesse Livermore prospered, and at the time was vilified in the press and made a public scapegoat. No surprise given the tragedies that befell many.

Livermore's own wife assumed that they had lost everything again, and had removed all the furniture and her jewellery from their 23 bedroom house, fearing the arrival of the bailiffs at any moment. It was only when he arrived home from his office that evening, he calmly announced to her that in fact this had been his most profitable day of trading, ever.

For these iconic traders, the ticker tape was their window on the world of the financial markets. Wyckoff himself referred to the ticker tape as a :-

*"method for forecasting from what appears on the tape **now**, what is likely to happen in the **future**"*

He then went on to say later in 'Studies in Tape Reading' :-

" Tape Reading is rapid-fire horse sense. Its object is to determine whether stocks are being accumulated or distributed, marked up or down, or whether they are neglected by the large interests. The Tape Reader aims to make deductions from each succeeding transaction – every shift of the market kaleidoscope; to grasp a new situation, force it, lightning-like, through the weighing machine of the brain, and to reach a decision which can be acted upon with coolness and precision. It is gauging the momentary supply and demand in particular stocks and in the whole market, comparing the forces behind each and their relationship, each to the other and to all.

A Tape Reader is like the manager of a department store; into his office are poured hundreds of reports of sales made by various departments. He notes the general trend of business – whether demand is heavy or light throughout the store – but lends special attention to the lines in which demand is abnormally strong or weak. When he finds difficulty in keeping his shelves full in a certain department, he instructs his buyers, and they increase their buying orders; when certain goods do not move he knows there is little demand (market) for then, therefore he lowers his prices as an inducement to possible purchasers.

As traders, surely this is all we need to know!

Originally developed in the mid 1860's as a telegraphic system for communicating using Morse code, the technology was adapted to provide a system for communicating stock prices and order flow.

These then appeared on a narrow paper tape which punched out the numbers throughout the trading day. Below is an original example of what these great traders would have used to make their fortunes.

Hard to believe perhaps, but what appears here is virtually all you need to know as a trader to succeed, once you understand the volume, price, trend and time relationship.

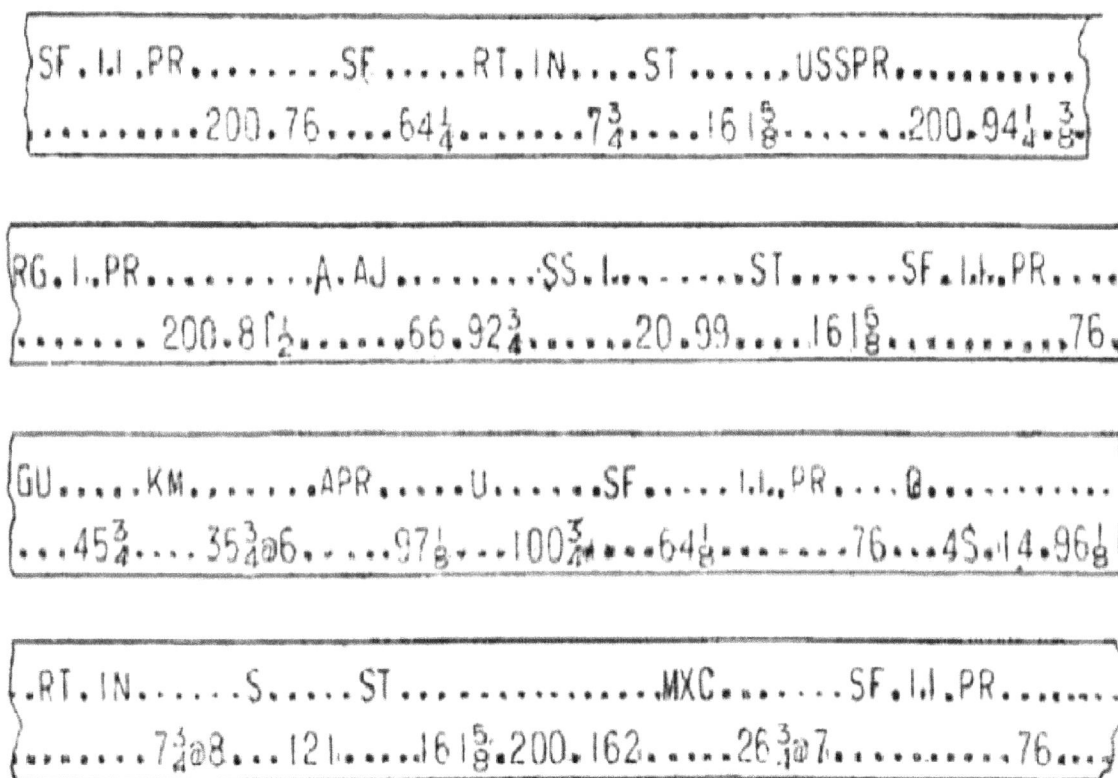

```
SF.LI,PR........SF.....RT.IN,...ST......,USSPR...........
..........200.76....64¼.......7¾....161⅝.......200.94¼.⅜

RG.I.,PR..........A.AJ.........SS.I.,-....ST......SF.LI,PR....
........200.81½......66.92¾......20.99....161⅝...........76

GU.....KM.,.....APR.....U......SF.....LI,PR....B..........
...45¾....35¾@6......97⅛...100¾...64½.......76...4S.14.96⅛

.RT.IN......S.....ST..............MXC........SF.LI,PR........
.......7¾@8...121....161⅝.200.162.....26¾@7...........76...
```

Fig 1.10 Example Of Ticker Tape

Fig 1.10 is a Public Domain image from the Work of Wall Street by Sereno S. Pratt (1909) - courtesy of HathiTrust www://www.hathitrust.org/

This is precisely what Charles Dow, Jesse Livermore, Richard Wyckoff, J P Morgan, and other iconic traders would have seen, every day in their offices. The ticker tape, constantly clattering out its messages of market prices and reactions to the buying and selling, the supply and demand.

All the information was entered at the exchanges by hand, and then distributed to the ticker tape machines in the various brokerage offices. A short hand code was developed over the years, to try to keep the details as brief as possible, but also communicate all the detailed information required.

Fig 1.11 is perhaps the most famous, or infamous example of the ticker tape, from the morning of the 29th October 1929, the start of the Wall Street crash.

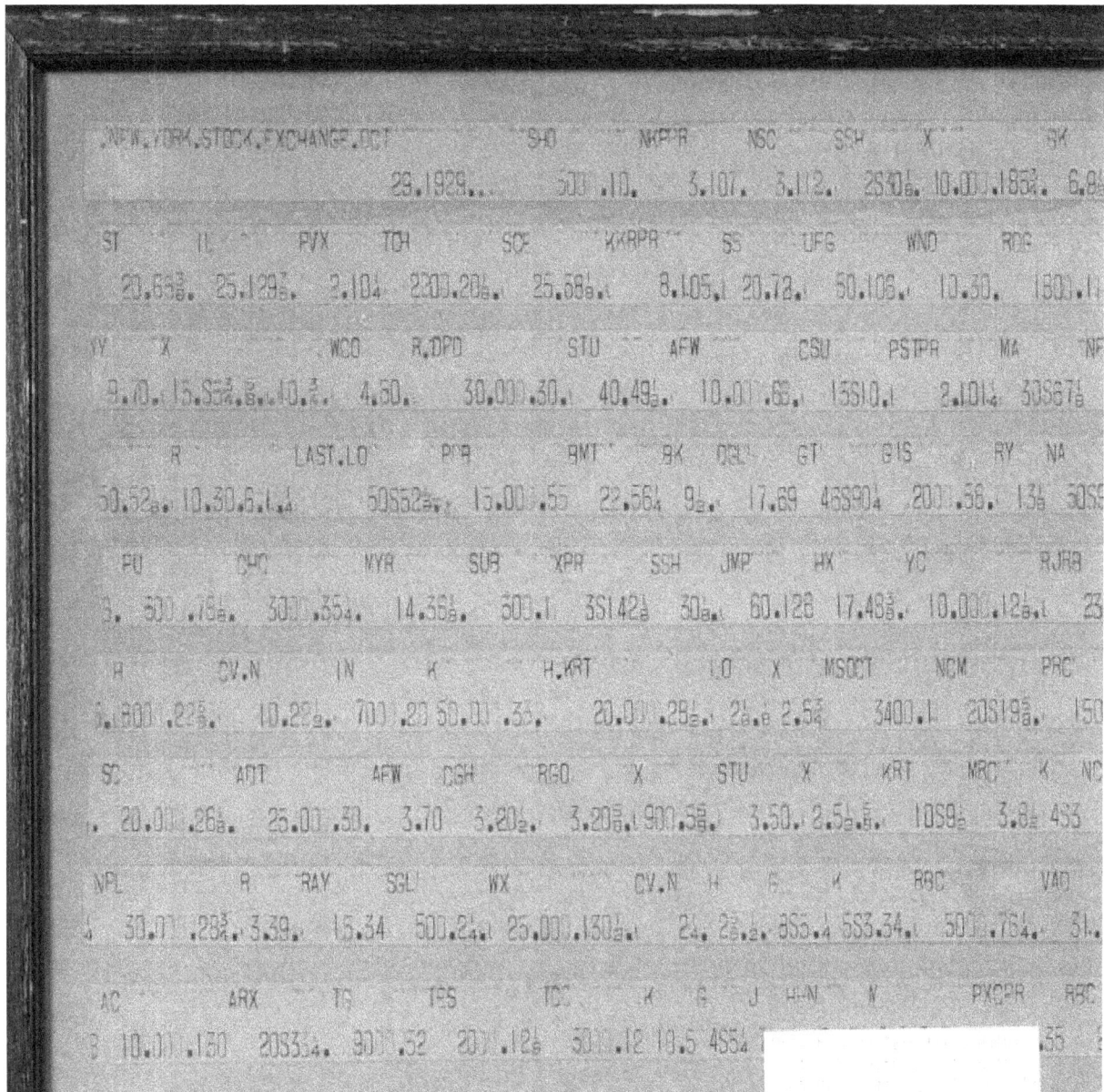

Fig 1.11 Ticker Tape Of Wall Street Crash

The image from Fig 1.11 is kindly provided from the resources of the Museum of American Finance where you can see the original.

On the top line is the stock ticker, with companies such as Goodyear Tyre (GT), United States Steel (X), Radio Corporation (R) and Westinghouse Electric (WX), with the notation PR alongside to show where the stock being sold was Preferred, rather than Common stock.

Below on the second line were printed all the prices and trading volumes, all in a short hand form to try to speed up the process. The character 'S' was often used in the prices quoted, to show a break between the number of shares being traded and the price quoted, but having the same meaning as a dot on the tape. Where 'SS' appeared, then this referred to an odd number of shares, generally less than 100. Finally, zeros were frequently left off quotes, once again for speed. So if we take US Steel (X) as an example from the above we can see on the first line of the ticker tape 10,000 shares at 185 ¾ and by the time we reach the end of the tape, the stock is being quoted as 2.5 ½. So 200 shares, but on such a day, was the price still 185, or had it fallen to 175 or even 165, as many shares did.

This then was the tape, that all these iconic traders came to know and understand intimately. Once they had learnt the language of the ticker, the tape had a story to tell, and one simply based on price and volume. For their longer term analysis, they would then transfer all this information across to a chart.

What has changed since? Well, the honest answer is actually very little.

We are fortunate in that our charts are electronic. All the price action and volume is delivered to us second by second, tick by tick, but just to prove that the ticker and its significance still remain, below is a more modern version of the same thing. The only difference is that this is electronic, but the information this portrays is the same.

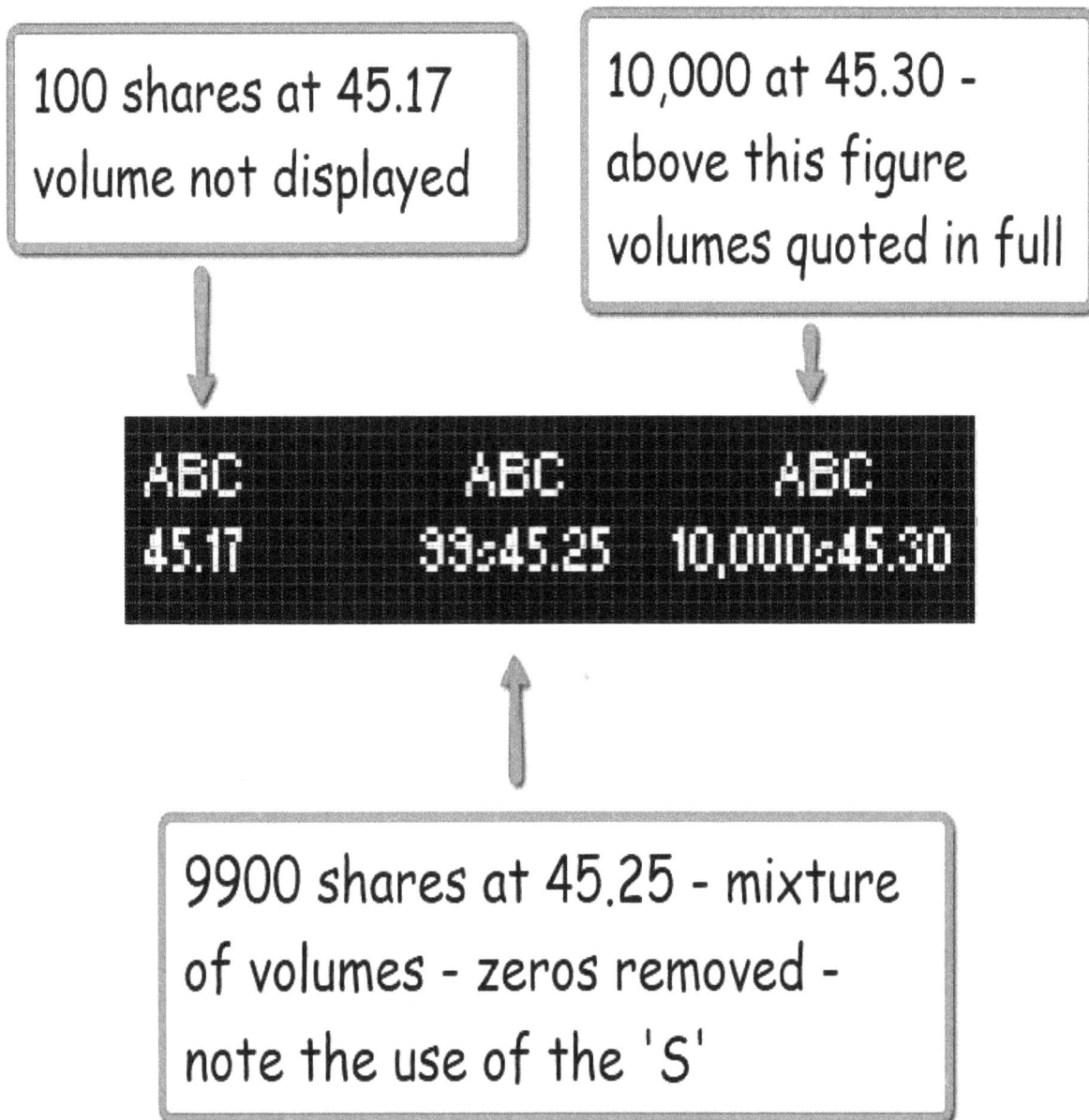

100 shares at 45.17 volume not displayed

10,000 at 45.30 - above this figure volumes quoted in full

9900 shares at 45.25 - mixture of volumes - zeros removed - note the use of the 'S'

ABC   ABC   ABC
45.17   9S:45.25   10,000:45.30

Fig 1.12 Electronic Ticker

Looks familiar doesn't it! And what do we see here in this very simple example in Fig 1.12

Well, we have a price that has risen from 45.17 to 45.30 supported by what appears to be strong volume. What we don't know at this stage is the time between these price changes, and whether the volumes for this instrument are low, above average or high. All key factors.

Whilst the two look similar, there is one HUGE difference, and that was in the timeliness of the information being displayed. For the iconic traders of the past, it is even more extraordinary to think that they managed to succeed despite the delays in the data on the ticker tape, which could be anything from a few minutes to a few hours out of date. Today, all the information we see is live, and whether on an electronic ticker, an electronic chart, or in an on screen ticker with level 1 and level 2 data, we are privileged to have an easy life when trading, compared to them.

Finally, in this introduction to volume and price analysis, let me introduce you to another of the trading 'greats' who perhaps will be less familiar to you. His legacy is very different to those of Dow, Livermore and Wyckoff, as he was the first to expose, a group he variously referred to as 'the specialists', 'the insiders' and what perhaps we would refer to as the market makers.

Richard Ney was born in 1916, and after an initial career in Hollywood, transitioned to become a renowned investor, trader and author, who exposed the inner workings of the stock market, as well as the tacit agreements between the regulatory authorities, the government, the exchanges and the banks, which allowed this to continue. In this respect he was similar to Wyckoff, and as an educator saw his role of trying to help the small investor understand how the game was rigged on the inside.

His first book, The Wall Street Jungle was a New York Times best seller in 1970, and he followed this up with two others, The Wall Street Gang and Making It In The Market. All had the same underlying theme, and to give you a flavour let me quote from the forward by Senator Lee Metcalf to The Wall Street Gang

"In his chapter on the SEC Mr Ney demonstrates an understanding of the esoteric operations of the Stock Exchange. Operations are controlled for the benefits of the insiders who have the special information and the clout to profit from all sorts of transactions, regardless of the actual value of the stock traded. The investor is left out or is an extraneous factor. The actual value of the listed stock is irrelevant. The name of the game is manipulation."

Remember, this is a Senator of the day, writing a forward to this book. No wonder Richard Ney was considered a champion of the people.

His books are still available today and just as relevant. Why? Because everything that Richard Ney exposed in his books, still goes on today, in every market, and let me say here and now, I am not writing from the standpoint of a conspiracy theorist. I am merely stating a fact of trading life. Every market that we either trade or invest in is manipulated in one way or another. Whether covertly by the market makers in equities, or in forex by the central banks who intervene regularly and in some cases very publicly.

However, there is one activity that the insiders cannot hide and that is volume, which is why you are reading this book. Volume reveals activity. Volume reveals the truth behind the price action. Volume validates price.

Let me give you one final quote from The Wall Street Gang, which I hope will make the point, and also lead us neatly into the next chapter. From the chapter entitled "The Specialist's Use of the Short Sale", Richard Ney says the following :

"To understand the specialists' practices, the investor must learn to think of specialists as merchants who want to sell an inventory of stock at retail price levels. When they clear their shelves of their inventory they will seek to employ their profits to buy more merchandise at wholesale price levels. Once we grasp this concept we are ready to posit eight laws:

1. *As merchants, specialists will expect to sell at retail what they have bought at wholesale.*

2. *The longer the specialists remain in business, the more money they will accumulate to buy stock at wholesale, which they will then want to sell at retail.*

3. *The expansion of communications media will bring more people into the market, tending to increase volatility of stock prices as they increase elements of demand-supply.*

4. *In order to buy and sell huge quantities of stock, Exchange members will seek new ways to enhance their sales techniques through use of the mass media.*

5. *In order to employ ever increasing financial resources, specialists will have to effect price declines of ever increasing dimensions in order to shake out enough stock.*

6. *Advances will have to be more dramatic on the upside to attract public interest in order to distribute the ever increasing accumulated inventories.*

7. *The most active stocks will require longer periods of time for their distribution.*

8. *The economy will be subjected to increasingly dramatic breakdowns causing inflation, unemployment, high interest rates and shortages of raw materials.*

So wrote Richard Ney, who correctly called consecutive market tops and bottoms throughout the 1960's 70's and 80's. He was the scourge of the SEC, and the champion of the small speculator and investor.

Therefore, volume reveals the truth behind the numbers. Whether you are trading in manipulated markets such as stocks or forex, or ones such as futures where we are dealing with the major operators, volume reveals that manipulation and order flow in stark detail.

The market makers in stocks cannot hide, the major banks who set exchange rates for the foreign exchange markets, cannot hide. In the futures markets, which is a pure market, volume validates price and gives us a picture of supply and demand coupled with sentiment and the flow of orders as the larger operators move in and out of the markets.

In the next chapter we are going to look at volume in more detail, but I am going to start with an article I wrote for Stocks and Commodities magazine, many years ago, and which echoes the eight laws of Richard Ney. It was written long before I came across Richard and his books, but the analogy is much the same and I include it here, to further reinforce the importance of volume in your trading. I hope I am getting the message across, but if not, the following 'parable' may convince you! I hope so.

Chapter Two

Why Volume?

The key is having more information than the other guy – then analyzing it right and using it rationally.
Warren Buffett (1930-)

This is the article that I wrote for Stocks and Commodities magazine many years ago. I called it the Parable of Uncle Joe. I have made some minor changes, but the essence of the article remains, as originally published.

One day after a particularly bad trading day, my Uncle Joe took me aside and consoled me with some hard facts about how the markets really work. And he told me this story.

You see, my Uncle Joe owns a unique company, which has given him an insider's perspective on how stock price movement is managed.

His company, Widgets & Co., is the only company in the state that distributes widgets, and it does so under license from the government. It has been buying and selling its unique widgets for many years. These widgets have an intrinsic value, they never break, and the number in circulation at any one time is much the same.

Being a reasonably clever man with many years of experience managing his business, my uncle soon realised that just buying and selling his widgets to customers was, in fact, rather dull. The amount of money he made each time he bought and sold was quite small, and the number of transactions per day was also low.

In addition, he also had all the running expenses of his office, his warehouse and his staff. Something would have to be done.

Having given the problem some thought, he wondered what would happen if he mentioned to a neighbour that widgets could soon be in short supply. He knew his neighbour was a terrible gossip, so this was almost as effective as putting an advertisement in the local paper. He also knew from checking his warehouse, that he had enough stock to meet any increased demand should his plan be successful.

The following day he met his neighbour outside, and casually mentioned his concerns, begging the man to keep it to himself. His neighbour assured him that he wouldn't breathe a word; his lips were sealed.

Several days passed and widget sales remained flat.

However, after a week or so, sales started to pick up with more customers coming to the warehouse and buying in larger quantities. It seemed his plan was starting to work and everyone was happy. His customers were happy as they knew that widgets would soon be in short supply, and so their value would increase. Uncle Joe was happy because he was selling more widgets, and making more money every day.

Then he started to think.

With everyone buying his widgets, what would happen if he raised his prices? After all, he was the only supplier and demand was high at the moment.

The following day he announced a price increase, but still believing there would soon be a widget shortage, his customers continued to buy in ever larger quantities!

As the weeks passed he gradually increased his prices higher and higher, but still the buying continued. A few of his more astute customers started to sell their widgets back to him, taking their profits, but Uncle Joe didn't mind as he still had plenty of willing buyers.

This was all good news for Uncle Joe, until one day, he suddenly realised with some alarm that his warehouse was now looking very empty indeed. He also started to notice that the volume of sales each day was decreasing. He decided to keep moving prices up, so everyone would think that the situation was unchanged.

But now he had a new problem. His original plan had been too successful.

How on earth was he going to persuade all his customers to sell widgets back to him, so that he could continue in business?

He pondered this problem for several days with no clear solution. Then, quite by chance, he met his neighbour again in town. The man drew him to one side and inquired whether the rumour he had heard was true? Inquiring into what that rumour might be, Uncle Joe learned that his neighbour had heard that another, much bigger widget distribution company was setting up business in the area.

Being clever, Uncle Joe realised that providence had given him the answer on a plate. Appearing crestfallen, he admitted that the rumour was true, and that his business would suffer badly. More importantly, widget values were likely to drop dramatically in price.

As they parted company, Uncle Joe chuckled to himself at having such good fortune, and such a helpful gossip for a neighbour.

Within days he had queues of customers outside his warehouse doors, begging him to buy back their widgets. With so many people selling, he dropped his prices quickly, making people even more desperate to sell before their widgets became worthless!

As the prices fell further, more and more people cracked under the pressure. Uncle Joe was now buying back an enormous volume of widgets. After several weeks the panic selling was over, as few people had been brave enough to hold out under the pressure.

Uncle Joe could now start to sell widgets again at their old levels from his warehouse full of stock. He didn't mind if it was quiet for a few months, as he has made a great deal of money very quickly. He could afford to take it easy. His overhead expenses were covered and he could even pay his staff a healthy bonus. Everyone soon forgot how or where the rumours had started and life returned to normal.

Normal that is until Uncle Joe started thinking one day. I wonder if we could do that again?

Uncle Joe's story is of course fiction. It was written before I discovered the work of Richard Ney, but it is interesting that we both use the same analogy to describe the insiders, the specialists, or what most people call the market makers.

It is my view, (and of Richard Ney) that this is one of the great ironies of the financial markets. Whilst insider dealing by individuals on the outside is punished with long prison sentences and heavy fines, those on the inside are actively encouraged and licensed to do so. The problem for the exchanges and governments is that without the market makers, who are the wholesalers of the market and provide a guarantee of execution of the stock, the market would cease to function. When we buy or sell in the cash market, our order will always be filled. This is the role of the market maker. They have no choice. It is their remit to fulfil all orders, both buying and selling and managing their order books, or their inventory accordingly.

As Ney said himself, the market makers are wholesalers, nothing more, nothing less. They are professional traders. They are licensed and regulated and have been approved to 'make a market' in the shares you wish to buy and sell. They are usually large international banking organisations, generally with thousands or tens of thousands of employees worldwide.

Some of them will be household names, others you will never have heard of, but they all have one thing in common - they make vast amounts of money. What places the market maker in such a unique position, is their ability to see both sides of the market. In other words, the supply and demand. The inventory position if you like.

Just like Uncle Joe, they also have another huge advantage which is to be able to set their prices accordingly. Now, I don't want you to run away with the idea that the entire stock market is rigged. It isn't. No single market maker could achieve this on their own

However, you do need to understand how they use windows of opportunity, and a variety of trading conditions to manipulate prices. They will use any, and every piece of news to move the prices, whether relevant or not. Have you ever wondered why markets move fast on world events which have no bearing. Why markets move lower on good news, and higher on bad news?

The above explanation is a vast over simplification but the principle remains true. All the major exchanges such as the NYSE, AMEX and the NASDAQ have specialists who act as market makers. These include firms such as Barclays plc (BARC) and Getco LLC that oversee the trading in shares and what is often referred to as The Big Board (shades of Jesse Livermore, perhaps). According to Bloomberg Business in 2012 *'exchanges are experimenting with ways of inducing market makers to quote more aggressively to attract volume'*. In addition, in the same article the US exchanges are very keen to increase the number of companies who can act as market makers. But, other than this, not much has changed since the days of Richard Ney.

Do these companies then work together? Of course they do! It goes without saying. Do they work in an overt way? No. What they will all see, is the balance of supply and demand in general across the markets and specifically in their own stocks. If the specialists are all in a general state of over supply, and a news story provides the opportunity to sell, then the market markers will all act pretty much in unison, as their warehouses will all be in much the same state. It really is common sense once you start to think about the markets in this way.

On the London Stock Exchange there are official market makers for many securities (but not for shares in the largest and most heavily traded companies, which instead use an electronic automated system called SETS).

However, you might ask why I have spent so much time explaining what these companies do, when actually you never see them at all. The answer is very simple. As the 'licensed insiders', they sit in the middle of the market, looking at both sides of the market. They will know precisely the balance of supply and demand at any one time. Naturally this information will never be available to you, and if you were in their position, you would probably take advantage in the same way.

The only tool we have at our disposal to fight back, is volume. We can argue about the rights and wrongs of the situation, but when you are trading and investing in stocks, market makers are a fact of life. Just accept it, and move on.

Volume is far from perfect. The market makers have even learnt over the decades how to avoid reporting large movements in stock, which are often reported in after hours trading. However, it is the best tool we have with which to see ' inside the market'

Volume applies to all markets and is equally valuable, whether there is market manipulation or not. Volume in the futures market, which is the purest form of buying and selling reveals when the market is running out of steam. It reveals whether buying interest is rising or falling on a daily basis. It reveals all the subtleties of pull backs and reversals on tick charts and time charts from minutes to hours. Volume is the fuel that drives the market. Volume reveals when the major operators are moving in and out of the market. Without volume, nothing moves, and if it does move and the volume is not in agreement, then there is something wrong, and an alarm bell rings!

For example, if the market is bullish and the futures price is rising on strong and rising volume, then this is instantly telling us that the price action is being validated by the associated volume. The major operators are buying into the move. Equally, if the market is falling and the volume is rising, then once again volume is validating price. It really is that simple. These principles apply whatever the market, whether it is bonds, interest rates, indices, commodities or currencies. What you will discover in this book is that the analysis of price and volume applies to every market, manipulated or otherwise. In the manipulated cash markets of stocks, it provides you with the ultimate weapon to avoid being suckered in by the market makers.

In the futures markets, it gives you the ultimate weapon to validate price, and to reveal the true market sentiment of buyers and sellers and to take action as the reversals in trend are signalled using volume. Here, we are following the major operators who will have the inside view of the market.

In the spot forex market we have a different problem. There is no true volume reported. Even if there were, would this be shown as trade size, or 'amounts of currency' being exchanged. Fortunately however, we do have an answer to volume in the world's largest financial market, and it's called tick volume.

However, tick volume is not perfect, nothing is in trading. First, the tick volumes on one platform will vary from the tick volumes on another, since tick data will be provided through the platform of an online broker. Second, the quality of the data will depend on several factors, not least whether the broker is subscribed directly to the interbank liquidity pool directly using one of the expensive wholesale feeds. Nevertheless, a quality FX broker will normally provide a quality feed.

But, is tick data valid as a proxy for volume?

The short answer is yes, and various studies over the years have shown that tick data as a proxy for 'volume' is 90% representative in terms of the true 'activity' in the market. After all, volume is really activity, and in this sense can be reflected in price, since tick data is simply changes in price. So, if the price is changing fast, then does this mean that we have significant activity in the market? In my opinion the answer is yes. To prove this point, we only need to watch a tick chart prior to, and just after a significant news release.

Take the monthly Non Farm Payroll, which every forex trader knows and loves! Assume we are watching a 233 tick chart. Prior to the release each 233 tick bar may be taking a few minutes to form. During the release and immediately after, each bar is forming in seconds, appearing as if being fired onto the screen using a machine gun! A chart that has taken an hour to fill with bars, is now a full frame within minutes.

This is activity, pure and simple, which in turn we can assume is representative of volume. There will always be market manipulation in the spot forex market. In many ways it is the most widely manipulated of all. We only have to consider the currency wars as evidence of this, but as traders, tick volume is what we have, and tick volume is what we use. Whilst it isn't perfect, I can guarantee you one thing. You will be considerably more successful using it, than not, and you will see why, once we start to look at the charts themselves across all the various markets.

If you are still not convinced? Let me give you an analogy, not perfect I accept, but which I hope will help.

Imagine that you are at auction, and suppose for argument's sake that it's an auction for furniture. It is a cold, wet and miserable day in the middle of winter, and the auction room is in a small provincial town. The auction room is almost empty, with few buyers in the room. The auctioneer details the next item, an antique piece of furniture and starts the bidding with his opening price. After a short pause, a bid is made from the room, but despite further efforts to raise the bidding, the auctioneer finally brings the hammer down, selling the item at the opening bid.

Now imagine the same item being sold in a different scenario. This time, the same item is being sold, but the auction house is in a large capital city, it is the middle of summer and the auction room is full. The auctioneer details the next piece which is our antique furniture, and opens the bidding with a price. The price moves quickly higher, with bidders signalling interest in the auction room, and phone bidders also joining in. Eventually tape bidding slows and the item is sold.

In the first example, the price changed only once, representing a lack of interest, and in our terms a lack of bidders in the room, in other words volume. In the second example the price changed several times and quickly with the price action reflecting interest, activity and bidders in the room. In other words volume.

In other words, the linkage between activity and price is perfectly valid. Therefore, as far as I'm concerned, using tick data as a proxy for volume data in the forex market is equally valid. Activity and volume go hand in hand, and I hope that the above analogy, simple and imperfect as it is, will convince you too.

The above simple analogy also highlights three other important points about volume.

The first is this. All volume is relative. Suppose for example this had been our first visit to this particular auction room. Is the activity witnessed average, above average or below average. We would not be able to say, since we have no yardstick by which to judge. If we were a regular visitor, then we could judge instantly whether there were more or less attendees than usual, and make a judgement on likely bidding, as a result.

This is what makes volume such a powerful indicator. As humans we have the ability to judge relative sizes and heights extremely quickly, and it is the relative aspect of volume which gives it such power. Unlike the tape readers we have a chart, which gives us an instant picture of the relative volume bars, whether on an ultra fast tick chart, an intra day time chart, or longer term investing chart. It is the relationship in relative terms which is important.

The second point is that volume without price is meaningless. Imagine an auction room with no bidding. Remove the price from the chart, and we simply have volume bars. Volume on its own simply reveals interest, but that interest is just that, without the associated price action. It is only when volume and price combine that we have the chemical reaction which creates the explosive power of Volume Price Analysis.

Third and last, time is a key component. Suppose in our auction room, instead of the bidding lasting a few minutes, it had lasted a few hours (if allowed!). What would this tell us then? That the interest in the item was subdued to say the least. Hardly the frenetic interest of a bidding war.

To use a water analogy. Imagine that we have a hosepipe with a sprinkler attached. The water is the price action and the sprinkler is our 'volume' control. If the sprinkler is left open, the water will continue to leave the pipe with no great force, simply falling from the end of the pipe. However, as soon as we start to close our sprinkler valve, pressure increases and the water travels further. We have the same amount of water leaving the pipe, but through a reduced aperture. Time has now become a factor, as the same amount of water is attempting to leave the pipe in the same amount of time, but pressure has increased.

It is the same with the market.

However, let me be provocative for a moment, and borrow a quote from Richard Wyckoff himself who famously said :

"….trading and investing is like any other pursuit—the longer you stay at it the more technique you acquire, and anybody who thinks he knows of a short cut that will not involve "sweat of the brow" is sadly mistaken"

Whilst this sentiment could be applied to almost any endeavour in life, it is particularly relevant in the study of price and volume.

As you are probably aware, or will not doubt find out when you begin trading, there are several free 'volume' indicators, and many proprietary systems you can buy. Whether free or paid, all have one thing in common. They have neither the capacity nor intellect to analyse the price volume relationship correctly in my view, for the simple reason, that trading is an art, not a science.

When I finished my two weeks with Albert, I then spent the next 6 months just studying charts, and learning to interpret the price and volume relationship. I would sit with my live feed and my two monitors, one for the cash market and the other for the equivalent futures market, watching every price bar and the associated volume and using my knowledge to interpret future market behaviour. This may not be what you want to read. And some of you may be horrified at how labour intensive this all sounds.

However, just like Wyckoff, I also believe there are no short cuts to success. Technical analysis, in all its aspects is an art, and interpreting the volume price relationship is no different. It takes time to learn, and time to be quick in your analysis. However, just like the tape readers of the past, once mastered is a powerful skill.

The technique is a subjective one, requiring discretionary decision making. It is not, and never will be, one that lends itself to automation. If it were, then this book would simply be more fuel for the fire.

Finally, (and I hope you are still reading and have not been put off by the above statements), one further aspect of volume is whose perspective are we using when we talk about buying and selling. Are we talking from a wholesalers perspective or from the retail perspective. So, let me explain.

As investors or speculators the whole raison d'etre for studying volume is to see what the insiders, the specialists are doing. For the simple reason that whatever they are doing, we want to follow and do as well! The assumption being, implied or otherwise, is that they are likely to have a much better idea of where the market is heading. This is not an unreasonable assumption to make.

So, when the market has moved sharply lower in a price waterfall and a bearish trend, supported by masses of volume, this is a buying climax. It is the wholesalers who are buying and the retail traders who are panic selling. A buying climax for us represents an opportunity.

Likewise, at the top of a bull trend, where we see sustained high volumes, then this is a selling climax. The wholesalers are selling to the retail traders and investors who are buying on the expectation of the market going to the moon!

So remember, when I write about volume throughout the remainder of this book, buying and selling is always from a wholesalers perspective as this is the order flow that we **ALWAYS** want to follow.

Now in the next chapter we're going to move on to consider the other side of the equation, which is price.

Chapter Three

The Right Price

No price is too low for a bear or too high for a bull.
Unknown

Now we turn to the counter balance of volume which is price, and forgive me for a moment if we return to Jesse Livermore and one of his many quotes which I mentioned at the start of this book:

"there is nothing new in Wall Street. There can't be because speculation is as old as the hills. Whatever happens in the stock market today has happened before and will happen again"

Now to use and paraphrase this famous quote, I would say that there is nothing new in trading. As I said in chapter one, Volume Price Analysis has been around for over 100 years. The same is true when we consider the analysis of price, and the only representation of price which truly changed how traders studied and analysed charts was in the introduction of candlestick charts in the early 1990's.

Fads come and go in trading. Something that was in 'vogue' a few years ago, is no longer considered valid, and some 'new' approach is then promoted. One approach which is being marketed heavily at the moment is 'price action trading' or PAT. This is as it sounds. Trading using an analysis of price, with no (or very few) indicators, which I find strange. And my reasons are as follows.

Imagine suggesting to Jesse Livermore, Charles Dow, Richard Wyckoff, and Richard Ney, that we had devised a new and exciting way to analyse the markets. The ticker tape print out would now ONLY show the price, but NO volume. I'm sure Jesse and the others would have been struck dumb at such a suggestion. But don't worry. In this book I explain price action trading, which is then validated with volume. So you get two approaches for the price of one here! Now that's what I call value for money!!

However, I digress. Living close to London as I do, and just a stone's throw away from The President, is the old LIFFE building, the London International Financial Futures and Options Exchange. As a frequent visitor to this part of London, I would often drive past this exchange, and at any time during the day, would see the traders in their different brightly coloured jackets, dashing out to grab coffees and sandwiches before rushing back to the floor of the exchange. Without exception these were generally young men, loud and brash, and in fact on the corner of Walbrook and Cannon Street there now stands a bronze statue of a floor trader, mobile phone in hand. These were the days of fast cars, and aggressive trading, and it was ironic that this was the world where I started my own trading career, with FTSE 100 futures orders filled on the floor of the exchange.

This was the world of adrenaline pumped traders, yelling and screaming using unintelligible hand signals, buying and selling in a frenetic atmosphere of noise and sweat. It was positively primordial where the overriding emotion emanating from the floor was fear, and obvious to anyone who cared to view it from the public gallery.

However, the advent of electronic trading changed all of this, and the LIFFE exchange was one of many casualties. All the traders left trading and moved away from the pit, and onto electronic platforms. The irony is, that most of the traders, and I have spoken to many over the years, failed to make the transition from pit trading, to electronic trading, for one very simple reason.

A pit trader, could sense not only the fear and greed, but also judge the flow of the market from the buying and selling in the pit. In other words, to a pit trader, this was volume or order flow. This is what a pit trader saw and sensed every day of the week, the flow of money, the weight of market sentiment, and the trading opportunities that followed as a result. In other words, they could 'see' the volume, they could see when the big buyers were coming into the market and ride on their coat tails. This is the equivalent of volume on the screen.

However, without being able to see, judge, and feel the flow in the pit, most of these traders failed to make a successful transition to screen trading. Some succeeded, but most were never able to make that move, from an environment where price action was supported by something tangible. Whether they would call it activity, order flow, sentiment, or just the 'smell of the market' this is what brought the price action to life for them, and why they struggled to succeed with the advent of the electronic era.

Pit trading still continues today, and if you do get the chance to view it in action, I would urge you to go. Once you have seen it for real, you will understand why volume is so powerful in supporting price, and why I believe the exponents of PAT are simply promulgating something different for the sake of it.

Whilst it is undoubtedly true to say that price action encapsulates all the news, views and decisions from traders and investors around the world, and that with detailed analysis we can arrive at a conclusion of future market direction, without volume we have no way of validating that price analysis. Volume gives us our bearings, it allows us to triangulate the price action and to check the validity of our analysis. This is what the pit traders of old were doing – they would see a price move, validate it by considering the order flow in the pit, and act accordingly. For us, it is the same. We simply use an electronic version of order flow which is the volume on our screens.

But, let me give you another example.

Returning to our auction again, only this time there is no physical sale room. Instead we are joining an online auction, and perhaps now you can begin to imagine the problems that the ex pit traders encountered. We have moved from the physical sale room, where we can see all the buyers, the number of people in the room, the phone bids and the speed of the bidding. In a physical sale room we also get a sense of where the price starts to pause. We see bidders become fearful as the price approaches their limit and they hesitate with the next bid, just fractionally, but enough to tell you they are near their limit. This is what the pit traders missed.

In an online auction we are logged in and waiting for the auction to start. An item we want to buy appears and we start bidding. We have no idea how many other bidders are there, we have no idea if we are playing on a level playing field. All we see is the price being quoted. The auctioneer, for all we know, could be taking bids 'off the wall' (fake bids in other words) which happens more often than many people think. The reason is that all good auctioneers like to encourage auction fever – it's good for business, so they use every trick in the book.

Meanwhile back to our online auction. We continue bidding and eventually win the item.

But, have we got our item at a good price? And, in this scenario we are only referring to price and not value, which is a very different concept. Besides, I hope by now, you are beginning to get the picture. In the online auction all we see is price.

Therefore, in a real online 'auction' of trading, do we really want to base our trading decisions solely on price? Furthermore, the great iconic traders of the past would have given us their answer, and it would have been a very emphatic NO.

Once again I accept it is an imperfect example, but one which I hope makes the point.

To me, a price chart with no volume is only part of the story. Price does encapsulate market sentiment at a given and precise moment in time, but with so much market manipulation prevalent in so many markets, why ignore such a valuable tool which is generally provided free.

Whilst price is a leading indicator, in itself, it only reveals what has gone before, from which we then interpret what is likely to happen next. Whilst we may be correct in our analysis, it is volume which can complete the picture.

In a manipulated market, volume reveals the truth behind the price action. In a pure market, volume reveals the truth behind market sentiment and order flow.

So, let's take a closer look at price, and in particular the effect that changes in technology have had on the four principle elements of a price bar, the open, the high, the low and the close. And the most significant change in the last few years has been the move to electronic trading, which has had the most profound effect on two elements of the four, namely the opening and closing prices.

Scroll back to the days of Ney and earlier, and the markets in those days only traded during a physical session. The market would open when the exchange opened, and close when the exchange closed at a prescribed time. Trading was executed on the floor of the exchange, and everyone knew when the market was about to open or close. This gave the opening and closing prices great significance, particularly on the open and close of the day. The opening price would be eagerly awaited by traders and investors and, as the closing bell approached, frenetic trading activity would be taking place as traders closed out their end of day positions. This is now generally referred to as regular trading hours (RTH), and is the time the exchange is physically open. Whilst this principle still applies to stock markets around the world, with the NYSE trading from 9.30am to 4.00pm, and the LSE open from 8.00 am until 4.30 pm, what has revolutionised the trading world is the advent of electronic trading.

The platform that really changed the game was Globex, introduced by the CME in 1992, since when virtually every futures contract can now be traded 24 hours a day. Whilst the cash markets, such as stocks, are restricted to the physical time set by the exchange, what has changed, certainly with regard to this market, has been the introduction of electronic index futures, which now trade around the clock. What this means, in effect, is that the opening and closing prices of the cash market are now far less important than they once were.

The reason is simply the introduction of Globex, as electronic trading has become the standard for index futures, which are derivatives of the cash market indices. The ES E-mini (S&P 500) was the first to be introduced in 1997, followed shortly afterwards by the NQ E-mini (Nasdaq 100) in 1999, and the YM E-mini (Dow Jones 30) in 2002. With these index futures now trading overnight through the Far East and Asian session, the open of the cash index is no longer a surprise with the futures signalling overnight market sentiment well in advance. By contrast, in the days before the advent of electronic trading, a gapped open, up or down, would have given traders a very strong signal of market intent. Whereas today, the open for the major indices is no longer a great surprise as it is forecast by the overnight futures markets.

Whilst it is certainly true to say that individual stocks may well react for a variety of reasons to sentiment in the broad index, generally all boats tend to rise on a rising tide, and therefore likely to follow suit. The open and the close for individual stocks is still significant, but the point is that the index which reflects market sentiment will be broadly known in advance, making the open less relevant than it once was.

The same could be said of the closing price. When the physical exchange closes, stocks are closed for the day in the cash markets, but electronic trading continues on the index future and moves on into the Far East session and beyond.

This facet of electronic trading also applies to all commodities, which are now traded virtually 24 hours a day on the Globex platform, and both currency futures, and currency spot markets also trade 24 hours a day.

The electronic nature of trading is reflected in the price chart. Twenty years ago, gap up or gap down price action would have been the norm, with the open of a subsequent bar closing well above or below the close of the previous bar. These were often excellent signals of a break out in the instrument, particularly where this was confirmed with volume. Such price action is now rare, and generally restricted to the equity markets, which then catch up when the physical exchange opens the next day. Virtually every other market is now electronic such as the spot forex market, and as we have just seen, indices catch up with the overnight futures as do commodities and other futures contracts.

The open of one bar will generally be at exactly the same price as the close of the previous bar, which reveals little. This is one of the many effects that electronic trading is now having on price action on the charts, and is likely to continue to have in the future. Electronic trading is here to stay, and the significance of these elements of price action in various markets will change as a result.

If the market is running 24 hours a day, then the open of one bar will simply follow the close of the previous bar, until the market closes for the weekend. From a price action trading perspective, this gives us little in the way of any valid 'sentiment' signals, which makes volume even more relevant in today's electronic world – in my humble opinion at any rate!

However, let's take a look at an individual bar in more detail, and the four elements which create it, namely the open, the high, the low and the close, and the importance of these from a Volume Price Analysis perspective. At this point I would like to say that the only price bars I use in the remainder of this book, and in my own trading are candlesticks. This is what Albert taught all those years ago, and it is how I learnt.

I have tried bar charts and thought I could dispense with candles. However, I have returned to candles and do not plan to use any other system, for the foreseeable future. I do understand that some traders prefer to use bars, line charts, Heikin Ashi, and many other. However, my apprenticeship in Volume Price Analysis was with candlesticks and I believe its true power is revealed when using this approach. I hope, by the end of this book you too will agree.

Therefore, I want to start by dissecting a typical candle and explain how much we can learn from it. In any candle, there are seven key elements. The open, high, low and close, the upper and lower wicks and the spread as shown in Fig 3.10. Whilst each of these plays a part in defining the price action within the time frame under consideration, it is the wicks and the spread which are the most revealing in terms of market sentiment, when validated with volume.

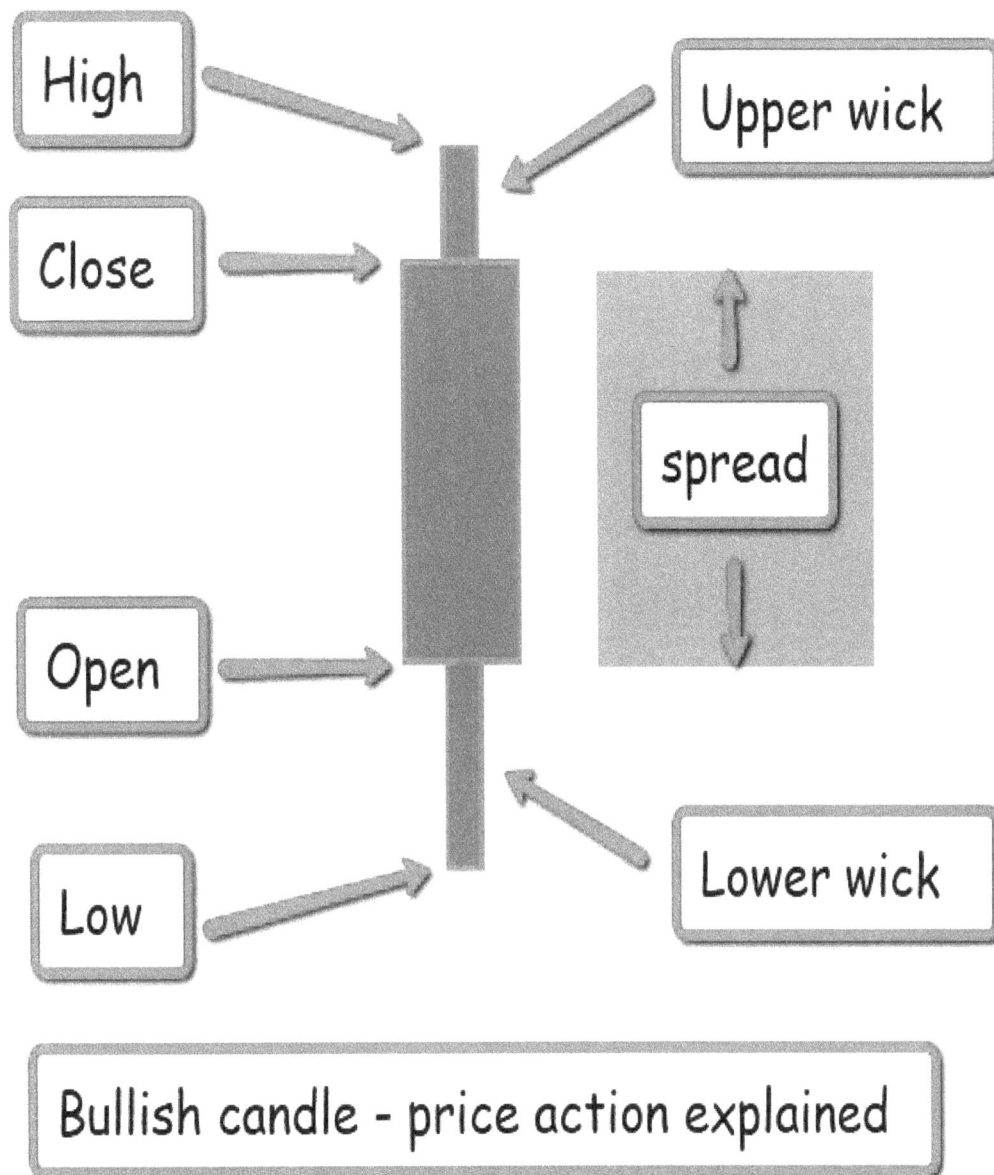

Fig 3.10 A Typical Candle

Perhaps the simplest way to visualise the price action contained within a candle, and is applicable regardless of timeframe (from a tick chart to a monthly chart), is to display the price action, as a sine wave, with the market oscillating back and forth, as buyers and sellers battle for supremacy.

The image in Fig 3.11 is a visual representation of this price action and in this case it is the buyers who are triumphant. However, the price action could have taken a different journey in creating this candle. It is the completed candle which is important.

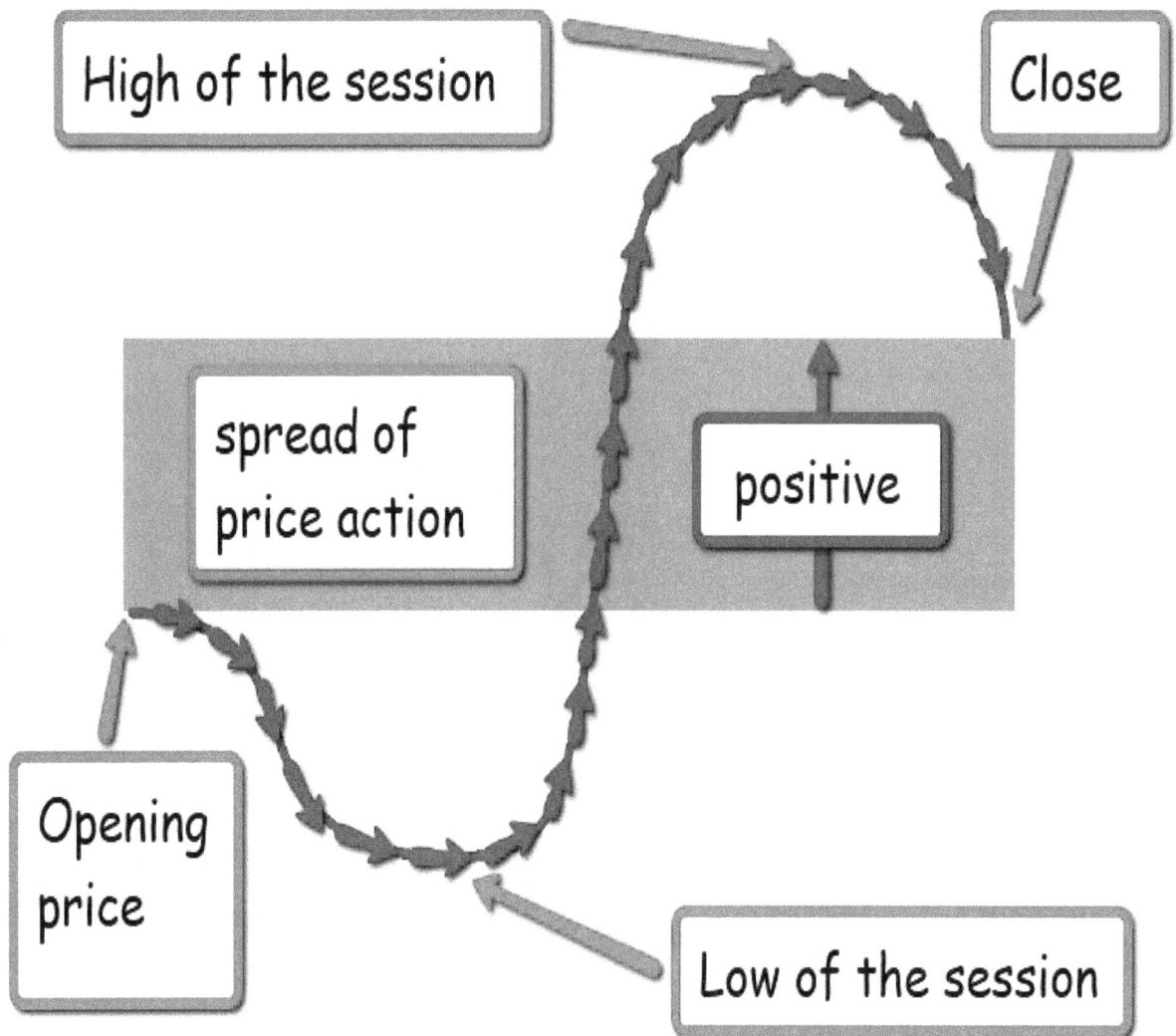

Fig 3.11 Price Action As A Sine Wave

Let's start with the spread which reveals the sentiment for that session.

A wide spread between the open and the close indicates strong market sentiment, either bullish or bearish, depending on whether the closing price finished above the opening price or below it.

A narrow spread between the open and the close indicates sentiment which is weak. There is no strong view one way or the other. The wicks to the top and bottom are indicative of change. A change in sentiment during the session. After all, if the sentiment had remained firm throughout, then we would have no wicks at all. This is the equivalent of our online auction, or physical auction, where the price opens at one level, and closes at a higher level once sold. The price action would simply create a solid candle with no wick to the top or the bottom, and in the context of trading, suggesting strong and continued sentiment in the direction of the candle.

This is the power of the wicks and why, when used in combination with the spread, reveal so much about true market sentiment. It forms the basis of price action trading, which is perfectly valid in it's own right.

However, why stop at this point and refuse to validate that price action with volume? This is something I simply cannot understand and perhaps any PAT traders reading this book can convince me otherwise. Just drop me an email as I am always happy to learn.

So, as you can see, the length and context of the wick, whether to the upside or the downside is paramount in Volume Price Analysis, and the easiest way to explain this is to consider some further visualisation examples, which will help to make the point.

Let's take two examples and the first is in Fig 13.12. Here we have a wick where the price has opened, the market has moved lower, and then recovered to close back at the open price. In the second example in Fig 13.13 we have a wick where the price has opened, the market has moved higher and then moved lower to close back at the open.

Let's analyse what's happening here with the price action and market sentiment. In both cases we can be certain that this is the profile of the price action, since the closing price has returned to the original opening price. So there is no guesswork. It is true that within the price action, there may have been ups and downs, pull backs and reversals, but at some point in the session, the price action hit a low, or a high and then returned to the original starting point.

Lower Wick Example

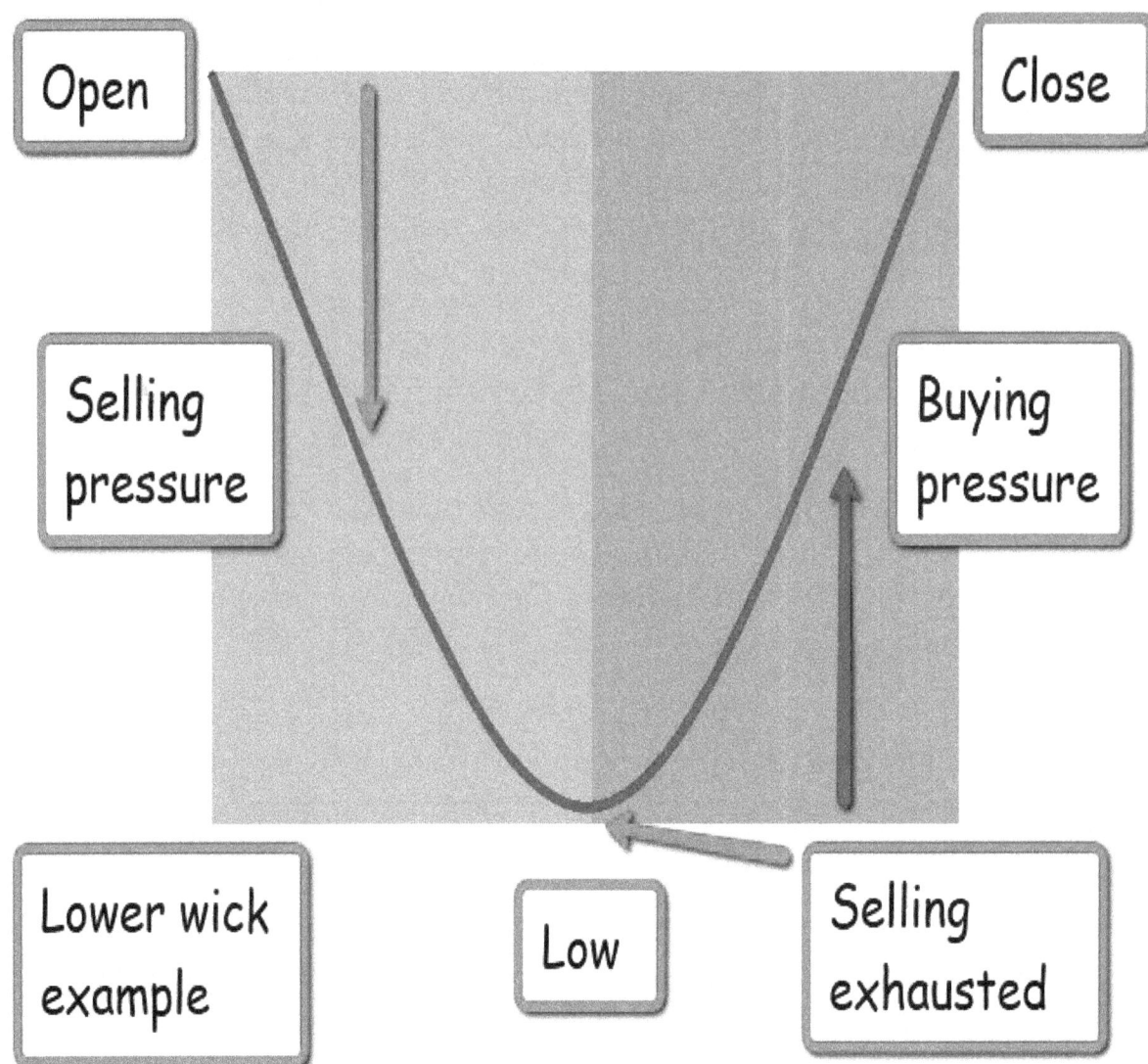

Fig 3.12 Lower Wick Example

Taking the lower wick example first, the price bar opened and almost immediately sellers were in the market forcing the price lower, and overwhelming the buyers. Perhaps within the move lower, there were pauses and brief attempts to rally, which would have been seen perhaps in faster time frames, and a key part of trading. However, in this session, as far as we are concerned, the sellers remained in control throughout the first part of the candle's creation.

At some point during the course of the session, the buyers started to come back into the market, wrestling control from the sellers as the market price had now become an attractive buying proposition. Gradually near the bottom of the price bar, the sellers finally give up, having been overwhelmed by the buyers who gradually take control. Now it's the turn of the sellers to be under pressure, as more and more buyers flood into the market, overwhelming the sellers and taking the price back higher once again, to finally close at the opening price.

But, what does this price action reveal? And the answer is two very important things.

First, that in this session, whatever the time frame may have been, there has been a complete reversal in market sentiment. Why? Because the selling pressure that was in evidence during the first part of the candle's creation, has been completely overwhelmed and absorbed in the second half.

Second, that the sentiment on the close of the bar is bullish – it has to be, since we know that the price action closed at the open, so at the instant of closure, the price must have been rising, supported by all the buying pressure underneath.

Does this mean that this is signalling a reversal in any trend? The short answer is no, and you will discover why once we start looking at volume, which will then give us the complete picture. At the moment we are simply considering price action which is only half the picture, but the point I want to make, is that the wick on a candle is **EXTREMELY** important, and a vital part of Volume Price Analysis, as is the spread. In this case the spread was zero, which is JUST as significant as any large spread of the candle.

I hope that the above example has helped to explain what is happening 'inside' the candle with the associated price action. This is a very simple example, with the price action split symmetrically into a 50/50 window. Nevertheless, the principle holds good. The price action may have been split into a 25/75 or even a 15/85, but the point is this – the sellers were overwhelmed by the buyers during the course of the session that the candle is representing.

This now brings me on to another area of volume analysis which we are also going to consider later in the book. I've already mentioned Volume Price Analysis or VPA several times so far, which is the relationship between volume and price over the entire life of the candle, but what happens within the life of the candle for example. Where is the buying and selling actually taking place, and this is called Volume At Price, or VAP for short.

Whilst VPA focuses on the 'linear relationship' between volume and price once the candle has closed, VAP focuses on the volume profile during the creation of the price bar. In other words, 'where' has the volume been concentrated within the associated price action.

We could say that VPA is our big picture of the volume price relationship on the outside of the candle, whilst VAP gives us the detail of the volume profile, 'inside' the candle. This helps to give us an additional perspective on our 'outside' view – two views of the same thing, but from different perspectives, with one validating the other. A further triangulation of the volume and price relationship.

Now let's look at our other example, which was the upper wick example.

Upper Wick Example

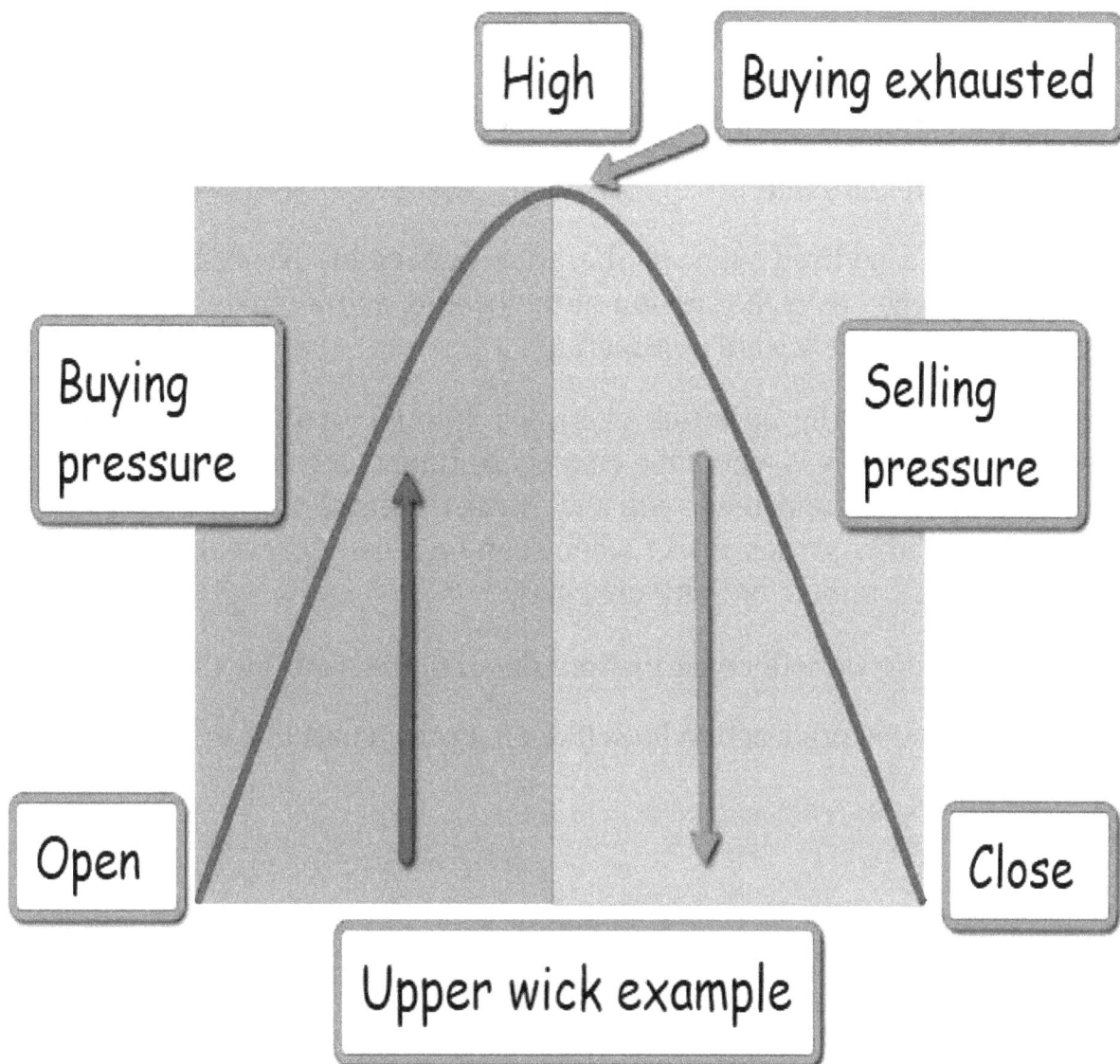

Fig 3.13 Upper Wick Example

In this example the market opened with the buyers immediately taking control, forcing the price higher, and overcoming the sellers, who are compelled to admit defeat under the buying pressure. However, as the session develops the price action reaches a point at which the buyers are beginning to struggle, the market is becoming resistant to higher prices and gradually the sellers begin to regain control.

Finally, at the high of the session, the buyers run out of steam and as the sellers come into the market, the buyers close out their profits. This selling pressure then forces prices lower, as waves of sellers hit the price action.

The candle closes back at the open price and the session closes. Once again, there are two key points with this price behaviour which are fundamental.

First, we have a complete reversal in market sentiment, this time from bullish to bearish. Second, the sentiment at the close is bearish, as the open and closing price are the same.

Again, this is a stylised view of the price behaviour. Nevertheless, this is what has happened over the session of the candle, and it makes no difference as to what time frame we are considering.

This could be a candle on a tick chart, a 5 minute chart, a daily chart or a weekly chart, and this is where the concept of time comes into play. This type of price action, accompanied with the correct volume profiles, is going to have a significantly greater effect when seen on a daily or weekly chart, then when seen on a 1 minute or 5 minute chart.

This is something we will cover in more detail in the next few chapters.

But, what does this price action look like on a price chart in candle form?

Lower Wick Example

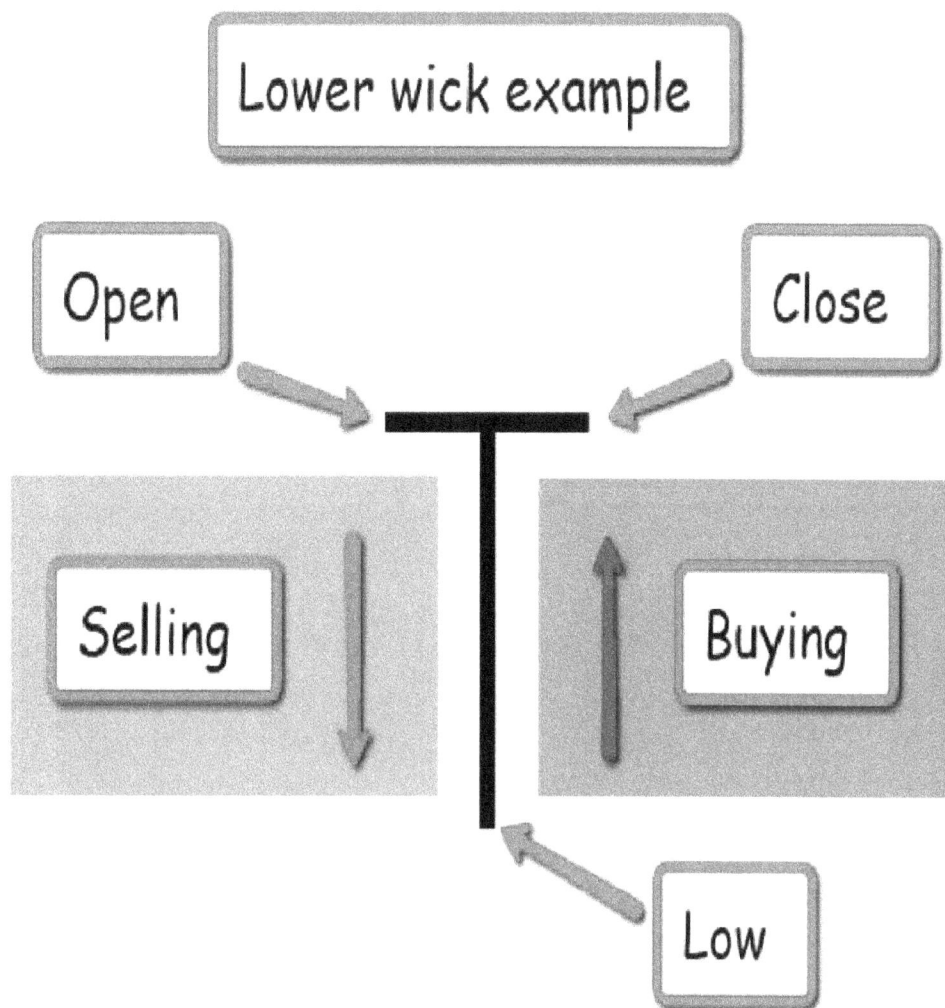

Fig 3.14 Candle From Lower Wick Example

Although the resulting candle doesn't look very exciting it actually represents one of the most powerful price actions that you will find on any chart, particularly when volume analysis is added to it. Price action and volume then tell us where the market is likely to go next.

And here is another, equally powerful candle.

Upper Wick Example

Once again, this is an extremely important price pattern, which we will return to time and time again throughout the book.

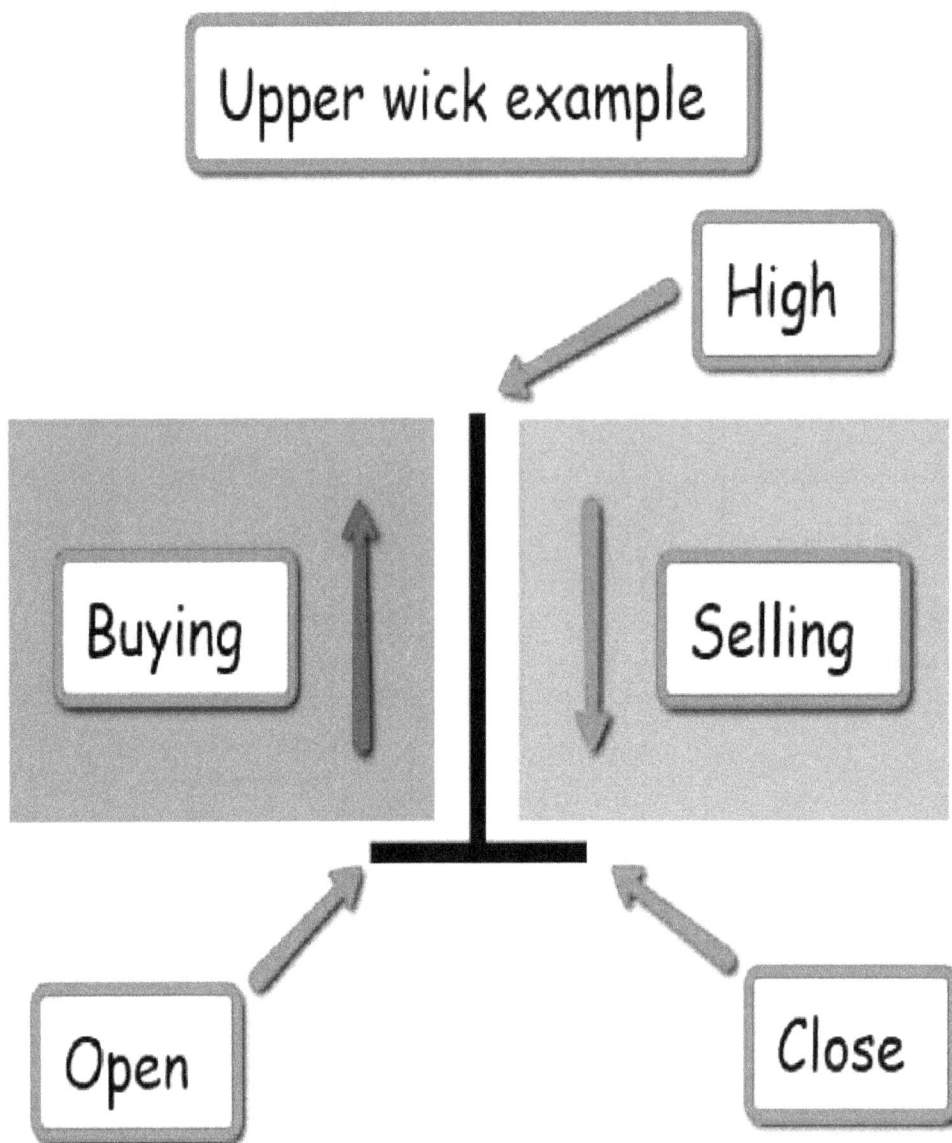

Fig 3.15 Candle Resulting From Upper Wick Example

Now this is where, for price action trading, the book might stop. After all, we can now visualise the buying and the selling simply from the price action of the wick on the candle. But what of course this does **NOT** reveal, is the strength of this price action, and perhaps even more importantly, whether this price action is valid. Is the price action genuine, or is it false, and if it is genuine, what is the strength of any consequent move likely to be. This is why I feel price action trading only tells half the story. It is volume which completes the picture. And in the next chapter we start to consider volume from first principles.

Chapter Four

Volume Price Analysis – First Principles

[On the continual learning in share investing] Wherever learning curves begin in this mercurial business, they never seem to end.
John Neff (1931-)

In this chapter I want to start with some basic tenets for Volume Price Analysis VPA, but first of all, let me set out what I believe are the guiding principles in order to be consistently successful as a trader using this approach. I must stress, these are the principles I use every day, and have been developed over 16 years, since I first started using this technique based on Albert's teaching. Despite the cost and surreal experience, I am eternally grateful to Albert for setting me (and my husband David) on the right trading road. And I hope this book will do the same for you.

Now, these are not rules, but simply guiding principles to help to put the rest of what you are about to learn into context. And just as an aside, for the remainder of the book I will be referring to Volume Price Analysis as VPA – it's quicker and easier for you, and for me!

Principle No 1: Art Not Science

The first principle to understand is that learning to read charts using VPA is an art, it is not a NOT a science. Moreover, it is not a technique that lends itself easily to automation or software. Although it does take a little while to become proficient, you will be rewarded for your effort and time. It can then be applied to any instrument in any market in any time frame. The reason software does not work with VPA, is simply that most of the analysis is subjective. You are comparing and analysing price behaviour against the associated volume, looking for confirmations or anomalies, whilst at the same time, comparing volume to judge its strength or weakness in the context of volume history.

A software program, does not have any subjectivity in its decision making. Hence it can never work.

The other advantage is that once you have learnt this technique, it is effectively free to use for life! The only cost is any data feed you may need for the live volume, and your investment in this book!

Principle No 2 : Patience

This principle took me some time to learn, so I hope that I can save you a huge amount of wasted effort here.

The financial market is like a super tanker. It does not just stop and turn on a dime or sixpence. The market always has momentum and will almost always continue beyond the candle or candle pattern which is signalling a potential reversal or an anomaly. When I first started, I always became very excited whenever I saw a trading signal, and would enter a position immediately, only to see the market continue on for a while before the signal was validated with the market duly changing course.

The reason for this is very simple to understand once you begin to think about what is happening in each price bar, and in terms of the reality of the market. So, let me use an analogy here to help illustrate this point.

The analogy is of a summer shower of rain. The sun is shining, then there is a change, the clouds blow in, and in a few minutes the rain begins to fall, lightly at first, then heavier, before slowing again, and finally stopping. After a few minutes the sun comes out again, and starts drying up the rain.

This analogy gives us a visual picture of what actually happens when a price reversal occurs. Let's take an example of a down trend where the market has been selling off over a period of several down candles. At this point we begin to see signs of potential buying coming into the market. The sellers are being overwhelmed by the buyers. However, they are NOT all overwhelmed immediately within the price action of the candle. Some sellers continue to hang on, believing that the market is going to move lower. The market does move a little lower, but then starts to tick higher and some more sellers are frightened out of the market. The market then drops back lower once again, before recovering, and in doing so shakes out the more obstinate sellers. Finally, the market is ready to move higher having 'mopped up' the last dregs of selling.

As I said before, the market never stops dead and reverses. It always takes time for all the sellers or all the buyers to be 'mopped up', and it is this constant whipsawing which creates the sideways congestion price zones that we often see after an extended trend move, higher or lower. This is where price support and resistance become so powerful, and which are also a key element of VPA.

The moral here is not to act immediately as soon as a signal appears. Any signal is merely a warning sign of an impending change and we do have to be patient. When a shower of rain stops, it doesn't stop suddenly, it gradually peters out, then stops. When you spill something, and have to mop it up with some absorbent paper, the 'first pass' collects most of the spill, but it takes a 'second pass' to complete the job. This is the market. It is a sponge. It takes time to complete the mopping up operation, before it is ready to turn.

I hope I have made the point! Please be patient and wait. The reversal will come, but not instantly from one signal on one candle.

Principle No 3 : It's All Relative

The analysis of volume is all relative and I only came to this conclusion once I stopped obsessing about my volume feed. When I first started I became obsessed with trying to understand every aspect of my volume feed. Where did it come from? How was the data collected? Was it accurate? How did it compare to other feeds? And was there something better that would give me more accurate signals, and so on. This debate continues to this day in the many trading forums with discussions centred around the provenance of the data.

After spending many months trying to compare feeds and back test, I soon realised that there was NOTHING to be gained from worrying about minor imperfections or discrepancies. As I wrote earlier, trading and VPA is an art, not a science. Data feeds will vary from broker to broker and platform to platform thereby creating slightly different candle patterns. If you compare a chart from one broker with another of the same instrument and time frame, then the chances are you will have two different candlesticks. And the reason for this is very straightforward. It is because the close of the candle will depend on a variety of things, not least the clock speed on your computer, where you are in the world, and at what time during the session the closing price is triggered. They all vary.

Data feeds are complex in how they calculate and present the data to you on the screen. They all come from different sources, and are managed in different ways. Even those from the cash markets will vary, spot forex feeds even more so. But, it's really not a big issue for one simple reason.

Volume is all relative, so it makes no difference as long as you are using the same feed all the time. This is what months of work proved to me.

This is why I lose patience with traders who say that tick data as a proxy for volume is only 90% accurate. So what? For all I care, it can be 70% accurate or 80% accurate. I am not interested in the 'accuracy'. All I am interested in is consistency. As long as the feed is consistent, then that's fine, because I am comparing my volume bar on my feed with previous volume bars, *on my feed* ! I am not comparing it with someone else's feed. I admit it did take time before it dawned on me that this common sense approach was perfectly valid.

Therefore, please don't waste as much time as I did. Volume is all relative because we are constantly comparing one volume bar with another, and judging whether this is high, low or average with what has gone before. If the data is imperfect, then it makes no difference whatsoever, as I am comparing imperfect data with imperfect data.

The same argument applies to tick data in the spot forex market. I do accept it is imperfect again, but we are only comparing one bar with another, and provided it is displaying activity, that's fine. It's an imperfect world and one we have to live and trade in. The free tick volume feed on a simple MT4 platform works perfectly – trust me. I've used it for years and make money every day using it. Furthermore it is provided, for free, by the broker.

Principle No 4 : Practise Makes Perfect

It takes time to become proficient in any skill, but once learnt is never forgotten. The trading techniques you will learn in this book work in all time frames, and are equally valid, whether you are a speculator or investor. As an investor you may be looking for a buy and hold over months, so will be considering the longer term charts of days and weeks, much like Richard Ney for example. Alternatively, you may be an intra day scalping trader using VPA on tick charts or fast time charts. So, take your time and don't be impatient. It is worth the time and effort you invest, and after a few weeks or months you will be surprised at how quickly you can suddenly start to interpret and forecast every twist and turn in the market.

Principle No 5 : Technical Analysis

VPA is only part of the story. We always use a variety of other techniques to confirm the picture and provide additional validation. The most important of these are support and resistance, for the reasons that I outlined in Principle No 2. This is where the market is pausing and executing its 'mopping up' operations, before reversing. Alternatively, it may simply be a pause point in a longer term trend, which will then be validated by our volume analysis. A breakout from one of these regions of consolidation, coupled with volume, is always a strong signal.

Trends are equally important, as are price pattern analysis, all part of the art form which is technical analysis.

Principle No 6 : Validation or Anomaly

In using VPA as our analytical approach, we are only ever looking for two things.

Whether the price has been validated by the volume, or whether there is an anomaly with the price. If the price is validated then that confirms a continuation of the price behaviour. By contrast if there is an anomaly, then this is sending a signal of a potential change. These are the only things we are constantly searching for in VPA.

Validation or anomaly. Nothing else. And here are some examples of validation based on single bars, before moving onto multiple bars and actual chart examples.

Examples Of Validation

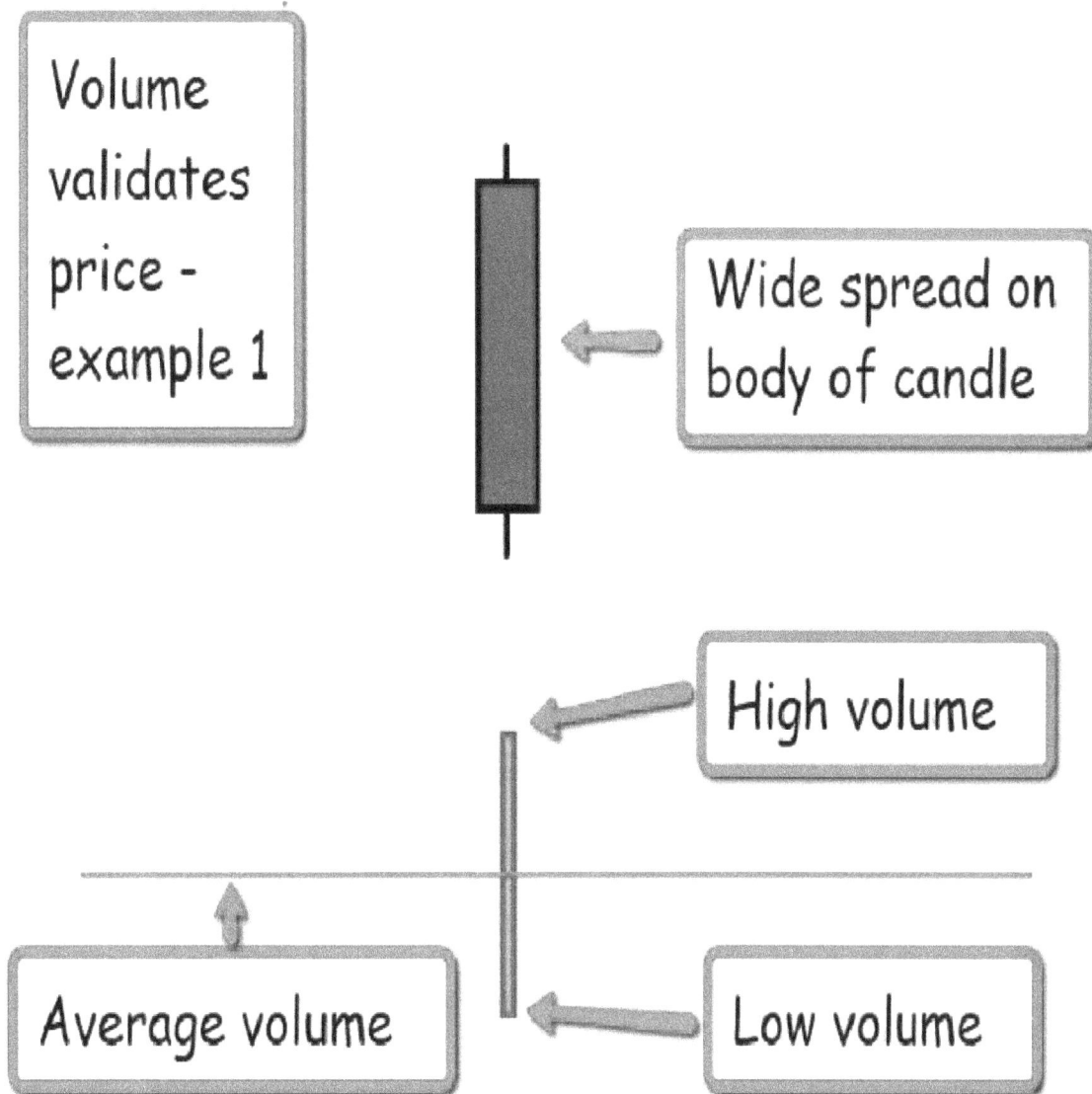

Fig 4.10 Wide Spread Candle, High Volume

In the example in Fig 4.10 of a wide spread up candle with small wicks to top and bottom, the associated volume is well above average, so the volume is validating the price action.

In this case we have a market which is bullish, and has risen strongly in the trading session closing just below the high of the session. If this is a valid move then we would expect to see the effort required to push the market higher, reflected in the volume.

Remember, this is also Wyckoff's third law of effort vs. result. It takes effort for the market to rise and also takes effort for the market to fall, so if there has been a large change in price in the session, then we expect to see this validated by a well above average volume bar. Which we have. Therefore, in this case the volume validates the price. And from this we can assume two things. First, that the price move is genuine, and has not been manipulated by the market makers, and second, that for the time being, the market is bullish, and until we see an anomaly signalled, then we can continue to maintain any long position that we may have in the market.

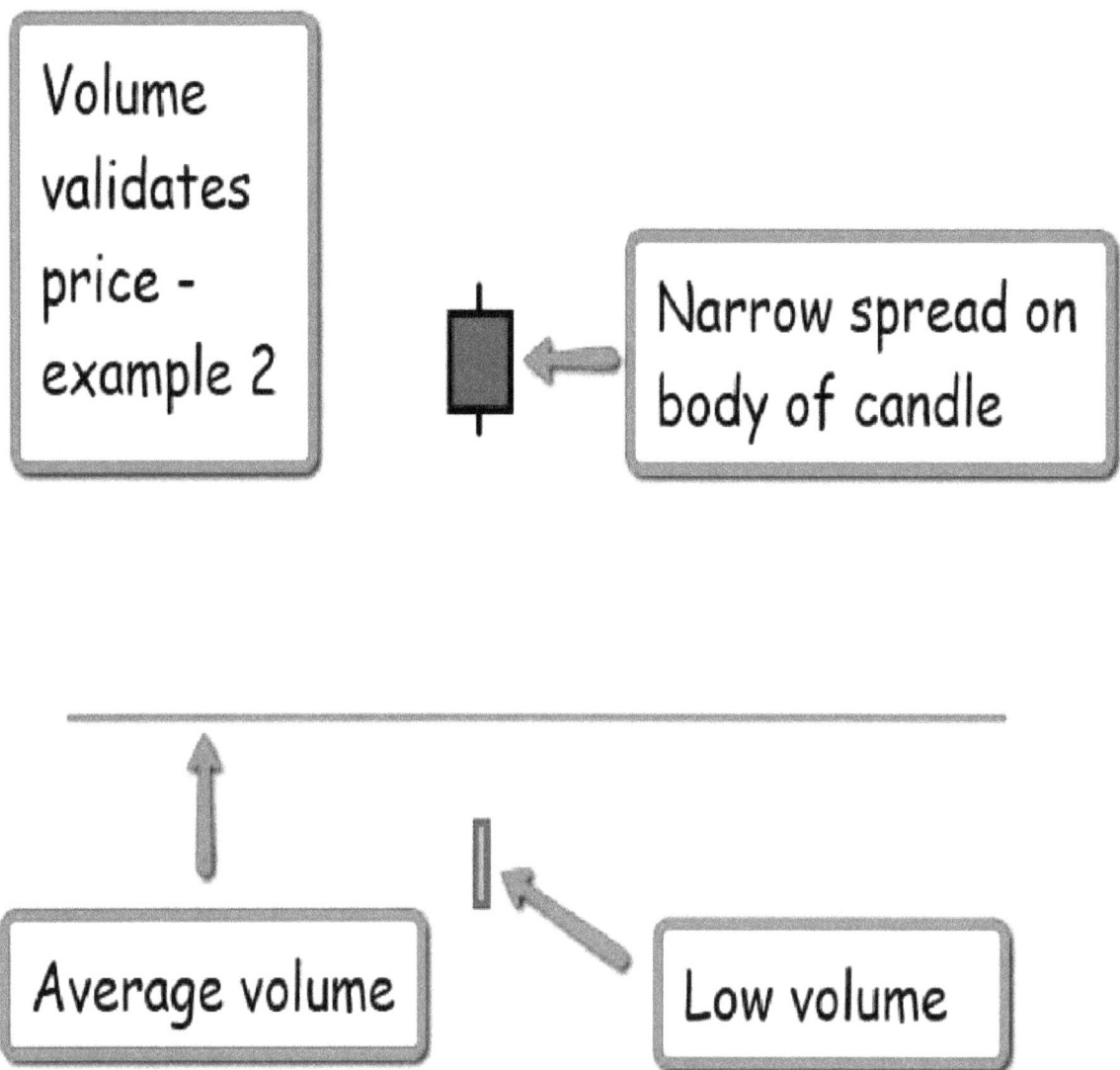

Volume validates price - example 2

Narrow spread on body of candle

Average volume

Low volume

Fig 4.11 Narrow Spread Candle, Low Volume

Fig 4.11 is an example of a narrow spread candle accompanied by low volume. In this case the price has risen, but only marginally higher, and the spread of the candle is therefore very narrow. The wicks to the top and bottom are once again small. The associated volume is well below average, and again the question that we have to ask ourselves is simple. Is the volume validating the price action, and the answer once again is yes. And the reason is again because of effort and result. In this case the market has only risen in price by a small amount, and therefore we would expect to see this reflected in the volume, which should also be low. After all, if effort and result validate one another, the effort required to move the market a few points higher (the result), should only warrant a small amount of effort (the volume). So once again, we have a true picture with the volume validating the price. Now let's look at these two examples again, but this time as anomalies.

Examples Of Anomalies

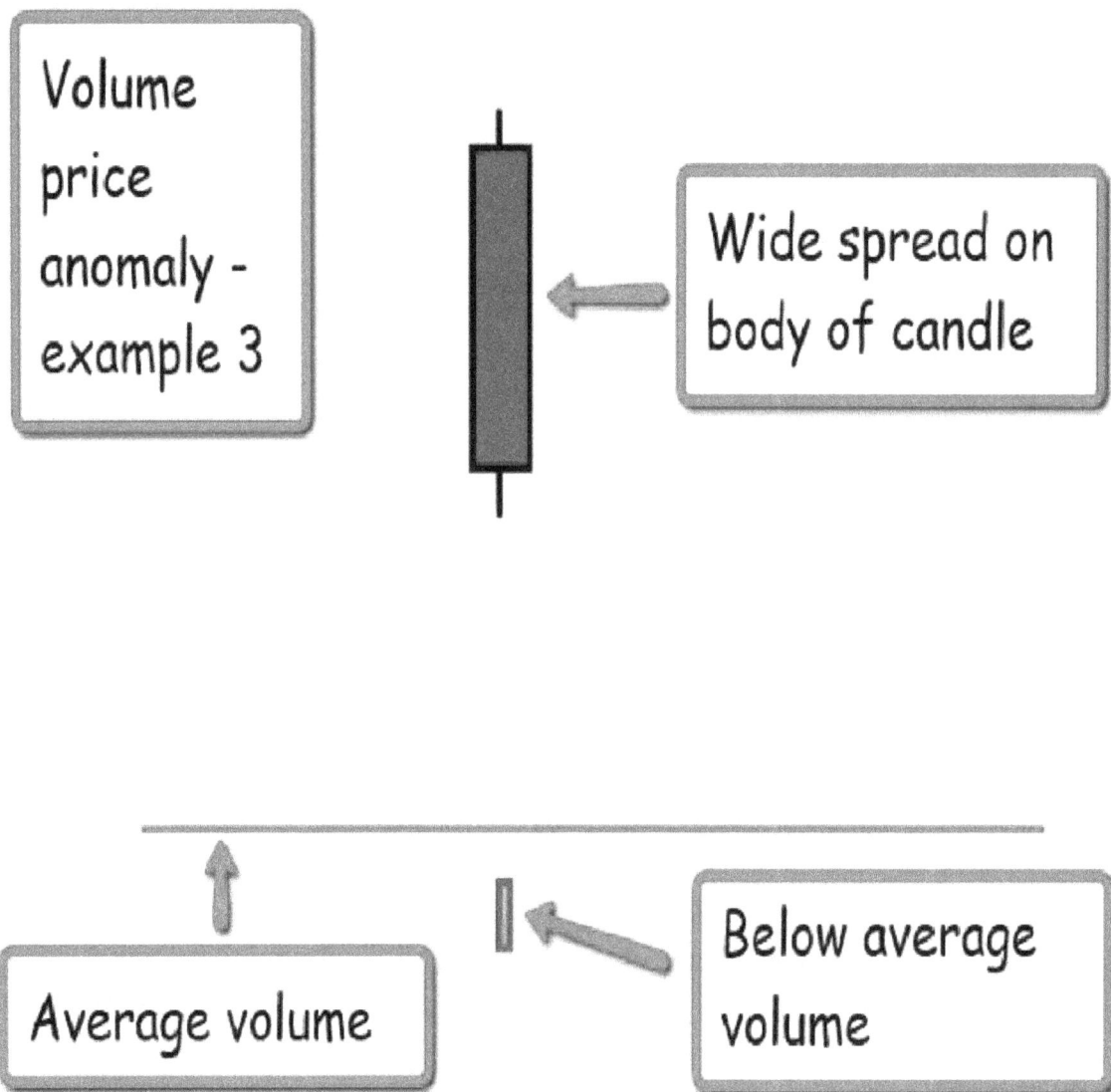

Fig 4.12 Wide Spread Candle, Low Volume

In Fig 4.12 we have our first anomaly which can be explained as follows. It is clear we have a wide spread up candle, and if we follow Wyckoff's third rule then this result, should be matched by an equal amount of effort. What we have instead is a big result, from little effort. This is an anomaly. After all for a wide spread up candle, we would expect to see a high volume bar, but here we have a low volume bar. Immediately the alarm bells start ringing, since something is not right here.

One question to ask is why do we have low volume when we should expect to see high volume. Is this a trap up move by the markets, or the market makers? Quite possibly, and this is where you can begin to see the power of such simple analysis. In one price bar, we can immediately see that something is wrong. There is an anomaly, because if this were a genuine move higher, then the buyers would be supporting the move higher with a high volume bar. Instead there is a low volume bar.

If we were in a long position in the market and this appeared, we would immediately start to question what is happening. For example, why has this anomaly appeared? Is it an early warning of a possible trap? This is a pattern which often occurs at the start of trading in equity markets. What is happening here is that the market makers are trying to 'feel out' the sentiment in the market. The above could be from a one minute chart for example. The market opens, then the price is pushed higher to test interest in the market from the buyers. If there is little or no buying interest, as here, then the price will be marked back down, with further price testing.

Remember from earlier in the book, that the futures index markets will have already been trading overnight on Globex, giving the market makers a clear idea of bullish or bearish sentiment. All that is needed is to test out the price level at which to pitch the price for the opening few minutes. Not only is this done for the main index, but also for each individual stock. It is extraordinary how easy this is to see, and is instantly visible with volume.

This is why I cannot understand the attraction of price action trading. Without volume a PAT trader would have no idea. All they would see is a wide spread up candle and assume the market was bullish.

This is very easy to prove and all we need to do is to watch a couple of charts from the opening bell. Choose the main index, and a couple of stocks. The anomaly will appear time and time again. The market makers are testing the levels of buying and selling interest, before setting the tone for the session, with an eye on any news releases due in the morning, which can always be used to further manipulate the markets, and never allowing 'a serious crisis go to waste' (Rahm Emanuel). After all, if they were buying into the market, then this would be reflected in a high volume bar.

The volume bar is signalling that the market is NOT joining in this price action, and there is a reason. In this case it's the market makers in equities testing the levels of buying and selling, and therefore not committing into the move, until they are sure buyers will come into the market at this price level.

The same scenario could equally apply in the forex market.

A fundamental item of news is released, and the market makers see an opportunity to take stops out of the market. The price jumps on the news, but the associated volume is low. Now let's look at another example of an anomaly.

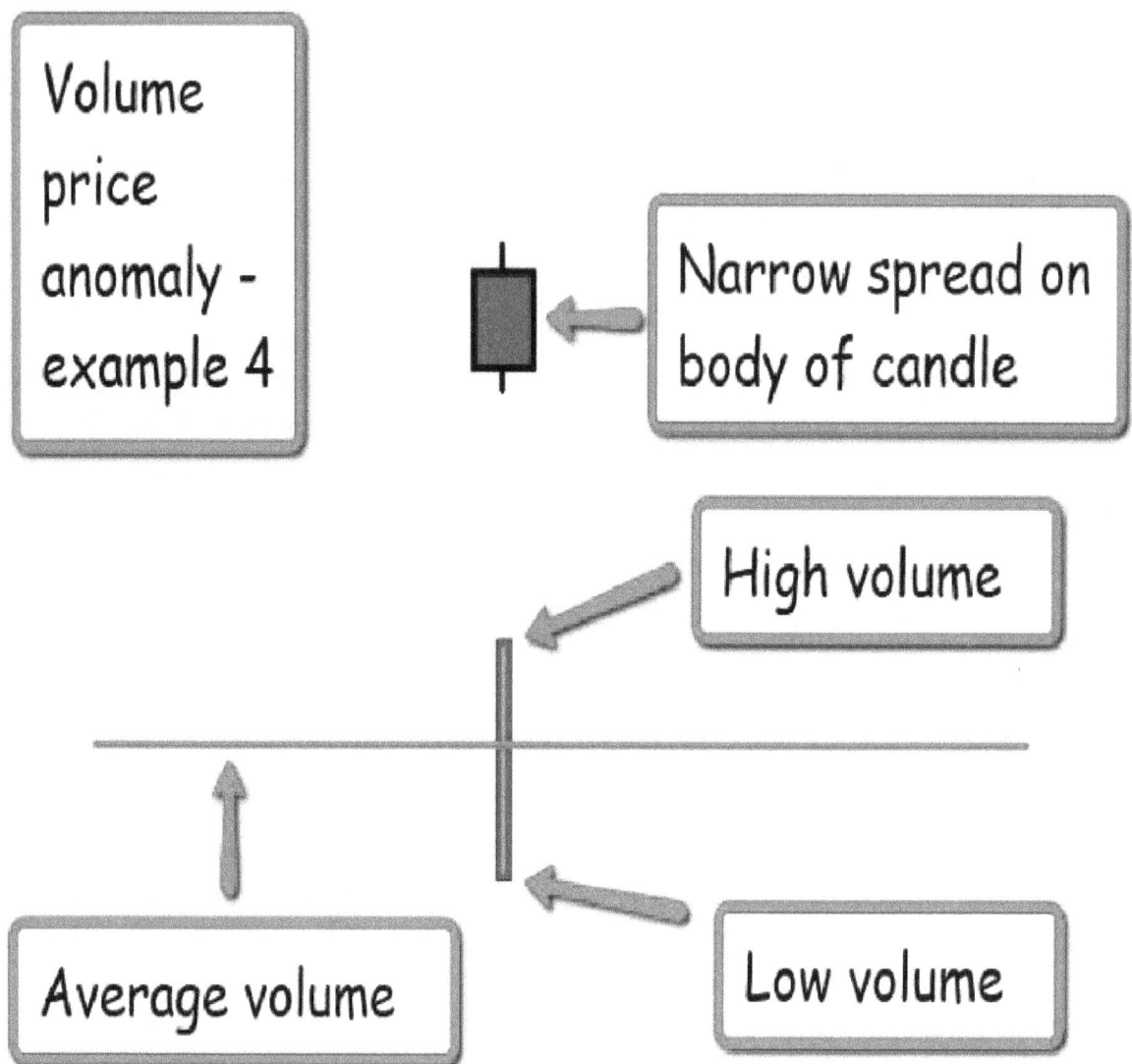

Fig 4.13 Narrow Spread Candle, Low Volume

Once again this is a clear signal of a potential trap. The move higher is NOT a genuine move but a fake move, designed to suck traders into weak positions, and also take out stops, before reversing sharply and moving in the opposite direction. This is why VPA is so powerful and once you have learnt this skill will wonder why you never discovered it before. Volume and price together reveal the truth behind market behaviour in all its glory.

In the example shown in Fig 4.13 we can see a narrow spread candle with high volume which, once again, is another anomaly.

As we saw earlier in Fig 4.11, a small increase in the price (result), should only require a small increase in volume (effort), but this is not the case here.

The small price increase has been generated by a huge amount of volume, so clearly something is wrong. Generally, we would expect to see this height of volume bar, accompany a wide spread candle with the volume driving the price higher. But, in this case the high volume has only resulted in a very small rise in the price.

There is only one conclusion we can draw. The market is starting to look weak, and is typical of a candle pattern that starts to develop at the top of a bullish trend, or the bottom of a bearish trend.

For example in an established bullish trend the market opens, and starts to rise a little, but the buyers (longs) are now starting to take their profits, as they have been in this trend for while and feel that this is the right time to close out. However, as these positions are closed out, more eager buyers come in, (as most traders and investors always buy at the top of markets), but the price never rises as the longs continue to liquidate and take their profits, before more buyers come in, and the cycle repeats throughout the session.

What is actually happening is that the market has reached a price at which further effort does not result in higher prices, as each wave of new buyers is met with longs selling out at this level and taking their profits, 'off the table'. So there is no sustained move higher in price.

In other words, what this combination of price and volume is revealing is weakness in the market. If we were to imagine a profile of the volume bar in terms of selling and buying volumes, the buyers would just outweigh the sellers, reflecting the narrow price spread.

This is akin to driving up an icy hill which is gradually increasing in steepness. At the start we can still move higher, but gradually as we try to move up the hill we have to increase the power, eventually getting to a stage where we are on full power and standing still, as the wheels spin on the ice. Perhaps not a perfect analogy, but one which I hope makes the point and cements this idea in place. In our car analogy, we are now stationary, halfway up the hill, engine on full power, wheels spinning and going nowhere! What happens next is we start sliding backwards, gaining momentum as we go and mirrors what happened in the price action described. The market reached a point where no matter how much more effort is applied, is now resistant to higher prices, and the sellers are knocking back the buying.

The reverse, also happens after a trend run lower. In this case, it is the selling which is absorbed by the buying, and once again signals a potential reversal point as the market runs out of steam. After all, if the selling had followed through, then we would have seen a wide spread down candle, and not a narrow spread candle.

Now this candle and volume relationship also raises another much deeper question, and here we go back to the insiders, and the market makers.

If we return to our bullish example again, with the narrow spread candle and the high volume, the question we might reasonably ask, is 'who is actually selling here?' Is it the investors and speculators, exiting the market after the trend run higher, or is it another group perhaps? Maybe it is the insiders and the market makers ? Who is it more likely to be? After all, we know that most investors and traders tend to buy at the top when in fact they should be selling, and sell at the bottom when they should be buying. Something which the specialists and market makers are well aware of in the psychology and make up of most traders and investors.

They also know this group is easy to frighten out of the market. Generally, they get in far too late after a bullish trend has been in place for some time, and only jump in when they feel it is safe, having watched the market move higher and higher, regretting the decision not to enter much earlier. As the late Christopher Browne once said ‘*The time to buy stocks is when they are on sale, and not when they are high priced because everyone wants to own them.* This sentiment applies to any instrument or market. Buying when ‘*on sale’* is always at the bottom of a trend, and not at a top!

'Missing an opportunity' is a classic trader (and investor) fear. The trader waits and waits before finally jumping in, just at the point when the market is turning and they should be thinking of getting out. This is what the insiders, specialists, market makers and big operators bank on, trader fear. Remember, they see both sides of the market from their unique and privileged positions.

Back to the question! The specialists have driven prices higher, but the market is now struggling at this level. They are selling to the market to clear their warehouse, but the buyers are not there in sufficient numbers to move the price higher, as it is constantly knocked back by longer term traders, selling out and taking their profits off the table. The specialists continue selling into the buying, but the volume of buyers is too small, in contrast to the number of sellers, to move the price significantly higher, as each attempt to push the market higher is hit with more selling, which in turn is replenished with more buyers.

What is actually taking place here is a battle. The first sign of a real struggle, with the specialists struggling to clear their warehouse before moving the market lower, and fast. The market is not receptive to higher prices, but the specialists cannot move the market lower until they are ready, and so the battle continues. I explain this in much greater detail later in the book. They maintain the price at the current level attracting more buyers in, who are hoping to jump into the trend and take some easy profits, but the sellers keep selling, preventing any real rise in price.

This is one of the many classic relationships to look for on your charts. As I have said many times before, this could be on a fast tick chart, or a slow time chart. The signal is the same. It is an early warning that the market is weak and struggling at this level, and therefore you should either be taking any profit off the table, if you have an existing position, or, preparing to take a position on any reversal in trend.

Moreover, it is important to remember that just as a candle can have a different significance, depending on where it appears in the trend, the same is true with VPA.

When an anomaly occurs, and we will start looking at actual chart examples, the first point of reference is always where we are in the trend, which will also depend on the time frame. However, this is one of the many beauties of this type of trading analysis. For example, on a 5 minute chart, a trend might be considered as one lasting an hour, or perhaps even two hours. Whereas on a daily chart, a trend could last for weeks or even months. Therefore, when we talk about a trend, it is important to understand the context of a trend. A trend is always relative to the time frame we are are trading. Some traders only consider a trend to be valid if it is over days, weeks and months, the super cycles if you like.

However, I don't subscribe to this view. To me a trend on a 1 minute or a 5 minute chart is just as valid. It is a price trend, which may be a short term pull back in a longer term trend, or it may be confirming the longer term trend. It makes no difference. All that matters is that the trend, is a trend in price. The price has moved the same way for some period of time, in that time frame.

Just remember. VPA applied to a 5 minute chart will yield just as many profitable and low risk trades as on a longer term daily or weekly chart. The analysis is the same.

The point I am making here is this – whenever we see an anomaly which sets the alarm bell ringing, the first step is to establish were we are in any trend. In other words, we get our bearings first. For example, are we at a possible bottom, where perhaps the market has been selling off for some time, but is now looking at a major reversal?

Or perhaps we are half way up or down a trend, and we are merely observing a minor pull back or reversal in the longer term trend. Deciding where we are in the trend, is where we bring in some of our other analytical tools which then help to complement VPA and gives us the 'triangulation' we need.

In judging where we are in the trend, and potential reversal points, we will always be looking at support and resistance, candle patterns, individual candles, and trend lines. All of this will help to give us our 'bearings' and help to identify where we are in the price action on the chart. A perspective if you like, and a framework against which to judge the significance of our analysis of volume and price.

Multiple Candle Examples

I now want to explain how we use VPA with multiple candles and volume, as opposed to single candles. The approach is identical as we are only ever looking for two things. Is the volume confirming the price action, or is this an anomaly?

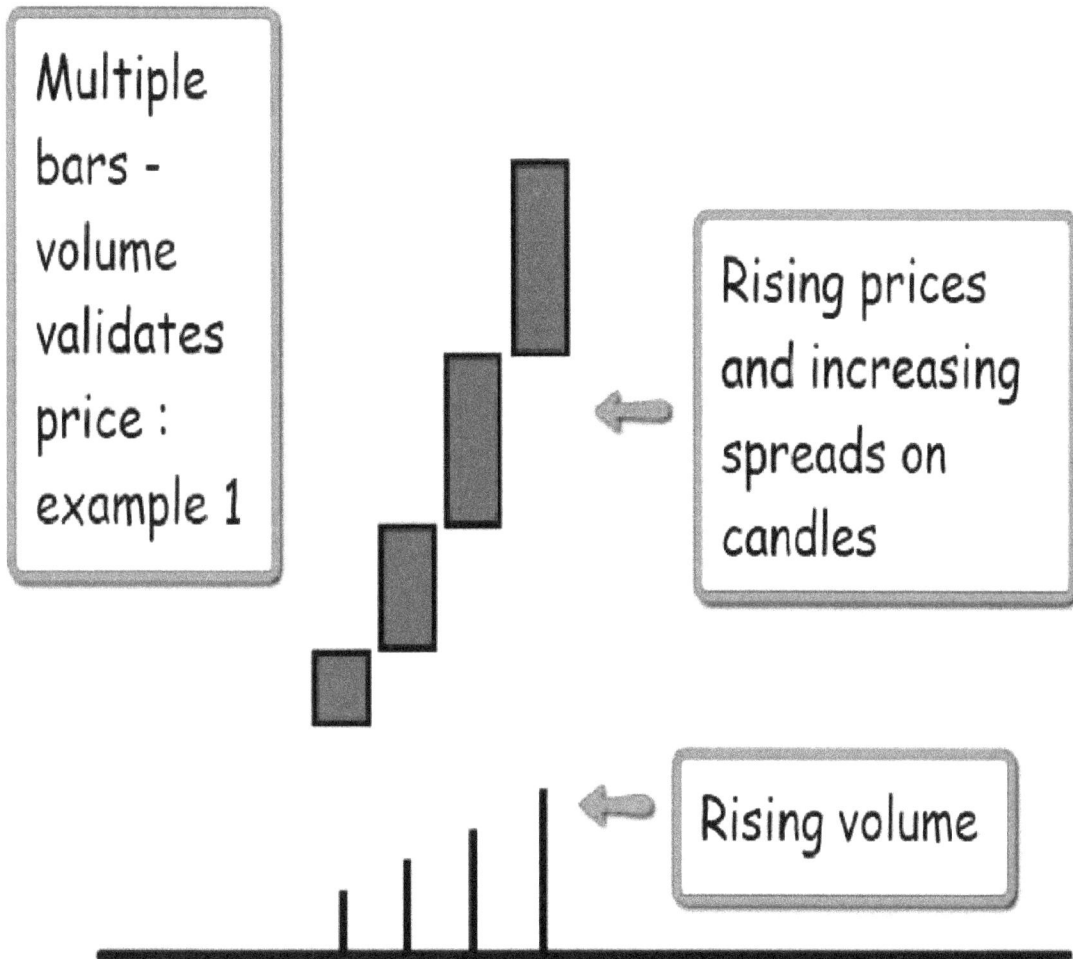

Fig 4.14 Multiple Bar Validation In Up Trend

In the first example in Fig 4.14 we have a bullish trend developing in a rising market, and what is obvious is that rising prices are accompanied by rising volume.

This is exactly what we would expect to see and furthermore having multiple volume bars also gives us a benchmark history, against which to judge future volume bars.

If we were watching this price action live, this is what we would see happening on our chart. The first candle forms, a narrow spread up candle with low volume, which is fine. The volume validates the price, no anomaly here. The second candle then begins to form, and on close inspection we note that the spread of this is wider than the first, and based on Wyckoff's rule, we expect to see greater volume that on the first bar, which is indeed the case. So the up trend is valid, the volume has validated the price on both candles.

By the time the third candle starts to form, and closes with a spread which is wider than both the first and the second, we should expect a volume bar which reflects Wyckoff's third law of effort vs result. The third law which states we have increased the result (price spread is wider than before) which should be matched by increased effort (volume should be higher than on the previous candle) – and so it is. Therefore, once again, the price action on the candle has been validated by the volume. But, in addition to that simple observation, the three candles themselves are now validating the price trend.

In other words, the price over the three bars has moved higher, developed into a trend, and the volume is rising and NOW validating the trend itself. After all, just as effort vs result applies to one candle, it also applies to a 'trend' which in this case consists of three candles. Therefore, if the price is moving higher in the trend, then according to Wyckoff's third law, we should expect to see rising volume as well. And this is the case.

The point is this. Effort vs result, applies not only to the individual candles we looked at earlier, but also to the trends which start to build once we put the candles together. In other words we have two levels of validation (or anomaly).

The first level is based on the price/volume relationship on the candle itself. The second level is based on the collective price/volume relationship of a group of candles, which then start to define the trend. It is in the latter where Wyckoff's second law of 'cause and effect' can be applied. Here the extent of the effect (price changes in trend) will be related to the size of the cause (the volume and period over which it is applied - the time element).

In this simple example, we have a very neat picture. The price action on each candle has been validated with the associated volume, and the overall price action has been validated by the overall volume action. This can all be summed as rising prices = rising volume. If the market is rising, and we see rising volume associated with the move, then this is a valid move higher, supported by market sentiment and the specialists. In other words, the specialists and insiders are joining in the move, and we see this reflected in the volume.

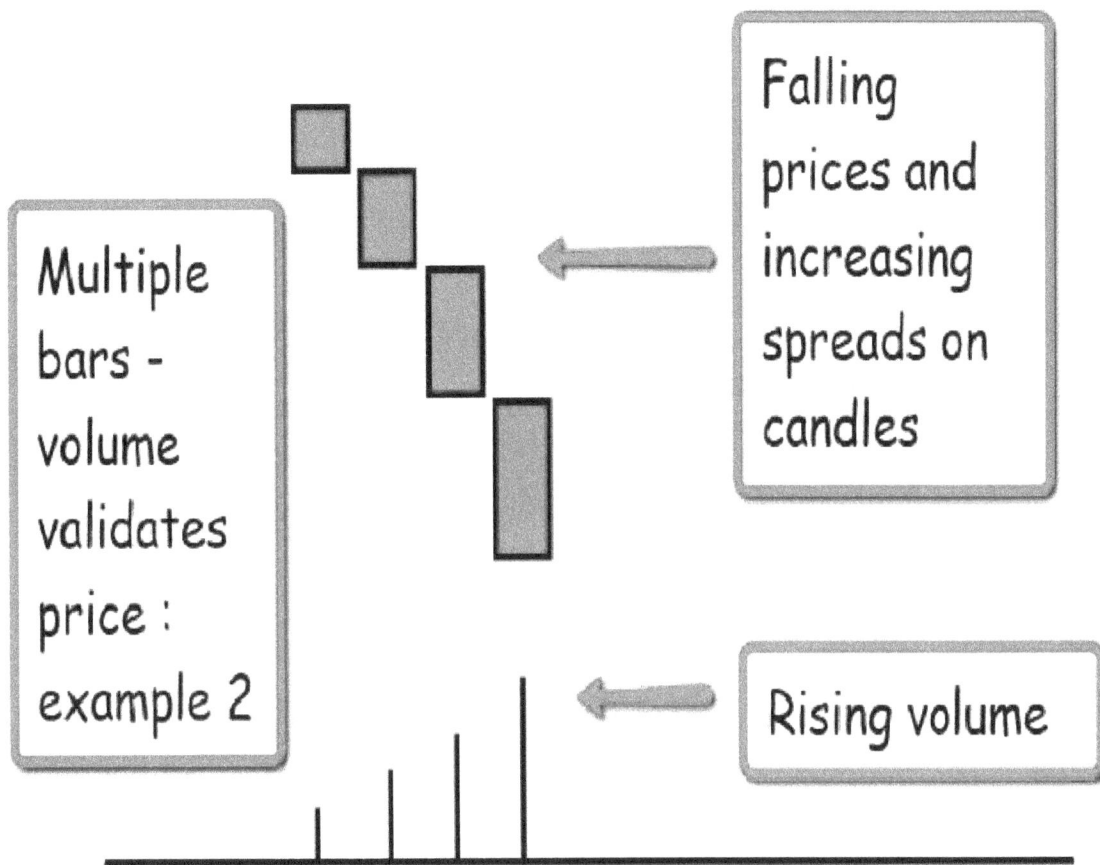

Fig 4.15 Multiple Bar Validation In Down Trend

I now want to examine the opposite, and look at an example where we have a market which is falling as shown in Fig 4.15.

In this case the market is moving lower, and perhaps this is where some of the confusion starts for new VPA students. As humans, we are all familiar with gravity and the concept that it takes effort for something to move higher. The rocket into space, a ball thrown into the air, all require effort to overcome the force of gravity. As traders, these examples of gravity are fine in principle when the market is moving higher, as in our first example. Where these examples using gravity fail, is when we look at markets which are falling, because here too we need rising effort (volume) for the market to fall.

The market requires effort to both rise AND fall, and it is easier to think of in these terms.

If the specialists are joining in the move, whether higher or lower, then this will be reflected in the volume bars. If they are joining a move higher, then the volume will be rising, and **equally** if they are joining a move lower, then the volume bars will **ALSO** be rising in the same way.

This is Wyckoff's third rule again – effort vs result, and whether the price action is higher or lower, then this rule applies.

Looking at the four candles in the example in Fig 4.15, the first down candle opens and closes with a narrow spread. The associated volume is small, and therefore validates the price action. The next bar opens and closes with a wider spread, but with higher volume than on the previous candle, so once again the price action is valid.

The third candle opens and closes with higher volume, as we expect, and finally we come to our last candle which is wider still, but the associated volume is also higher than all the previous candles. Once again, not only has volume validated each individual candle, it has also validated the group of four candles as a whole.

Again we have two levels of validation. First, we check the individual candle and the associated volume for validation or anomaly. Second, we check to see a validation or anomaly in the trend itself.

One of the questions that hasn't been answered in either of the above examples is this – is the volume buying or selling? And, this is the next question we ALWAYS ask ourselves as the market moves along.

In the first example in Fig 4.14, we had a market that was rising nicely with the volume also rising to support the price action, so the volume here must all be buying volume, after all, if there were any selling volume, then this would be reflected somewhere in the price action.

We know this because there are no wicks on the candles, as the price moves steadily higher, with the volume rising to support the price action and validating the price. It can only be buying volume and a genuine move. Therefore, we can happily join in, knowing that this is a genuine move in the market. We join the insiders and buy!

But perhaps much more importantly – it is also a low risk trading opportunity. We can enter the market with confidence. We have completed our own analysis, based on volume and price. No indicators, no EAs, just price and volume analysis. It's simple, powerful and effective, and reveals the true activity within the market. Market sentiment is revealed, market tricks are revealed and the extent of market moves are also revealed.

Remember, there are only two risks in trading. The financial risk on the trade itself. This is easy to quantify and manage using simple money management rules, such as the 1% rule. The second risk is far more difficult to quantify, and this is the risk on the trade itself. This is what VPA is all about. It allows you to quantify the risk on the trade using this analytical technique, and when combined with all the other techniques you will learn in this book, is immensely powerful, and even more so when combined with analysis in multiple time frames.

As a result, you will become much more confident as a trader. Your trading decisions will be based on your own analysis, using common sense and logic, based on two leading indicators, namely price and volume.

To return to our second example in Fig 4.15 and the questions we ask ourselves here. Is the volume buying or selling, and should we join the move?

Here we have a market which is moving firmly lower, with the volume validating the candles and the overall price action. We have no wicks to any candles, and the market is falling with rising volume. Therefore, this must be a valid move and all the volume must be selling volume, as the specialists are joining in the move and selling. Market sentiment is firmly bearish.

Again, another low risk opportunity to enter the market, based on common sense, logic and an understanding of the price and volume relationship.

I now want to round off this chapter on the first principles of VPA by considering multiple candles with an anomaly. In the examples that follow, there is more than one anomaly, as we are considering the concept of VPA on two levels. The first level is that applied to each candle, the second level is to the overall trend.

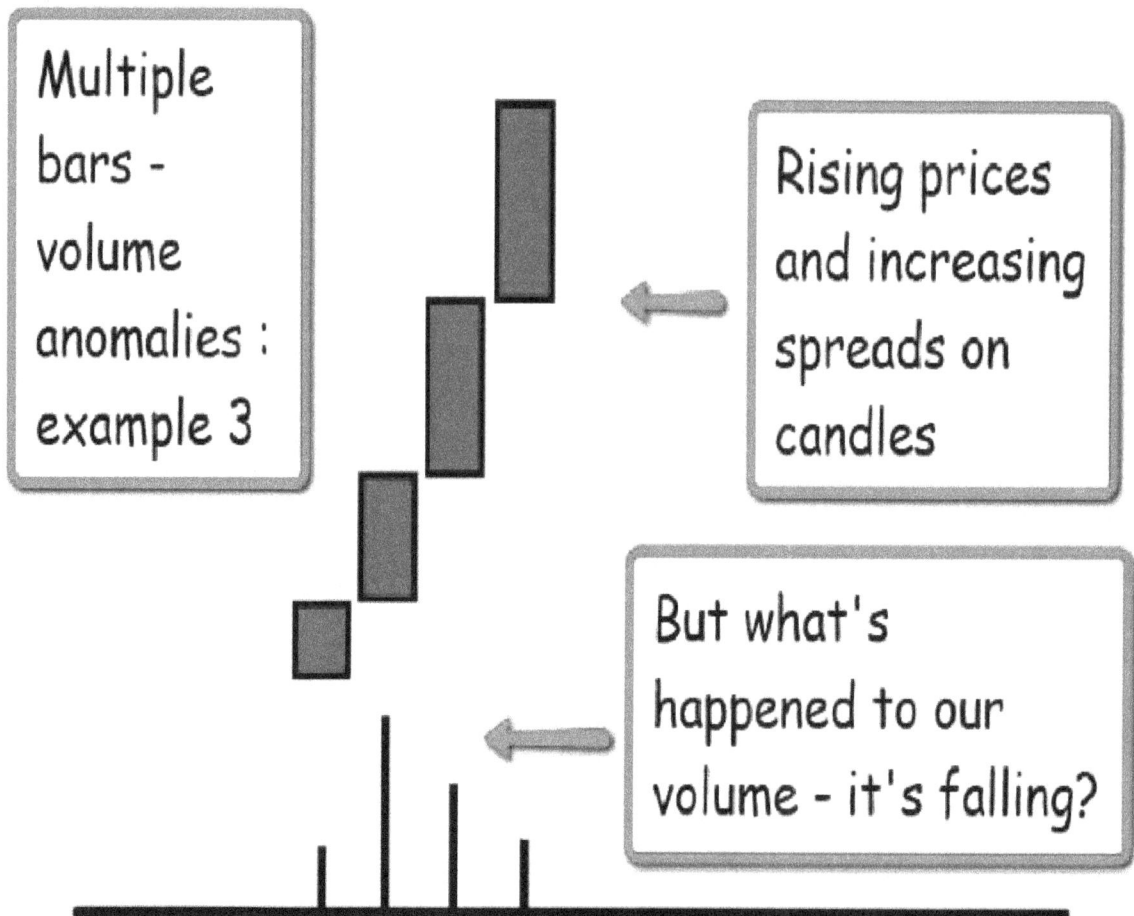

Fig 4.16 Multiple Bar Anomalies In An Uptrend

Fig 4.16 is the first example, and here we have what appears to be a bullish trend, with the first narrow spread up candle accompanied by relatively low volume. This is fine as the volume is validating the price and is in agreement. The second candle then forms and on the close we have a slightly wider spread candle than the first, but with high volume.

From experience and looking back at previous bars, this appears to be an anomaly. With high volume we would expect to see a wide spread candle. Instead, we only have a candle which is marginally wider in price spread than the previous candle, so something is wrong here. An alarm bell is now ringing!

Remember Wyckoff's third law, effort vs result? Here the effort (the volume) has not resulted in the correct result (the price), so we have an anomaly on one candle, which could be an early warning signal, and the alarm bells should now be starting to ring!

The third candle then forms, and closes as a wide spread up candle, but with volume that is lower than on the previous candle. Given the spread of the bar, it should be higher, not lower. Another warning signal.

The fourth candle then forms and closes as a very wide price spread up, but the volume is even lower! We now have several anomalies here, on candles two three and four.

Candle 2 Anomaly

This is an anomaly. We have a modest spread in price, but high volume. The market should have risen much further given the effort contained in the volume bar. This is signalling potential weakness, after all the close of the bar should have been much higher given the effort. The market makers are selling out at this level! It is the first sign of a move by the insiders.

Candle 3 Two Anomalies!

This is two anomalies in one. The price spread is wider than the previous candle, but the volume is lower. The buying pressure is draining away. Second, we have a market that is rising, but the volume has fallen on this candle. Rising markets should be associated with rising volume, NOT falling volume. This is also signalling clearly that the previous volume is also an anomaly, (if any further evidence were required).

Candle 4 Two Anomalies Again!

Again, we have two anomalies in one, and is adding further confirmation that the volume and price on this trend are no longer in agreement. Here we have a wide spread up candle and even lower volume than on previous candles in the trend. Following the effort vs result rule, we would expect to see significantly higher volume, but instead we have low volume.

Second, the falling volume is confirming that we have an anomaly on the trend, as we expect to see rising volume with a rising trend, whereas here we have falling volumes on a rising trend. The alarm bells would be ringing loud and clear now.

What are the conclusions we can draw from these four candles? The problems start with candle two. Here we have effort, but not an equivalent result in terms of the associated price action. This is therefore the first sign of possible weakness. The market is what is known as 'over bought'. The market makers and specialists are starting to struggle here. The sellers are moving into the market sensing an opportunity to short the market. This creates the resistance to higher prices at this level, which is then confirmed on the third and fourth candles, where volume is falling away.

The specialists and market makers have seen this weakness, and are selling out themselves at this level, preparing for a move lower, but continue to mark prices higher, to give the appearance of a market that is still bullish. It is not. This may only be a temporary pause, and not a major change in trend, but nevertheless, it is a warning of potential weakness in the market.

The high volume is as a result of an increasing number of sellers closing out their positions, and taking their profits, whilst the remaining buyers do not have sufficient momentum to take the market higher. The specialists and market makers are also selling out at this level adding to the volumes, as they have seen the weakness in the market. This is the reason that volumes fall on the next two candles, as they continue to mark the market higher, but are no longer involved in the move themselves. They have withdrawn and are trapping traders into weak positions.

The initial weakness appeared on candle two, which was then FURTHER confirmed by candles three and four. This is often the sequence of events that unfolds.

Initially we see an anomaly appear using the single candle analysis. We then wait for subsequent candles to appear, and analyse them against the initial anomaly. In this case, the anomaly was confirmed, with prices continuing to rise on falling volumes.

Now we have a market which is apparently weak, and confirmed as such. The next step is to move to the final level in our analysis which is to consider the analysis in the broader context of the chart. This will determine whether what we are seeing is a minor pull back, or the pre-cursor to a change in trend.

This is where Wyckoff's second rule comes into effect, the law of cause and effect. If this is simply a minor pull back or reversal, then the cause will be small, and the effect will be small.

In point of fact, the anomaly we have seen here, might be enough to result in minor short term weakness, a pull back due to one weak candle. The cause is weak, so the effect is weak. Before expanding further on this latter in the book, let us look at one more example of multiple bar anomalies.

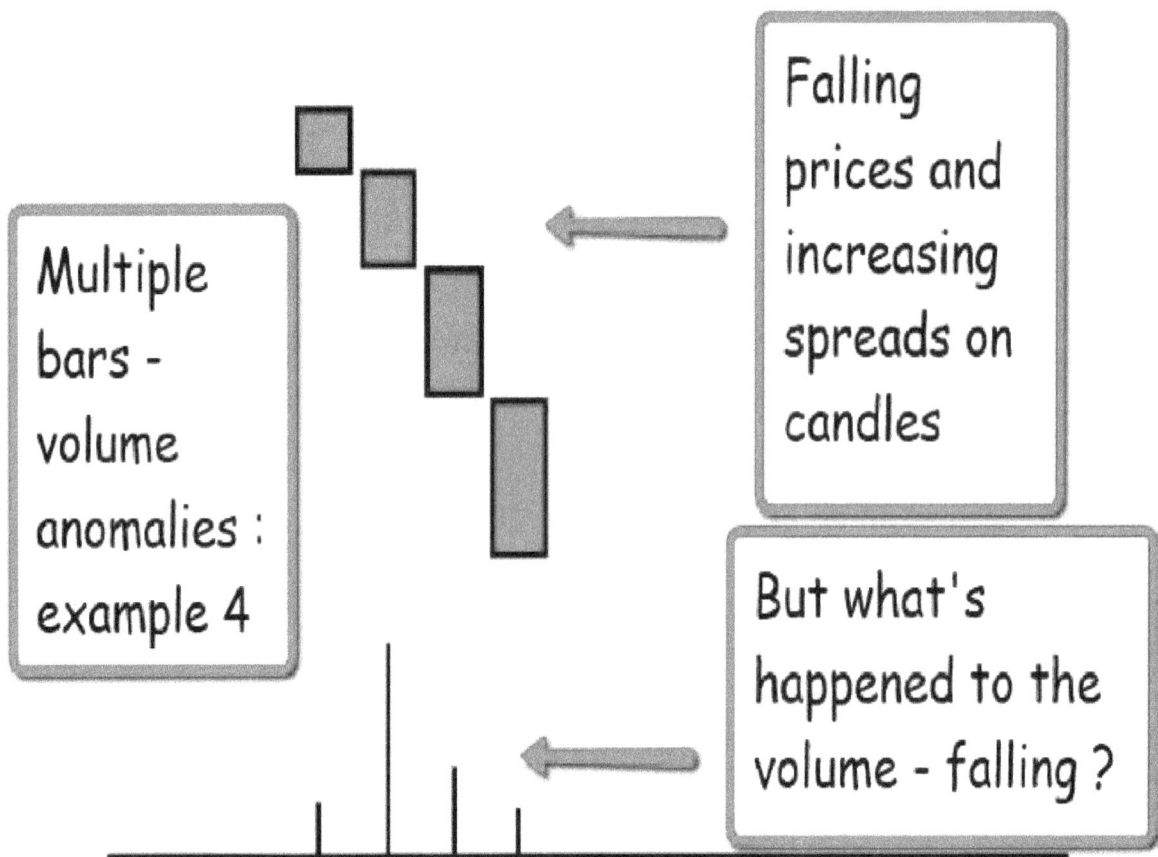

Fig 4.17 Multiple Bar Anomalies In A Downtrend

In the example in Fig 4.17 we have what is known as a price waterfall, where the market sells off sharply.

The first candle opens and closes, and is associated with low or relatively low volume, which is as we expect. We then start to see the anomalies starting with the second price bar in the waterfall.

Candle 2 Anomaly

The candle has closed with a marginally wider spread than the previous bar, but the volume is high or very high. What this is signalling is that the market is clearly resistant to any move lower. After all, it this was NOT the case, then the price spread would he been much wider, to reflect the high volume.

But, this is not the case, and is therefore an anomaly. And, just as in the previous example, the alarm bells are now ringing. What is happening here is that bearish sentiment is draining away with the sellers now being met with buyers at this level. The market makers and specialists have seen the change in sentiment with the buyers coming in, and are moving in themselves, buying the market at this price point.

Candle 3 Two Anomalies

Now we have two anomalies, similar to the example in Fig 4.16. First, we have a wide spread candle, but with only average to low volume. Second, the volume is lower than on the previous bar – in a falling market we expect to see rising volume, NOT falling volume. With falling volume the selling pressure is draining away, something that was signalled in the previous bar.

Candle 4 Two Anomalies Again!

Once again we have two anomalies here. First, we have a wide spread down candle, accompanied by low volume. The volume should be high, not low. Second, we now have falling volume over three candles in a market that is falling. Again, this is an anomaly as we should expect to see rising volume in a falling market.

As with the example in Fig 4.16, the first candle too in Fig 4.17 closes, and the volume validates the price. All is well! However, it is on candle 2 that the first alarm bells rings. Once again we have effort (volume), but not an equivalent result in terms of the associated price action. This is, therefore, the first sign of possible weakness. The market is what is known as 'over sold'. The market makers and specialists are starting to struggle here. The buyers are moving into the market in increasing numbers, sensing an opportunity to buy the market. This creates the resistance to lower prices at this level, which is then confirmed on the third and fourth candle, where volume is falling away.

The specialists and market makers have seen this weakness on candle 2 and moved in, but continue to mark prices lower, to give the appearance of a market that is still bearish. Once again, it isn't! This may only be a temporary pause, and not a major change in trend, but nevertheless, it is a potential warning of strength coming into the market.

The high volume is as a result of an increasing number of sellers closing out their positions, and taking their profits, whilst the remaining sellers do not have sufficient momentum to take the market lower. The specialists and market makers are now buying at this level adding to the volumes, as they have seen the strength coming into the market, and are happily absorbing the selling pressure. This is the reason that volumes fall on the next two candles, as they continue to mark the market lower, but are no longer involved in the move themselves. They have bought their stock on candle 2, and are now simply trapping additional traders into weak short positions in candles 3 and 4.

The initial signal appeared on candle two, as in the previous example, which was then FURTHER confirmed in candles three and four. The insiders have shown their hand on candle two in both of the above examples, and all from the volume and associated price action!

In both of these examples we would now be ready and waiting for any further signals, to give us clues as to the likely extent of any reversal in trend, or whether this might simply be a minor pull back. Even if it were merely a minor change in a longer term trend, this would still offer a low risk trade that we could enter in the knowledge that the position would only be open for a short time.

This brings me neatly to the point I mentioned earlier, namely the framework of Wyckoff's second law, the law of cause and effect.

In learning to base our trading decisions using VPA, the analytical process that we go through on each chart is identical. The description of this process may sound complicated, but in reality once mastered only takes a few minutes to execute. In fact, it becomes second nature. It took me around 6 months to reach this level by chart watching every day. You may be quicker or a little slower – it doesn't matter, as long as you follow the principles explained in the book. The process can be broken down into three simple steps:

Step 1 – Micro

Analyse each price candle as it arrives, and look for validation or anomaly using volume. You will quickly develop a view on what is low, average, high or very high volume, just by considering the current bar against previous bars in the same time frame.

Step 2 - Macro

Analyse each price candle as it arrives against the context of the last few candles, and look for validation of minor trends or possible minor reversals.

Step 3 - Global

Analyse the complete chart. Have a picture of where the price action is in terms of any longer term trend. Is the price action at the possible top or bottom of a longer term trend, or just in the middle? This is where support and resistance, trend lines, candle patterns, and chart patterns all come into play, and which we will cover in more detail shortly.

In other words, we focus on one candle first, followed by the adjacent candles close by, and finally the entire chart. It's rather like the zoom lens on a camera in reverse – we start close in on our subject, and then gradually zoom out for the complete picture.

I now want to put this into the context of Wyckoff's second law, namely the law of cause and effect, as this is where the elements of time come into our VPA analysis.

As I mentioned in the introduction, one of the classic mistakes I made time and time again when first starting all those years ago was to assume that as soon as I saw a signal, then the market would turn. I was caught out repeatedly, getting in too early, and being stopped out. The market is like the proverbial oil tanker – it takes time to turn and for all the buying or selling to be absorbed before the insiders, specialists and market makers are ready. Remember, they want to be sure that when they make their move, then the market will not be resistant. In the simple examples above, we just looked at four candles, with the insiders moving in on just one. In reality, and as you will see shortly, there is a great deal more to it than this, but this sets the basic principle in place, which is what this chapter is all about.

Therefore, on a daily chart this 'mopping up' phase could go on for days, weeks and sometimes even months, with the market continuing to move sideways. Several consecutive signals of a reversal could appear, and whilst it is clear that the market will turn, it is not clear when this will occur. The longer this period of consolidation, then the more extended any reversal in trend is likely to be. And, this is the point that Wyckoff was making in his second law, the law of cause and effect. If the cause is large, in other words the period over which the market is preparing to reverse, then the more dramatic and long lasting will be the consequent trend.

Let's try to put this concept into context as this will also explain the power of using VPA combined with multiple time frames.

If we take one of the simple examples above, where we were looking at four candles, and the associated volume bars. This is really step two in our three step process. Here we are at the macro level, and this could be on any chart from a tick chart to a daily chart. All we know is that over this four bar period there is a possible change being signalled. However, given the fact that this is only over a handful of candles, any reversal is unlikely to last long as any potential change is only based on a few candles. In other words, what we are probably looking at here in the micro stage, is a minor pull back or reversal. Nothing wrong with that, and perfectly acceptable as a low risk trading opportunity.

However, step back to the global view on the same chart, and we see this in the context of the overall trend, and immediately see that this four bar price action is in fact being replicated time and time again at this level, as the market prepares to reverse. In other words, the cause is actually much greater than a simple reversal and we are therefore likely to see a much greater effect as a result. Therefore, patience is now required and we must wait. But, wait for what? Well, this is where the power of support and resistance comes into play, and which I cover in detail in a later chapter.

Returning to Wyckoff's second law of cause and effect and how this principle can be applied to multiple time frames, the strategy I would like to share with you is one I use in my own trading. It is based on a typical set of charts on MT4 and uses the 5, 15 and 30 minute charts. This trio of charts is for intra day forex scalping and trades are taken on the 15 minute chart. The 5 minute chart gives me a perspective closer to the market, whilst the 30 minute chart, gives me a longer term view on a slower chart. The analogy I always use in my trading rooms is that of a three lane highway. The 5 minute chart is in the middle while the two charts either side acting as 'wing mirrors' on the market. The faster time frame, the 5 minute chart, tells us what is happening in the 'fast lane', whilst the 30 minute reveals what is happening in the 'slow lane', the slower time frame.

As the sentiment in the fast time frame changes, if it ripples through to the slower time frames, then this will develop into a longer term trend. For example, if a change occurs on the 5 minute chart, which then ripples through to the 15 minute chart, and ultimately through to the 30 minute chart, then this change has now developed into a longer term trend.

Returning to our VPA analysis. Imagine that on the 5 minute chart we see an anomaly of a possible change in trend which is then confirmed. This change in trend is also reflected in the 15 minute chart. If we take a trade on the analysis seen here, and the trend ultimately ripples through to the 30 minute chart, this reversal is likely to be more developed as a result, as it has taken longer to build, and is therefore likely to have further to run. The analogy I use here is of a clockwork model car.

If we only wind the mechanism by a few turns which takes a few seconds, then the car only runs a small distance before stopping. If we spend a little longer and add a few more turns to the mechanism then the car runs further. Finally, if we take a few minutes and wind the mechanism to the maximum, the car will now run the farthest distance possible. In other words, the time and effort we put in to define the strength of the cause, will be output in terms of the strength of the effect.

This is the power of VPA when used in multiple time frames and in conjunction with Wyckoff's second rule. It is immensely powerful, and combines two of the most dynamic analytical techniques into a unified single approach. It is an approach that can be applied to any combination of time frames from fast tick charts to higher time frame charts. It does not differentiate as to whether you are a speculator or an investor.

The approach is simple and straightforward, and is like the ripples in a pond when a stone is thrown. As the stone lands in the centre of the pond the ripples move outwards. This is like the ripples of market sentiment which move across time frames outwards from the fastest to the slowest. Once the ripples appear in the slowest time frame, then this is likely to have the greatest longer term impact as the move has taken the longest time to build, giving additional momentum to the move. To return to our clockwork car, when fully wound the car will travel further and a perfect expression of cause and effect.

In the following chapters, I would now like to build on these first principles and extend them out into actual examples, using real charts from a variety of markets.

Chapter Five

Volume Price Analysis: Building The Picture

Mistakes are the best teachers. One does not learn from success.
Mohnish Pabrai (1964 -)

In the previous chapter we looked at some of the basic building blocks of VPA, and how to apply our analysis first to single candles, and then to use this knowledge in relation to small groups of candles. This really took us through the first two steps of VPA in our three step process. The three step process which begins with a close up look at one candle, then gradually zooms out, to step 2 which is the candles in close proximity to the latest candle. Finally, we zoom out to bring the complete chart into focus, which is what we are going to focus on in this chapter, and in doing so, I hope will also help to reinforce the basic skills we learnt in the previous chapter.

In addition in this chapter, I'm also going to introduce some new concepts which I hope will help to put everything into context, and pull the various strands of VPA together. I think this is probably the best place to start, and then we can begin to look at a variety of examples, and I can walk you through each chart as the price action unfolds.

So let me start with five concepts which lie at the heart of VPA, and these are as follows:

1. Accumulation

2. Distribution

3. Testing

4. Selling Climax

5. Buying Climax

The simplest way to understand these terms, and for me to explain them to you, is to go back to our analogy of the warehouse, which was also used by

Richard Ney in his books to explain this concept. This is what he said:

*"To understand the specialists' practices, the investor must learn to think of specialists as merchants who want to sell an **inventory of stock** at **retail** price levels. When they **clear their shelves** of their inventory they will seek to employ their profits to **buy more merchandise** at **wholesale price levels.**"*

I used the same analogy in my article for Working Money magazine many years later, which was the Parable of Uncle Joe.

The easiest way to think of volume in terms of the market price action, and this applies to all markets, is to use the wholesaling analogy. However, in order to keep things simple, let's just refer to the specialists, the market makers, the large operators, the professional money, as the insiders from now on. So, the insiders are the merchants who own the warehouses of stock and their primary goal is to make money buy buying at wholesale prices and then selling at retail prices.

Remember also, in the following explanations, that in my VPA Principle No 2, the market always takes time to turn in a dramatic way, and this is also borne out in Wyckoff's second law of cause and effect. We are always going to see small changes up and down, as the market pulls back or reverses in a longer term trend. But, for the major changes in trend to occur, (and remember, a 'major change' can appear on a 5 minute chart or a 1 day chart) this takes time. The longer the time taken, (the cause), the greater the change (the effect). However, this does vary from market to market. Some markets may take days, weeks or even months, before they are ready to turn dramatically, whilst other markets may take just a few days. I will be covering this later in the book, once we start to look at the various nuances which apply to specific markets, as they all behave slightly differently.

The key principles described here still apply. It's just the time frames and speed at which events occur that changes dramatically, and is due to the different structure of each market, the role of the insiders in that market, and the role that each capital market plays as an investment or speculative vehicle.

The first term we need to understand is accumulation.

Before the insiders can begin to do anything, they need to make sure they have enough stock, or inventory, to meet demand. Think of this as a wholesaler, about to launch a major advertising campaign for a particular product. The last thing any wholesaler would want to do is to spend time, effort and money launching a campaign, only to discover that after a few days there was no more stock. This would be a disaster. Well, funnily enough, it's the same for the insiders. They don't want to go to a great deal of trouble, only to find that they have run out of stock. It's all about supply and demand. If they can create the demand, then they need the supply to meet this demand.

But, how do they fill their warehouses before starting any campaign? This is where accumulation comes in, and just like a real warehouse, takes time to fill. Naturally it's not possible to stock a large warehouse with one lorry load of goods. It may take several hundred loads to completely fill, and remember, at the same time, there are goods simultaneously leaving the warehouse. Just as filling a warehouse takes time in the real world, so it takes time in our financial world.

Accumulation then, is the term used to define an 'accumulation phase' which is the period that the insiders go through to fill up their warehouse, prior to launching a major marketing campaign on selling their stock. So accumulation is buying by the insiders, and depending on which market we are considering, can go on for weeks or months, depending on the instrument being acquired.

Now the next question, is how do the insiders 'encourage' everyone to sell. It's actually very simple, and it's called the media. The news media, in all its various forms, is manna from heaven as far as the insiders are concerned. Over the centuries they have learnt every trick in the book to manipulate each news release, every statement, natural disaster, political statement, war, famine and pestilence, and everything in between. The media is an avaricious monster, and demands 'new' and fresh news items daily. The insiders simply take advantage of the constant fear and greed which is generated by this stream of news stories, to manipulate the markets, for many different reasons, but not least to shake market participants out of the market.

These are the words of Richard Wyckoff on the subject written in the 1930s

"The large operator does not, as a rule, go into a campaign unless he sees in prospect a movement of from 10 to 50 points. Livermore once told me he never touched anything unless there were at least 10 points in it according to his calculations. The preparation of an important move in the market takes a considerable time. A large operator or investor acting singly cannot often, in a single day's session, buy 25,000 to 100,000 shares of stock without putting the price up too much. Instead, he takes days, weeks or months in which to accumulate his line in one or many stocks."

The word campaign is an appropriate one. Just like a marketing campaign or a military campaign, the insiders plan each phase with military precision, with nothing left to chance. Each phase is planned and executed using the media to trigger the selling. But how does an accumulation phase play out? In practice, it goes something like this:

An item of news is released which is perceived as bad for the instrument or market. The insiders grab the opportunity to move the market lower fast, triggering a waterfall of selling, as they start their accumulation phase, buying inventory at the lowest prices possible, the wholesale price if you like.

The markets then calm as the bad news is absorbed, before starting to move higher, which is largely as a result of the buying by the insiders.

Two points here. First, the insiders cannot frighten everyone too much, or no one would ever buy. If there is too much volatility, with dramatic swings, this would frighten away many investors and traders, which would defeat the object of the exercise. Each move is carefully planned with just enough volatility to frighten holders of stock into selling. Second, the buying by the insiders may push prices back up higher again too quickly, so they take great care in ensuring that inventory is purchased in 'manageable' volumes.

Too much buying, would force prices higher quickly, so great care is taken, and is a further reason why the accumulation phase takes time to complete. It would simply not be possible to fill the warehouse with just one move lower. It simply would not work because the numbers are too large. Our simple examples in the previous chapter, were just to introduce the basic principles.

What happens next is that anyone who survived the first wave of selling is relieved, believing the market will recover and they continue to hold. After a period of calm, more bad news arrives, and the insiders take prices lower once again, shaking more holders out of the market. As they buy again there is a consequent recovery in the price.

This price action is then repeated several times, each time the insiders accumulating more and more stock for their warehouse, until finally the last stock holders give up, and admit defeat. What does this look like on the price chart?

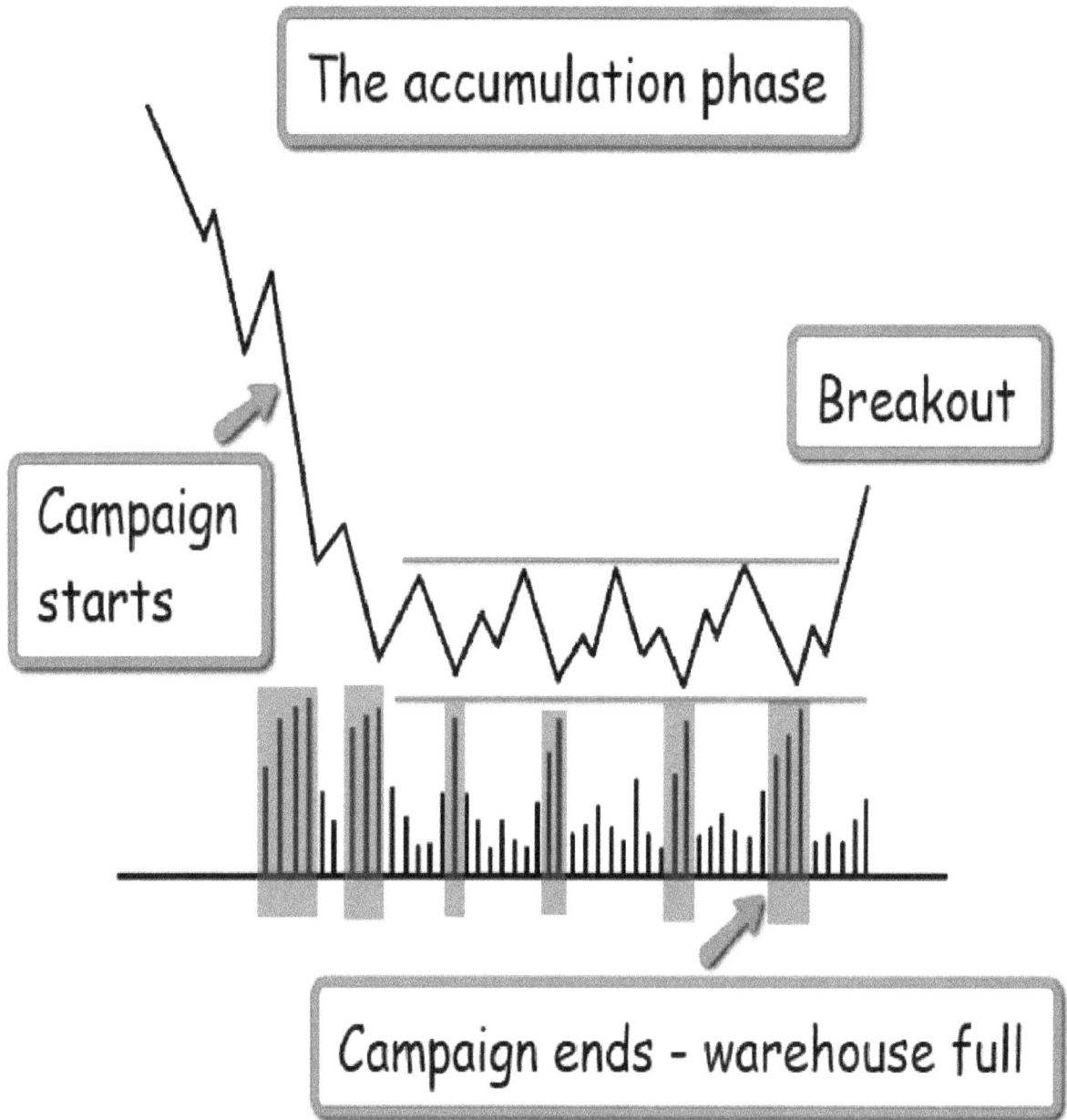

Fig 5.10 The Accumulation Phase

Whilst Fig 5.10 is a graphical representation of the price action, nevertheless I hope it gives a sense of what this looks like on a real chart. The repeated buying by the insiders is highlighted in blue.

I have deliberately avoided using a scale on the chart, either in terms of price or time, as I believe it is the 'shape' of the price and associated volume bars which is important. This is the price action which creates the classic price congestion which we see in all time frames, and which is why this 'shape' is so powerful, when associated with volume. This is what gives price action, the three dimensional perspective using VPA.

Once the campaign has begun, the price action then follows this typical pattern, where the market is repeatedly moved higher and lower. This type of price action is essential to 'shake' sellers out of the market. We can think of this as shaking fruit from a tree, or as we do in Italy, harvesting the olives! The tree has to be shaken repeatedly in order for all the crop to fall. Some of the crop is more firmly attached and takes effort to release. This is the same in the financial markets. Some holders will refuse to sell, despite this constant whipsaw action, but eventually they give up after several 'false dawns', generally on the point when the campaign is almost over, with the insiders preparing to take the market higher with fully stocked warehouses. So the campaign comes to an end. It is all over, until the next time!

This is repeated over and over again, in all time frames and in all markets. If we take the cause and effect rule of Wyckoff, the above price action could be a 'secondary' phase in a much longer term cycle, which is something I cover in more detail once we start to look at multiple time frames.

Everything, as Einstein said, is relative.

If we took a 50 year chart of an instrument, there would be hundreds of accumulation phases within the 50 year trend. By contrast an accumulation phase in a currency pair, might last a few hours, or perhaps only a few days.

And the reason for this difference is to do with the nature and structure of market. The equity market is a very different market to bonds and commodities. In equities for example, this phase might last days, weeks or months, and I cover this in detail when we look at the characteristics of each market and its internal and external influences, which create the nuances for us as VPA traders.

The key point is this. Just recognise the price action and associated volume for what it is. This is the insiders manipulating the market in preparation for an extended price move higher. It may be a small move (cause and effect) based on a short time period, or a more significant move based on a longer phase. And if you think that perhaps this is a fantasy, let me just quote from Richard Ney again, and this time from his second book, The Wall Street

Gang.

"On November 22, 1963, the day President Kennedy was assassinated, specialists used the alibi provided by the tragedy to clean out their books down to wholesale price levels. After they had accumulated large inventories of stock, they closed shop for the day and walked off the floor. This prevented public buy orders from being executed at the day's lows. The specialist in Telephone, for example, dropped his stock on November 22 from $138 to $130. He opened it on the 25th at $140! Sacrificing accuracy for expediency, he admitted to making $25,000 for his trading account."

Any news, provides the perfect excuse to manipulate the market, and nothing is exempt. In US equities it is the quarterly earnings season reports which provide the perfect opportunity. Economic data is also a rich source, whilst natural disasters can be used for longer term triggers. On an intra day basis, accumulation is made very easy with the constant round of comments from politicians, central banks, coupled with the daily stream of economic data. Life is very easy for the insiders, and to be honest, if we had the opportunity, we would probably do the same thing as well!

The Distribution Phase

The distribution phase is the exact opposite of the accumulation phase. In the accumulation phase, the insiders were filling their warehouses, in preparation for the next phase of the operation, and as I said earlier, the word campaign is perfect. This is a military campaign with nothing left to chance, as we will see shortly when I explain about testing.

With a full warehouse, the insiders now need to start moving the price higher, to encourage the somewhat nervous and jaundiced buyers back into the market. This is one reason why the insiders dare not frighten everyone too much, as they simply cannot afford to kill the goose that lays the golden egg!

Whilst the key emotional driver in 'shaking the trees' in the accumulation phase was fear, the fear of a loss, the key driver that is used in the distribution phase is also fear, but this time the fear of missing out on a good trade. The timing here is critical, as the insiders know that most investors and speculators are nervous, and like to wait for as many confirming signals as possible, before jumping into a market, fearing they will miss out on a big move higher. This is the reason most traders and investors buy at a top and sell at a bottom.

At the top of a bullish trend, traders and investors have seen the market move higher slowly, then gather momentum, before rising fast, and it is at this point that they buy, fearful of missing out on any 'quick profits'. This is precisely the point at which the insiders are preparing to pause and reverse. The same happens at the bottom of the accumulation phase. The investors and speculators can take no more pain and uncertainty, they have seen the market move lower slowly, then gather pace before dropping fast, which triggers waves of panic sales. Calm is then restored and the market starts to move into the accumulation phase. Here hope of a recovery is restored, before being dashed, then restored, then dashed again. This is the way that the insiders manipulate trader fear, and in many ways we could argue that it is not the markets they manipulate at all, but trader emotions, which are much easier.

So what is the typical pattern for our distribution phase, and how is it managed?

First, the market breaks out from the end of the accumulation phase, moving higher steadily, with average volume. There is no rush as the insiders have bought at wholesale prices and now want to maximise profits by building bullish momentum slowly, as the bulk of the distribution phase will be done at the top of the trend, and at the highest prices possible. Again, given the chance we would do the same.

The move away from the accumulation phase is now accompanied by 'good news' stories, changing sentiment from the 'bad news' stories which accompanied the falling market.

The market continues to rise, slowly at first, with small pull backs, but nothing too scary. Gradually the market picks up speed, as the bullish momentum gathers pace, until the target price area is reached. It is at this point that the distribution phase starts in earnest, with the insiders starting to clear their warehouses, as eager traders and investors jump in, fearful of missing out. The good news stream is now constant and all encompassing as the market continues to climb.

The insiders now have a willing supply of victims to whom they happily sell to in ever increasing numbers, but careful never to sell the market too hard. Prices therefore trade in a narrow range, sucking in more buyers on each dip. Finally, the warehouse is empty, and the campaign comes to an end. Fig 5.11 illustrates the typical price action and volume schematic of the distribution phase.

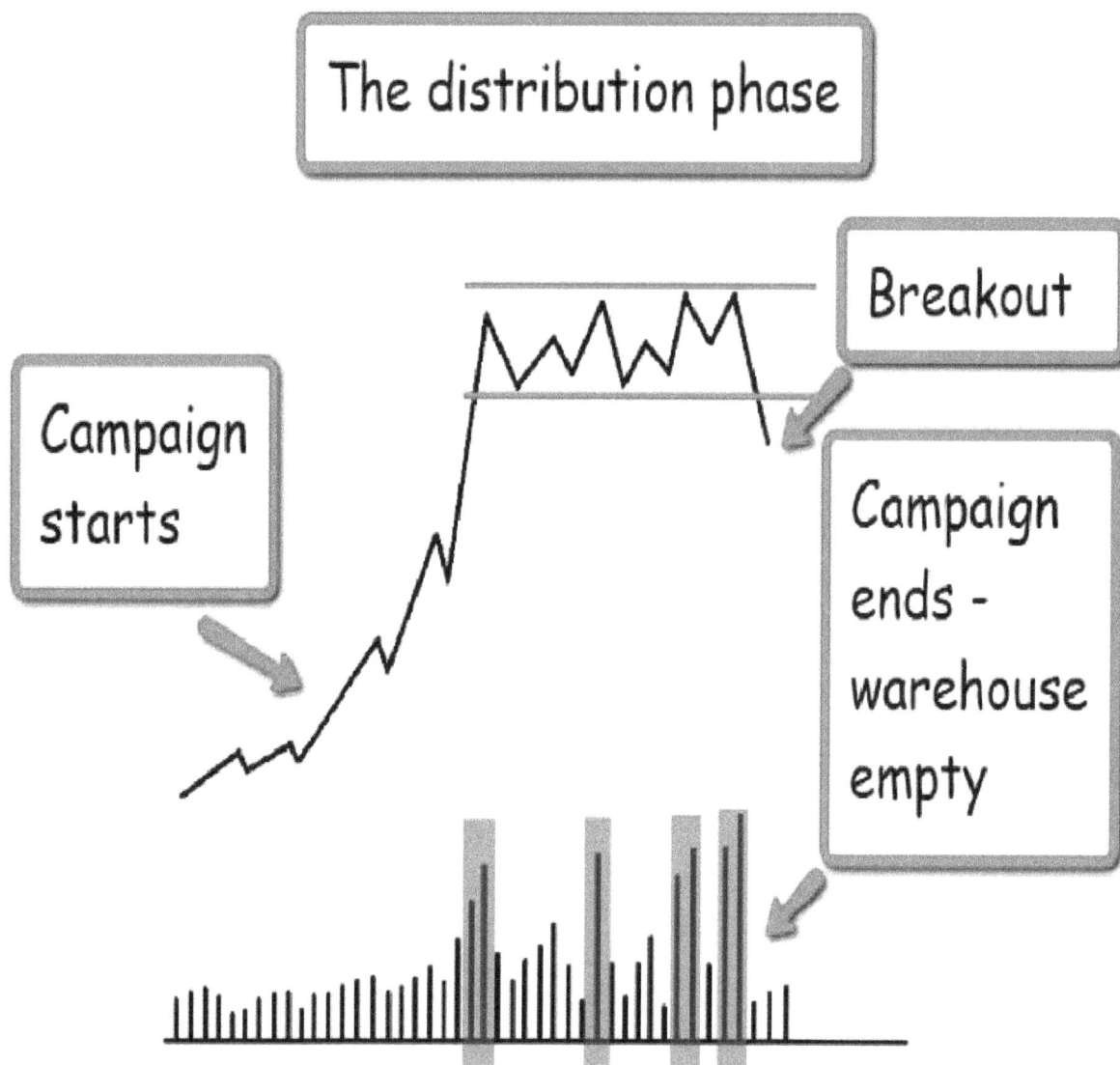

Fig 5.11 The Distribution Phase

The example in Fig 5.11 gives us a picture of what is happening here, and once we begin to think of this behaviour in terms of a full or empty warehouse, then it will start to make sense. It is very logical, and if we had our own warehouse of goods we wanted to sell at the highest price, we would go about this in much the same way.

First we would ensure we had enough stock and then start a marketing campaign to create interest. Next we would increase the marketing and hype the sales message – perhaps using celebrities, testimonials, PR, media, in fact anything to get the message across. A recent and classic example of marketing hype has been Acai berries (instant and massive weight loss with no effort – just eat the berries and wait for the results).

This is all the insiders are doing, they are simply playing on the emotions of the markets which are driven by just two. Fear and greed. That's it. Create enough fear and people will sell. Create enough greed and people will buy. It's all very simple and logical, and to help them, the insiders have the ultimate weapon at their disposal – the media.

This cycle of accumulation and distribution is then repeated endlessly, and across all the time frames. Some may be major moves, and others minor, but they happen every day and in every market.

Testing Supply

One of the biggest problems the insiders face when mounting any campaign is they can never be sure that all the selling has been absorbed, following an accumulation phase. The worst thing that could happen is they begin to move the market higher, only to be hit by waves of selling, which would drive the market lower, undoing all the hard work of shaking the sellers out of the market. How do the insiders overcome this problem? And the answer is that just as in any other market, they test!

Again, this is no different to launching a marketing campaign to sell a warehouse full of goods. Not only do the items have to be correctly priced, but also that the market is receptive, primed and ready if you like. Therefore a small test marketing campaign is used to confirm if we have the right product at the right price, and with the right marketing message to sell in volume.

The insiders also want to test, and once they have completed the accumulation phase, they prepare to move the market higher to begin the selling process. At this stage, they are generally moving back into price regions which have only recently seen heavy selling, so they execute a test to gauge market reaction and check that all the selling has been absorbed in the accumulation phase. The test is as shown in the schematic below:

Fig 5.12 is a schematic to explain this principle which is common sense when we think about it logically.

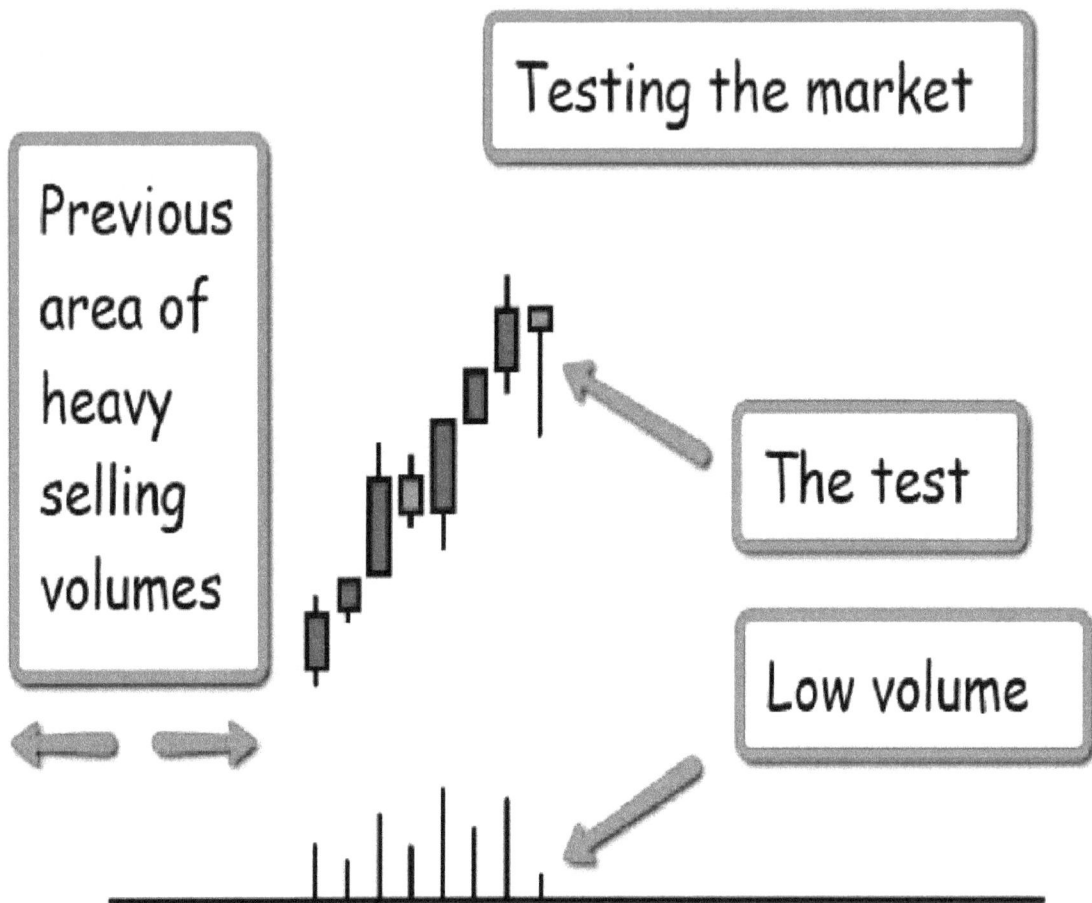

Fig 5.12 Low Volume Test – Good News!!

The phase of price action we are looking at here follows the accumulation phase, and prior to this, the insiders will have frightened everyone into selling by moving prices down fast. Panic selling follows with high volumes in this area. The insiders then begin to shake the trees for the more obstinate 'fruit' before they slowly begin to push the market out from this region and to start the gentle upwards trend, which will ultimately develop into the distribution phase at the top of the bull trend.

At this point the insiders are moving the market back through an area of recent heavy selling, and the worst thing that could happen, is for this selling pressure to return, bringing the campaign to a shuddering halt. The answer is to execute a test in the rising market which is shown in the schematic in Fig 5.12.

The market is marked lower, possibly on the back of a minor item of bad news, to test to see if this is likely to flush out any remaining sellers. If the volume remains low, this instantly tells the insiders that there are few sellers left, and that virtually all the selling has been absorbed in the accumulation phase of the campaign. After all, if the sellers were still in the market in any number, then the candle would have closed lower on above average volume. The volume is low, as the insiders move the candle back near the opening price with a 'good news' story, before continuing higher, happy with this positive result.

These so called 'low volume' tests occur in all time frames and in all markets, and is a simple way for the insiders to gauge the balance of supply in the market. They are, after all, trying to create demand here, but if there is an over supply in the market then this will bring the bull campaign to a halt.

In this case the test was successful and confirms that any selling pressure has been removed. The precise formation of the candle is not critical, but the body must be a narrow spread, with a deep lower wick. The colour of the body can be either bullish or bearish.

With the test now confirmed the insiders can move the market higher to the target distribution level, confident that all the old selling has now been absorbed.

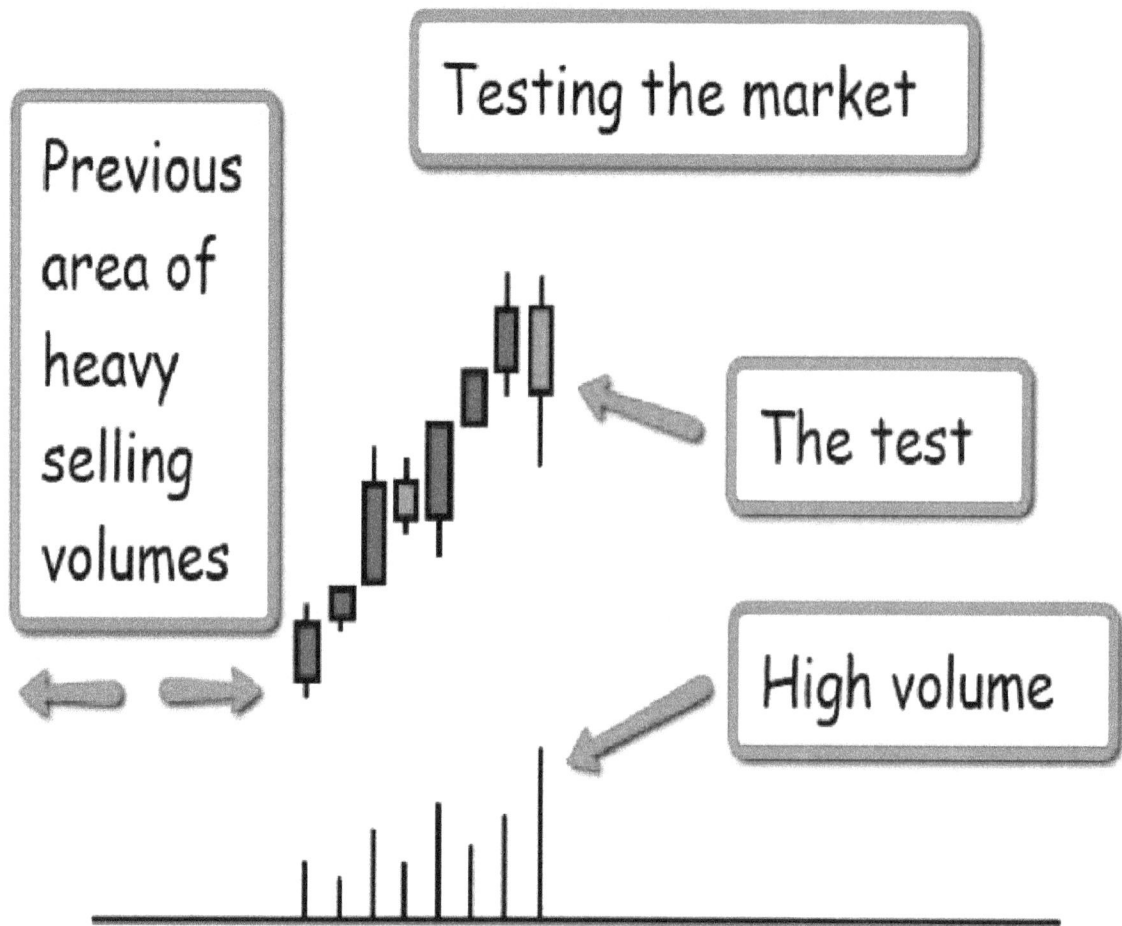

Fig 5.13 High Volume Test – Bad News !!

However, what if the test fails and instead of low volume appearing there is high volume, which is a problem. In starting to move the market away from the accumulation area, and executing the first part of the test by marking prices lower, this has resulted in sellers returning in large numbers and forcing the price lower.

Clearly on this occasion, the selling from the old trading range has not been absorbed in the accumulation phase, so any further attempt to take the market higher may struggle or fail.

A failed test means only one thing. The insiders will have to take the market back lower once again, and quickly, to shake these sellers out. The market is not ready to rise further, and the insiders therefore have more work to do, before the campaign can be re-started. This is equivalent to a failed test in an advertising campaign. Perhaps the pricing of the product is not quite right, or the marketing message is not clear. Either way, the test has shown that something isn't right and needs to be addressed. For the insiders it's the presence of too many sellers still in the market.

The original 'mopping up' campaign needs to be restarted, to absorb these old positions. The insiders will then relaunch their campaign again, and re-test the supply as the market begins to rise. On a failed test we can expect to see the insiders take the market back into the congestion area once again, to flush out this selling pressure before preparing to breakout again, with a further test. Any subsequent test on low volume will then confirm that selling pressure has now been removed.

Testing is one of the key tools that the insiders use, in all markets. Like everything else in VPA, it is a simple concept, based on simple logic, and once we understand the concept of accumulation and the structure on the chart, we will begin to see tests occurring in all time frames and in all markets. It is one of the most powerful signals you will see, as it is the insiders sending a clear message that the market is about to break out and move higher.

In the example in Fig 5.13 the insiders were testing for any residual selling pressure, often referred to as 'supply', following the accumulation phase. With a full warehouse they were all set to roll out the campaign and the last step was to check that all the selling in the price levels immediately ahead had all been absorbed. In this case it hadn't! However, once the test has been repeated and confirmed with low volume, the market will move higher.

Testing Demand

But what of the reverse scenario, where we are coming to the end of a distribution phase. The last thing the insiders want is to start a campaign to begin filling their warehouses again, move back into an area which has seen high demand (buying pressure) only for the buyers to take the market in the opposite direction.

Once again a test is employed to make sure that all the buying (demand) pressure has been absorbed in the distribution phase, and this is done with a test of demand as the campaign gets under way.

In this case the distribution campaign has been in progress for some time. The insiders have moved the market from the wholesale price level, to their target level for retail prices, and are now happily selling on waves of bullish news. The investors and speculators are rushing in and buying, fearing that they are missing out on a golden opportunity, and motivated by greed. The insiders pull in more demand by whip sawing the prices and gradually emptying their warehouses of all the inventory of stock.

Finally, when the campaign is complete, it's time to start the next phase of moving the market lower, and as the trend starts to develop, the price action moves back into areas which only recently had seen high volume buying. Once again a test is required, this time to test demand. If the demand is low, then all the buying has been absorbed in the distribution phase as we can see in the schematic in Fig. 5.14.

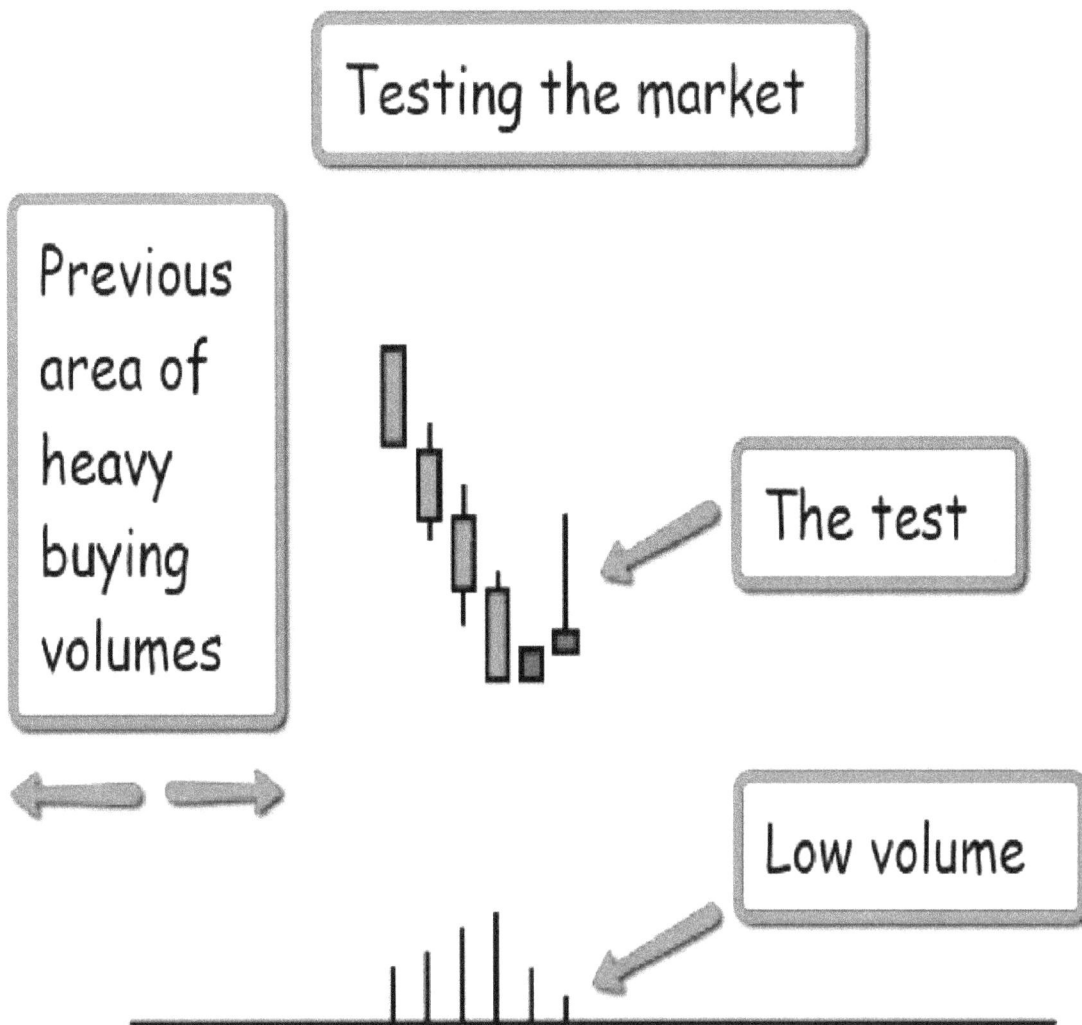

Fig 5.14 Low Volume Test – Good News !

Here we have the end of the distribution phase. The warehouses are empty, and the next stage is a sharp move lower, to repeat the process and move into an accumulation phase once again.

As the distribution phase ends, the insiders want to make sure that there is no demand still remaining in price areas which, until recently, had seen strong buying during the entry into the distribution phase. Once again, they test. The market is marked higher using some news, and if there is no demand, closes back near the open, with very low volume. This is what the insiders want to see. No demand, as shown by the low volume. They are now safe to start moving the market lower, and fast, as they now need to replenish their warehouses again.

Fig 5.15 is definitely NOT what the insiders want to see as they prepare to move away from the distribution price region. The market is marked higher and buyers flood in, thinking that the bullish trend is set to continue and move higher still. As before, a failed test stops the campaign in its tracks, and the insiders have to move back into the distribution price area, and clear these buyers out of the market, using the same processes as before. Once complete, then a further test is made, and if on low volume, then the trend lower will gather pace, and move quickly away from the distribution region, trapping traders into weak positions at this level.

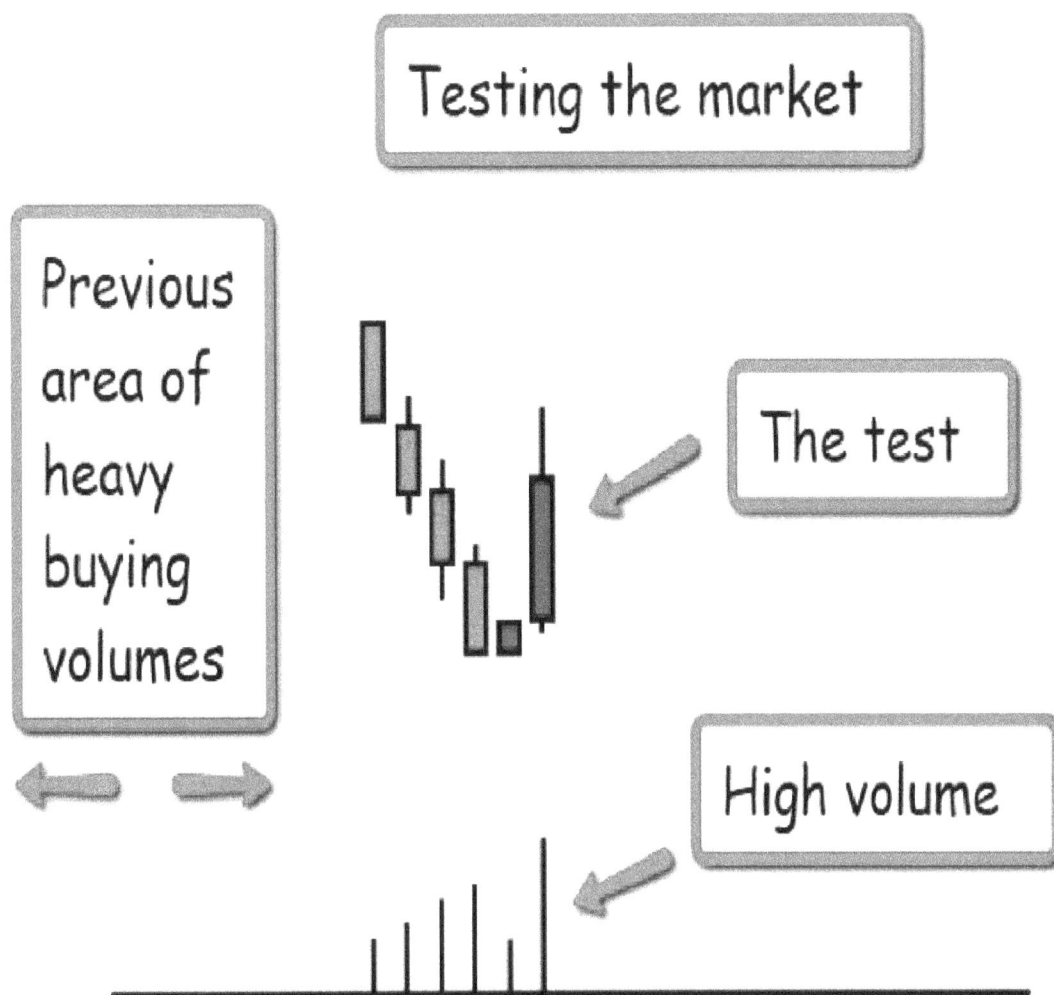

Fig 5.15 High Volume Test – Bad News !

Now we know what to look for, you will see testing occurring ALL the time, ONCE this has been preceded by an accumulation or a distribution phase. We may even see a series of tests, perhaps the first has low volume, followed by a second or third which have lower volume still. This is simply confirming that the insiders are preparing the next phase of a campaign, and the key is simple. Once prices break away from the congestion areas created during these two phases, we can be assured that the next stage is then under way.

Before moving on to consider the selling climax and the buying climax, at this point in the book I think it's appropriate to answer a couple of questions which sometimes puzzles both traders and investors.

The first question is – why do markets take longer to rise than to fall, and is this something to do with the insiders?

The second question is – over what time frames do these cycles of filling and emptying the warehouse typically last?

Let me answer the first, which also leads into the second. Market insiders only have two objectives. The first is make us fearful and the second is to make us greedy. They have no purpose in life, other than to create emotional responses which will ensure that we always do the wrong thing at the wrong time, but they always do the right thing at the right time.

A quote from the late great John Templeton who wrote:

"Heed the words of the great pioneer of stock analysis Benjamin Graham: 'Buy when most people…including experts…are pessimistic, and sell when they are actively optimistic.'"

Let's think about this logically and try to answer the first question. The markets have been in free fall, with panic selling by investors and traders. Then comes a period of calm as the market moves sideways into the accumulation phase, as the warehouses are stocked up ready for the move higher.

Now at this stage, remember, that from an insiders point of view, they have just frightened everyone to death, and the last thing they want to do, is to suddenly send the market soaring in the opposite direction. This would soon drive every investor and speculator away. After all, there is only so much emotion that traders can take, and too much too soon would quickly kill the goose that lays the golden egg. A calm approach is required. The tactic now is to quietly start to build confidence back up, moving prices higher steadily, without frightening anyone out of the market, and gradually drawing the buyers back in.

Soon, the panic selling is forgotten as the markets recover and confidence is slowly restored. This also suits the insiders, as they have a full inventory to sell, and want to take their time, and certainly don't want to see large volume buying as they move the market higher. At this stage, it is is about maximising profits, and the biggest profits are to be made once the distribution target price levels are reached at the retail level. It would be madness to suddenly mark up the market to the retail level, as many investors would then feel they had missed out on the move, and not join in later.

The strategy here is one of confidence building by taking the market higher slowly, and then gradually to move faster, generating the belief in the investor or speculators mind that this is a market with momentum, which is gathering pace all the time, and is an opportunity not to be missed to make some easy money.

The upwards trend then starts to gather pace, moving higher in steps, pausing, reversing a little, drawing in buyers, tempting others, then moving higher still, until close to the distribution area, the market picks up speed as buyers crack under the emotional pressure of missing out, and jump in.

Throughout the upwards journey, the inventory is gradually reduced, but topped up in minor reversals with sellers taking their profits, and helping to maintain levels for the final phase of the campaign.

This is the emotional journey that the insiders have mastered. It is the reason markets move higher in a series of higher highs and higher lows, with pauses and minor reversals along the way. It is a confidence building exercise, designed to restore confidence after the fear, and replace it with another emotion – greed. These are the two levers that the insiders have, and they are used to devastating effect, and the only weapon that you have in your armoury is VPA.

After greed comes fear – again!

With their warehouses now empty, the insiders need to get back to the 'bottom' and fill them up as quickly as possible. Again, we would do exactly the same thing in their position.

However, the insiders have nothing to sell now, and the only way to make money fast is to refill the warehouse again and begin another campaign. The market crashes lower, panic selling ensues, fear is triggered and the warehouses are filled once more. And so the cycle repeats, time and time and time again. The best analogy I can think of here is of an old fashioned helter skelter that we might see at a fair ground. It takes effort to get to the top, walking up all the steps, but the slide down on a mat is very quick! That's how the markets work. Up in stairs and down in elevators. The old fashioned board game of 'snakes and ladders' expresses this effect perfectly, it's up on the ladders, and then a slide all the way back down on the snake!

I hope this is now beginning to make sense, as it is only once we start to think of the markets in these terms that we begin to realise how anyone, other than the insiders, ever makes money. This is another point. The insiders have to be careful, for the simple reason that if the price action was continually and unrelentingly volatile, then traders and investors would look elsewhere for investing and speculating opportunities.

Just like Goldilocks and her porridge, the motto here is 'not too hot and not too cold'. The insiders have learnt their craft and honed their skills over decades. Most investors and speculators lose. You are lucky. By the end of this book you will become a VPA expert and be able to see and recognise all the tricks they play. They are there in plain sight and all we have to do is interpret the signals and then follow the insiders. It really is that simple.

Moving to the second question which was how often is this cycle repeated? And here I will let you into a secret. This was a question I wanted to ask Albert Labos all those years ago as we sat in a rusty cabin on the President learning all about the market makers (as he referred to them) and their tricks. I actually wrote down the question and asked my neighbour in the class, but he didn't know the answer either.

What I thought at the time was this. I understood about the accumulation and distribution phases which made perfect sense to me, but then I started to think. Also, remember that at the time we were really looking at trading indices, so essentially long cycles. I thought to myself that if the cycle was perhaps 10, 15, or 20 years, then this was a long time for a market maker to wait to make a profit from his (or her) buying and selling. Perhaps it was longer, and from one big market crash to another. Perhaps it was decades? I didn't dare ask the question at the time, and now I wish I had!

The answer to the question is that these cycles occur on all time frames from tick charts, to 1 minute charts, to 15 minute and hourly charts, and to daily, weekly and monthly charts. The best way to think of this is to imagine a set of nested Russian dolls.

The smallest doll, fits inside a slightly larger doll, which fits inside a larger doll, and so on. In the context of these cycles, we can imagine the same thing with a chart. An accumulation and distribution cycle on a one minute chart, may last a few hours, and be part of a larger cycle on a slower time frame chart, which in turn itself will be part of a larger cycle and so on. This is an important concept to grasp, as it brings in two important aspects of market behaviour.

First, that these cycles happen in ALL time frames, and second that by watching price action across multiple time frames you will start to see these cycles developing and unfolding and confirming one another as a result. A cycle that has already started on a one minute chart, will be setting up on 5 minute chart, and possibly just developing on the 15 minute chart.

Let me quote from Richard Ney again and his book The Wall Street Gang, books every trader and investor should try to read. They contain a wealth of information, and they give us a broad perspective on volume and price, along with an excellent view on how the specialists manipulate the markets. Whilst the books primarily focus on stocks, the principles are identical and relevant to all markets. In equities it's the specialists, insiders or market markets, in futures it's the large operators, and in spot forex it's the market makers again.

This is what he says about time frames :

"The specialist's objectives can be classified in terms of the short, intermediate and long term. Thus we can see that there are three broad classifications into which we can place the market's price movements.

He then goes on to say

"The short term trend. This can last from two days to two months. Within this trend there can be even shorter term trends lasting no more than several hours. The importance of the short term trend is that it is within this context that the specialist resolves his day to day inventory problems with his intermediate and long term objectives always in view. It is as though the short term trend is the spade with which the specialist digs the investor's

intermediate and long term grave."

"The ticker tape provides us with a microscopic view of the techniques of big block distribution at the top and big block accumulation at the bottom on behalf of the specialist's inventory."

"It is impossible to look solely at the tape as it passes in review and hope to determine longer term trends in the market. One can understand the tape and decipher its code of communication only when experience is shaped through memory – or through the use of charts. In a manner of speaking short and long term charts provide both a microscopic and a telescopic view of what has happened. In the final analysis, we need both in order to make financially rational decisions."

The reason that I have quoted this section from his book here, is that it neatly sums up the points I am trying to convey in this chapter.

Remember, this book was published in 1974, when the ticker tape was still in use, but we can replace the ticker tape with an electronic chart, on a short time scale. The concepts and principles are the same. We use the fast or ultra fast time frame as our microscopic view on the market, and then zoom out to our longer term time frames to give us that broader perspective on the volume and price relationship.

Now again, this is all relative, so for a scalping trader, this might be a 5 minute, 15 minute and 60 minute chart. A swing trader may consider a 60 minute, 240 minute and a daily chart. A trend trader may utilise a 4 hour, daily and weekly chart.

Therefore, regardless of the trading strategy and market, equities, commodities, bonds or forex, the point is that to succeed as a speculative trader or as an investor, the VPA relationships should be used in conjunction with multiple time frames. On a single chart VPA is immensely powerful, but when the analysis is 'triangulated' using slower time frames, this will give you a three dimensional approach to the market.

There is nothing wrong with focusing on one chart, but remembering the analogy of our three lane highway, where we are sitting in the middle lane with our wing mirrors on either side giving us a view on the fast and slow lanes, this will help to build confidence levels, while learning, and more importantly once you start to trade live.

To round off this chapter, I now want to focus on the the last two concepts of insider behaviour, namely the selling climax and the buying climax, before putting the whole cycle together in some simple schematics to help fix the broad principles.

The Selling Climax

As I outlined earlier in the book there is a degree of confusion about these two concepts, so let me try to explain. In the past, most people who have written about this subject, have done so from a personal perspective. In other words, when we buy or when we sell in the market. However, in the context of the insiders it is what they want us to do. Their sole objective is to get us to buy in the distribution phase, and to sell in the accumulation phase.

In terms of 'who is doing what' during these two phases, in the accumulation phase, the 'public' are selling and the insiders are buying, and conversely in the distribution phase the 'public' are buying and the insiders are selling.

This book is written from the perspective of the insiders, the specialists, the big operators and the market makers, and hopefully like me, you want to follow them! I hope so at any rate. As Albert used to say, we want to buy when they are buying, and sell when they are selling. Simple! Which is really what this book is all about.

When I describe and write about a selling climax, to me, this is when the insiders are selling and occurs during the distribution phase of the campaign. A buying climax is when the insiders are buying during the accumulation phase. To me, this just makes more sense. It may be a question of semantics, but it is important, and I would like to clarify it here, as many people refer to these events the other way round!

Just to be clear, a selling climax appears at the top of the bullish trend, whilst the buying climax appears at the bottom of a bearish trend, and reflects the actions of the insiders, and NOT the public!

The selling climax is the 'last hurrah' before the insiders take the market lower. It is the culmination of all their efforts, and is the point at which the warehouse is almost empty and requires one last big effort to force the market higher, drawing in those nervous traders and speculators who have been waiting and waiting for the right time to jump in, and can finally wait no longer. They give in to the fear of missing out, and buy.

This happens two or three times on high volume with the market closing back at the open, and at the end of the distribution phase. Following the selling climax, the market then breaks lower, and fast. This tranche of buyers, along with all the others, is then trapped at this price level, as the insiders move the market away from this region and back down the helter skelter to begin the process again.

Let's look at a typical example of what we might see as the selling climax marks the end of the distribution phase, and we can think of it in terms of fireworks – this is a firework display which marks the end of the event!

Once again, Fig 5.16 is simply a schematic of what to expect in the selling climax. Here the insiders have taken the market to their target level, at which they are selling inventory at retail prices, to happy buyers who believe that this market is going to the moon.

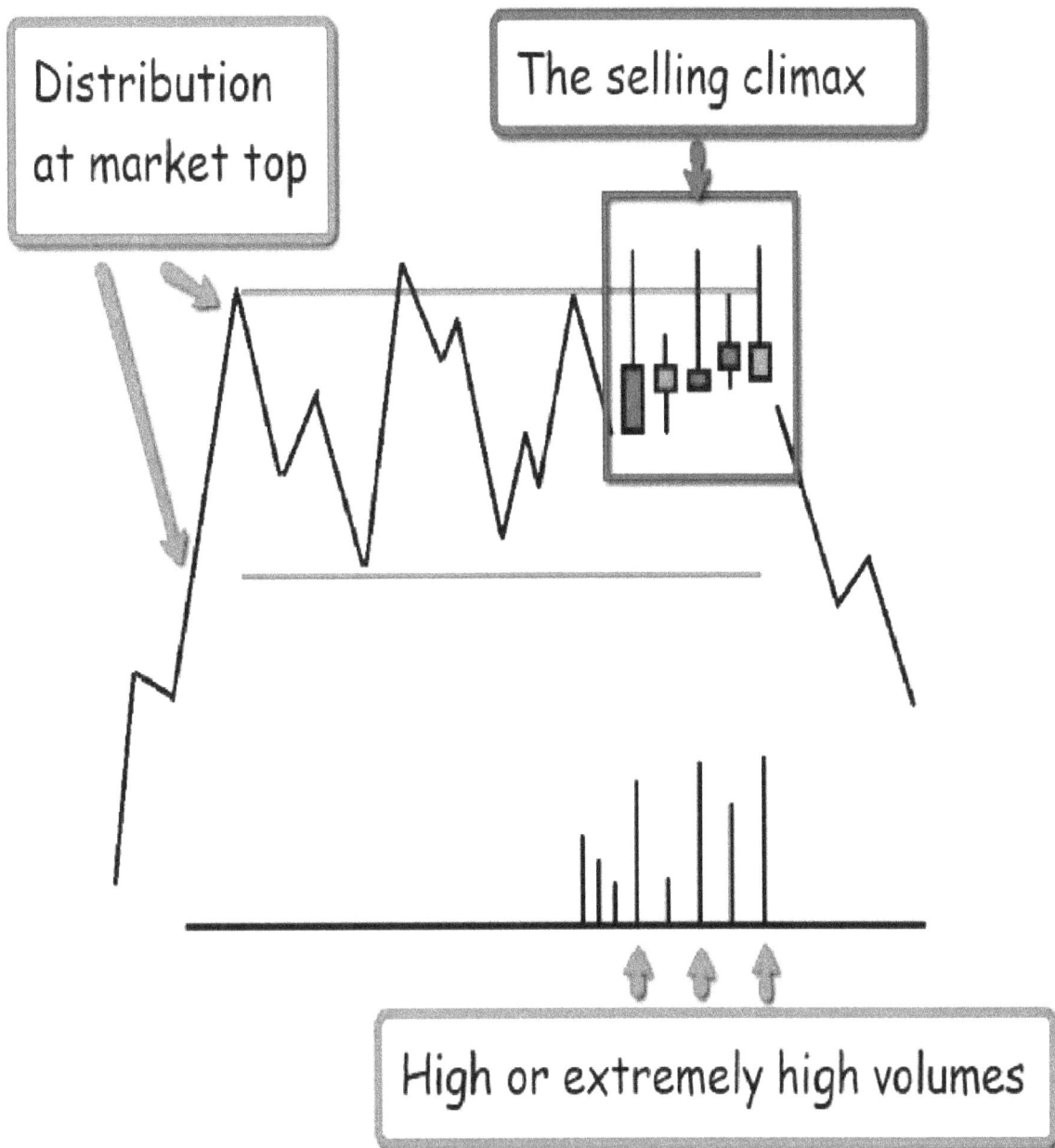

Fig 5.16 The Selling Climax – Firework Show

The insiders are happy to oblige, selling into the demand, moving the market lower, then back higher drawing in more demand, until they are close to clearing their inventory.

At this stage the price action becomes more volatile with surges higher followed by a close back to the open price, with increasing volumes of buyers flooding into the market, fearing they will miss out on the next leg up in the bullish trend. The next leg is in the opposite direction.

Finally, the inventory is cleared and the market sells off, moving lower and back out of the distribution phase. The clues for us, as VPA experts, are there to see.

Here we will see high volume coupled with a candlestick which has a deep upper wick and narrow body, and is one of the most powerful combinations of price action and volume we will ever see on a chart. Naturally, I will be covering this in detail later in the book.

These are the 'upper wick' candles that we looked at in chapter 3, and as I explained there, they are immensely powerful and reveal so much, particularly when combined with volume. The insiders are having one last effort to clear their inventory and mark prices higher early in the session. Buyers flood in, taking the market higher, fearful of missing out, with high or ultra high volumes, before the insiders take the market lower to lock these traders into weak positions, helped lower by profit taking. Some traders will sense that the market is 'over bought' at this level.

This price action is repeated several times, with the insiders selling into the demand, each time the price is pushed higher, before closing the candle lower at or near the opening price, helped by profit takers closing out.

The colour of the body of the candle is unimportant. What is important, is the height of the wick, the repeated nature of this price action, and the associated high volumes. This is sending a clear signal that the market is ready to move fast, and as the warehouses are all empty, the reaction will be quick. The insiders are now jumping on their mats, and heading off down the helter skelter, back to 'square one' to begin the process once again with an accumulation phase. When we see this price action, following a distribution phase, it's best to be in front of your screen – ready and waiting! Now let's look at the opposite of the selling climax, which is the buying climax. This is the firework party that marks the end of the accumulation phase, and signals the start of the bullish trend higher.

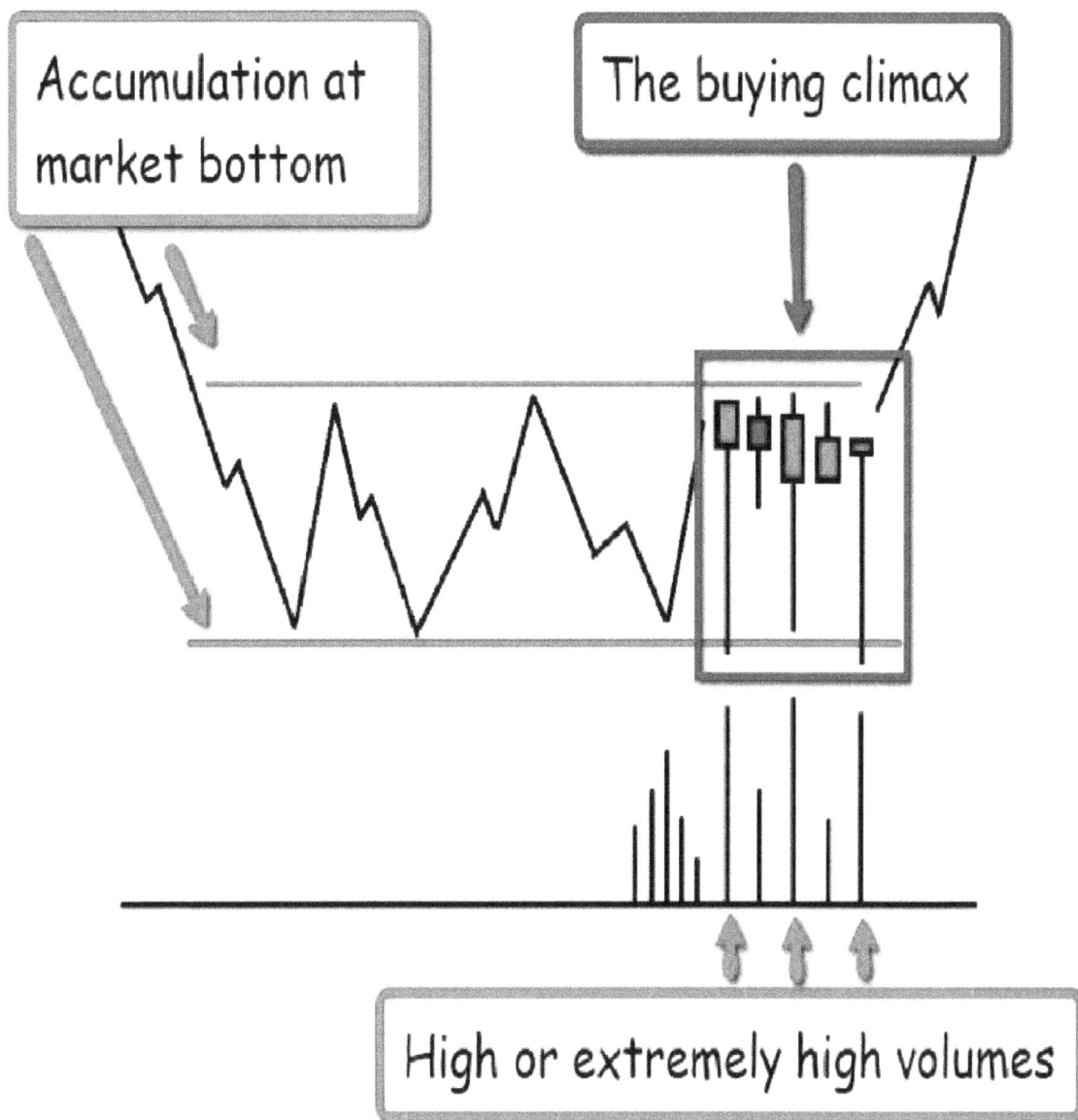

Fig 5.17 The Buying Climax – Firework Show (Again!)

The buying climax is simply a selling climax in reverse. The insiders have taken the market lower, panic has been triggered and fearful sellers are closing positions. See Fig 5.17.

The insiders then move into the accumulation phase to restock the warehouse, and move prices back and forth in a tight range, to shake out any last remaining tenacious sellers.

Towards the end of this phase, the insiders than mark prices down rapidly, flushing out more sellers, before moving the price higher later in the session to close somewhere near the opening price, helped higher by their own buying in the market, with bargain hunters also sensing that the market is 'over sold' at this level.

This is repeated several times, with panic selling continuing as frightened investors and speculators can take no more. They capitulate and throw in the towel. This is the last hurrah.

The insiders are now ready, with warehouses over flowing with stock, to start the march north, and begin the bullish trend higher, in nice easy steps, towards the target price for distribution.

Once we accept the fact that all markets are manipulated in one way or another, then the rest of the story simply fits into place.

The above is very logical, and common sense, but don't be misled into thinking that this is simply not possible with the current legislative authorities now in place. Nothing much has changed since the days of Wyckoff and Ney, and here let me quote from 'Making it in the Market' published in 1975.

This was a telephone conversation that Richard Ney had with an SEC (Securities and Exchange Commission) official. The SEC is supposed to regulate the financial world in the US.

Remember, this is 1975, and this it what was said on the telephone call, when the official was asked about checks on specialists and how they are regulated:

"specialists are under the Exchange. We don't get too concerned with them. They're not directly regulated by the Commission. They all operate under self regulation. They make their own rules – the Commission just O.K's them. Only if the Commission feels there is something not proper does it take exception. We check broker-dealers but we never go onto the Exchange to check out specialists."

So has anything changed?

In reality very little, except to say that trading is now largely electronic, and one of the many problems faced today by the SEC is HFT or High Frequency Trading.

There are the usual cases, where individuals and firms are taken to task to prove that the SEC and others have some sort of control and to assuage the public, that the markets are regulated in a fair and open way.

Sadly, as I hope the above shows, and in using VPA live will quickly prove to you, this is most certainly NOT the case. The insiders are FAR too experienced and wily to allow their golden goose to be killed off. They simply devise new and more elegant ways to manipulate prices for their own ends.

Let me quote from a recent release from the SEC in response to the issue of HFT :

"There are a number of different types of HFT techniques, and an SEC Concept Release [6] broke them down to four main types of strategies:

Market making: like traditional market making, this strategy attempts to make money by providing liquidity on both sides of the book and earning the spread.

Arbitrage: Trading when arbitrage opportunities arise (e.g. from mis-pricing between Indices, ETF's or ADRs and their underlying constituents.

Structural: These strategies seek to take advantage of any structural vulnerabilities of the market or certain participants, and include latency arbitrage or quote stuffing.

Directional: These strategies attempt to get ahead of – or trigger – a price move, and include order anticipation and momentum ignition."

And the date of this report? - late 2012.

I don't wish to labor the point, but I am conscious that some people reading this book may still consider me to be a 'conspiracy theorist'. I can assure you, I am not.

As Ney himself points out :

" most of those in government doing the investigating are beholden to the Stock Exchange in one way or another (via campaign contributions or through their law firms), or hope (if they are commissioners and chairmen of the SEC) to be employed in the securities industry at some not too distant date, nothing ever comes of these investigations."

Let me round off this chapter by creating a simple schematic, which I hope will help to put all of this into perspective.

Here it is, the complete market cycle, or as I like to call it – 'another day at the office' for the insiders, and this should hold no surprises. See Fig 5.18

The first campaign is the accumulation phase. The insiders start to fill their warehouses, which are empty following the sharp move lower, at wholesale prices.

Once the warehouses are almost full, the buying climax then begins, with some volatile price action to draw in more stock, but once complete, they then exit from the price region and test for supply. If all the selling has been absorbed, the insiders can start marking the market higher in steps, building confidence back into shell shocked investors and speculators who are still recovering.

As confidence returns, so the trend starts to gather momentum, drawing in buyers who now believe that the market will 'go to the moon'. Even cautious investors succumb and buy, just as the price is reaching the target area for retail prices.

With the market now at the retail level, more buyers are sucked in as the distribution phase starts in earnest, with prices moved higher to draw in more buyers, then lower to lock them in to weak positions. Finally the selling climax begins, with volatile price action, and the remaining inventory is cleared from the warehouses. Once empty, the market breaks lower, through this price area, and once again a test is executed, this time of demand. If the test confirms that buying in this region has been absorbed then the campaign is complete, and the market is moved lower fast.

The cycle is complete, and it only remains for the insiders to count their profits and repeat the exercise, again, and again, and again and … well I'm sure you get the picture.

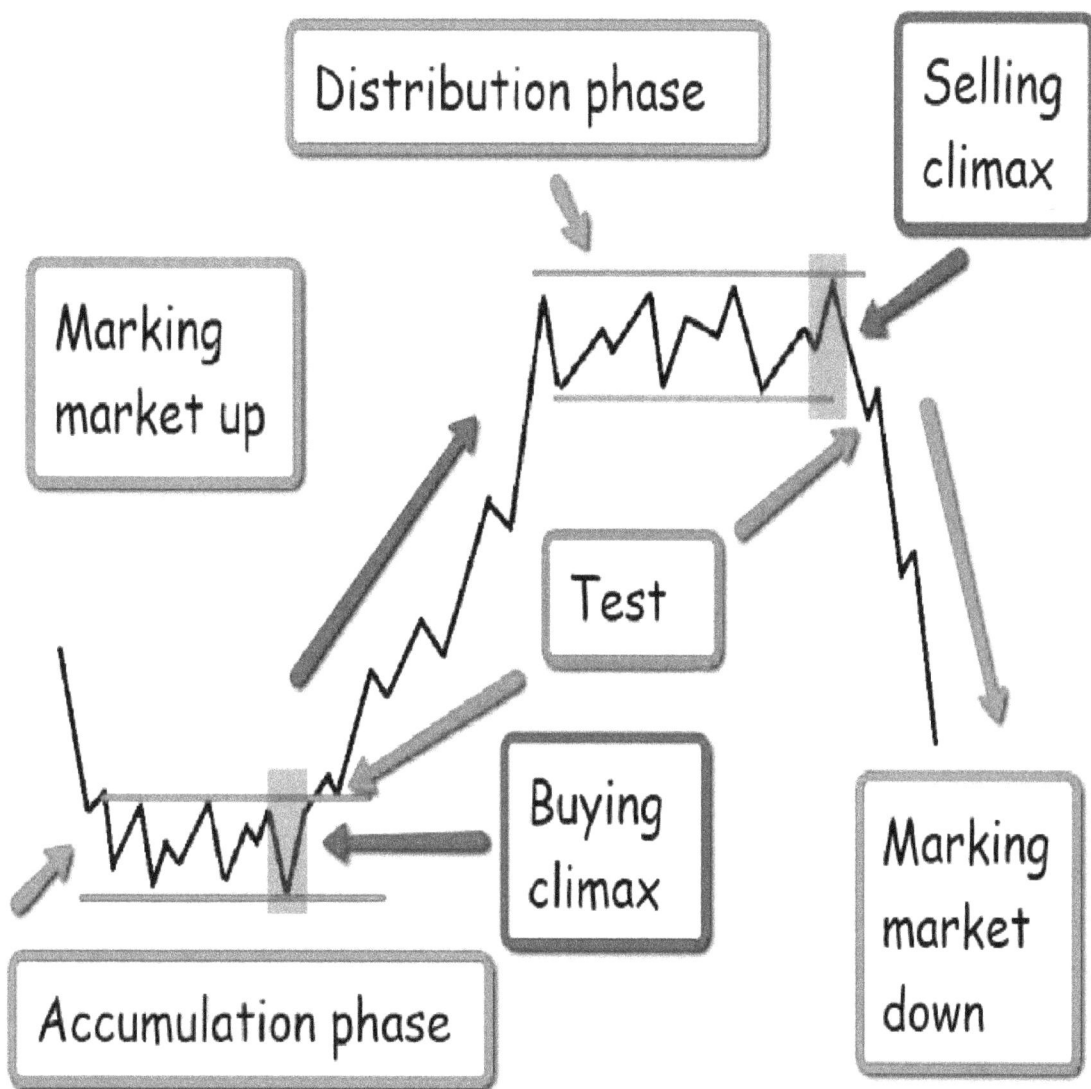

Fig 5.18 The Market Cycle – Another Day At The Office!

The important point to remember here, is that this cycle could be in any time frame and in any market. The above could be on a 5 minute chart for example of a currency pair, and perhaps over a few hours. It could equally be on a daily chart of a stock, and perhaps last weeks or even months. It could be on an hourly chart for a futures contract, and in this case the insiders would be the large operators, with the cycle perhaps lasting a few days or a week. The time scale is unimportant, other than in remembering Wyckoff's rule of 'cause and effect'.

Once we begin to study charts in detail we start to see this cycle occurring repeatedly, and armed just with the information in these early chapters, is enough to help traders and investors truly understand how the markets work and trade with confidence, as a result.

However, for a VPA trader it is just the starting point.

Before moving on to the next chapter let me try to 'frame' the context of what I have covered so far, not least because it is something that took me some time to absorb when I first started studying Volume Price Analysis.

Therefore, what I want to do here is to summarise what has been covered so far, starting with the concept of market manipulation, and try to explain what we mean by this phrase. Do we mean the insiders are free to simply move prices higher and lower at random and whenever it suits them to do so. The answer is NO. What I mean by market manipulation, which is perhaps different to other peoples view, is that this simply means using every available resource, to either trigger fear or greed in the retail traders mind. This means using every piece of news in the media to influence the buying and selling, and to move the market in the direction that the insiders require, either higher to a distribution phase, or lower to an accumulation range.

This is what I consider to be market manipulation. It is the creation of an environment, which in turn creates either fear or greed in the mind of the investor or the speculator. As I said earlier, market manipulation is not so much about manipulating the price, but manipulation of the twin emotions of fear and greed. Fear triggers selling and greed triggers buying, and the media in all its forms, is the perfect tool to create both.

Next, whilst the insiders all work together, this is NOT a cartel. There are many hundreds of specialists and market makers, and this simply would not be feasible. What does happen however, is that the insiders will all see strength and weakness at the same time. They have the advantage of seeing both sides of the market, all the buy orders and all the sell orders, and therefore true market sentiment.

What they cannot hide is volume, which is why it is so powerful. It is the only way we have of seeing when the insiders are involved in the price action, and if they are, whether they are buying or whether they are selling. When they are buying in the buying climax, we see it, because we have high volumes. When they are selling in the selling climax, we see it, because the volumes are high, and this is what you have to understand. It is the volume which is important not the manipulation element of the VPA, which brings me to another point.

I am often asked how the insiders decide on the target levels for accumulation and distribution, and this was something I struggled with myself. Are these just arbitrary levels decided in advance, or is there some logic that can help us to make sense of this aspect of price behaviour. Well the 'make sense' element is really this, which also helps us to understand the price behaviour that we see at these levels.

On any price chart, there are levels of price congestion that create the natural levels at which markets could be considered to be 'over sold' or 'over bought', terms which I introduced earlier in the chapter. These price levels are absolutely fundamental to the principles of VPA for two reasons. First, they represent areas where the market is either likely to find support, or is equally likely to struggle. They define barriers, areas where the market has paused in the past, and either moved on or reversed from these regions. I will explain these in more detail shortly, but for the time being accept the fact they exist, and are created during the phases of accumulation and distribution, as the market moves into sideways consolidation.

Now these 'phases' of price action appear all over our charts and in every time frame, and the insiders will be well aware of where these are and whether they are well developed areas, or simply minor areas where price in the past has perhaps paused before moving on. In preparing any campaign, the insiders therefore target these regions, as potential natural points for accumulation and distribution. This also explains the price action once we finally arrive at these areas.

Let's start with the distribution phase and consider what is actually happening during the selling climax?

The market has risen higher and accelerated on bullish news, and has arrived at the target area, which is potentially one where the market can be considered to be 'over sold', in other words, potentially weak and/or exhausted. We know this because these are the areas that insiders target before a campaign starts. Following the bullish trend higher, which has been supported with positive news, and increasing numbers of buyers entering the market, the insiders now pause at this level, and begin the job of distribution.

The initial phase of the distribution is executed purely from the momentum already driven into the market by the insiders, so the volume here will be high but not excessive. On any 'up' candles the volumes here will represent 'natural' buying by investors and speculators. In other words the insiders are not having to 'force' the market higher at this stage. They are simply selling into demand that has been created during the trend higher, and buyers are now in the 'greed' mindset. Any selling at this level, at this stage is again, 'natural' selling, as holders who have bought into the trend earlier, perceive that the market is perhaps struggling at this level, and decide to take their profits. The key point here is that the associated volumes during this phase are likely to be well above average but not excessive.

There will certainly be signals of weakness as we will see shortly, once we start to study the charts in detail, but this first phase of distribution, is what I call the 'natural' phase. This is the insiders simply meeting demand from greedy investors and speculators. Any selling is absorbed back into their inventory, and resold. The news is then used to move the market higher and lower in this range as the warehouse stock continues to dwindle.

The final phase is the selling climax, and this is where effort is required by the insiders. Now the market is very weak at this level. Perhaps the news is not quite so bullish as before, and the insiders are having to 'force' the price higher, using whatever news they can to pull in more buyers.

But with a weak market the buyers are now becoming overwhelmed with the sellers, which is why we see the price action reflected in the candles during the selling climax. The insiders now have a real struggle on their hands, desperately trying to keep the market propped up, forcing it higher, desperately selling in large volume to buyers, but as the volumes of selling increase, this in turn leads to falling prices, adding downwards pressure on the market.

This is the problem that all campaigns have eventually. The problem is simple. Sell in large enough volumes and ultimately the price will fall, working against you. It is this battle to keep the price high, but also to move inventory in volume that we are seeing played out in this final dramatic scene. It is the battle that insiders have to face at this stage.

The problem is one of moving large volumes fast, without moving the price down fast, undoing all the good work of earlier in the campaign. It is a fine balance, and this is the balance that you see in those last few candles at the end of the selling climax. The insiders are battling to force prices higher, supply the demand in ever increasing volumes without letting the price collapse, which is why we see the price behaviour in these candles. Let's take another look.

The Selling Climax

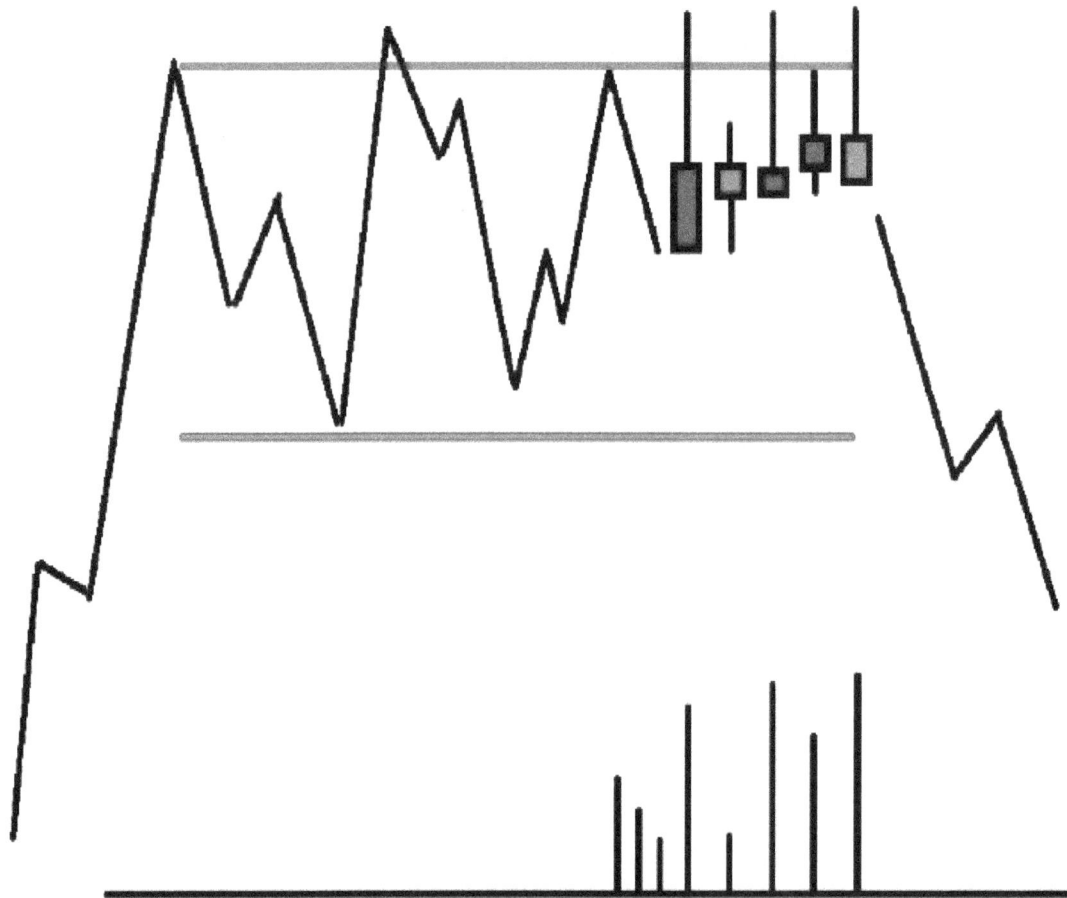

Fig 5.19 Selling Climax

What is happening here in Fig 5.19 is that in trying to meet demand by selling in large volumes, the selling by the insiders, is forcing the price back down again. We really only have to equate this to some real life examples. Scarcity in a product increases its value. Think of designer goods, branded items, luxury goods. If we want to increase the value of something then we make a 'limited edition'. This allows us to sell the item at a higher price, as there are fewer available and they are therefore more desirable. By contrast the price of a mass market product will be much lower by virtue of the numbers made, and the market unlikely to stand any increase in price.

Whenever large institutions have to sell large blocks of stock at the top of the market, they don't just place one order for the entire block. This would drive the price down and reduce the profit on the sale, so in order to overcome this problem there is a facility which many large companies use called 'dark pools'.

Now I did say at the start of this book that volume was the only activity that could not be hidden. Well this is not strictly true. Large institutions use dark pools to hide large transactions, and the details are not made public until after the trade has been completed.

There is no transparency, and once again, is something few traders or investors are ever aware of. It's not a huge issue for us, and anyway, there is little than can be done about it.

However, this does reinforce the point. When a large block has to be sold, executing this in one order would drive the price down too far, so the alternative is to either break the order into smaller blocks and sell in smaller volume, or to use the dark pool to hide it completely.

The same problem occurs in the buying climax, where the insiders are buying in large volume, which in turn starts to raise the market as a result. Nick Leeson, the rogue trader who bankrupted Barings Bank had the same problem. His positions were so large, that it was impossible to unwind them without moving the market against his own buying and selling.

Finally, another example is when trading an illiquid stock, or currency. Buying in volume will very quickly put the price up against you. Sell in volume and the price will move lower. This is the problem that the insiders face, when they are selling or buying in large volume. The price will always move against them as a result, which is why they cannot simply complete all their selling or buying in one session.

It has to be done over two, three or four, and is another reason why the distribution process, the selling climax and the buying climax have to be spread over a period. This was one of the issues I struggled with for some time when I first started, but I soon learnt we simply have to be patient, and wait for the climax to complete. Remember it takes time to sell large volumes quickly!

The Buying Climax

It is the same problem with the buying climax. It is the sheer scale of their own buying which results in the market price rising, coupled with short holders closing positions. But, the predominant effect, once the insiders enter the market is the volume effect on price. If we go back to our buying climax example once more :

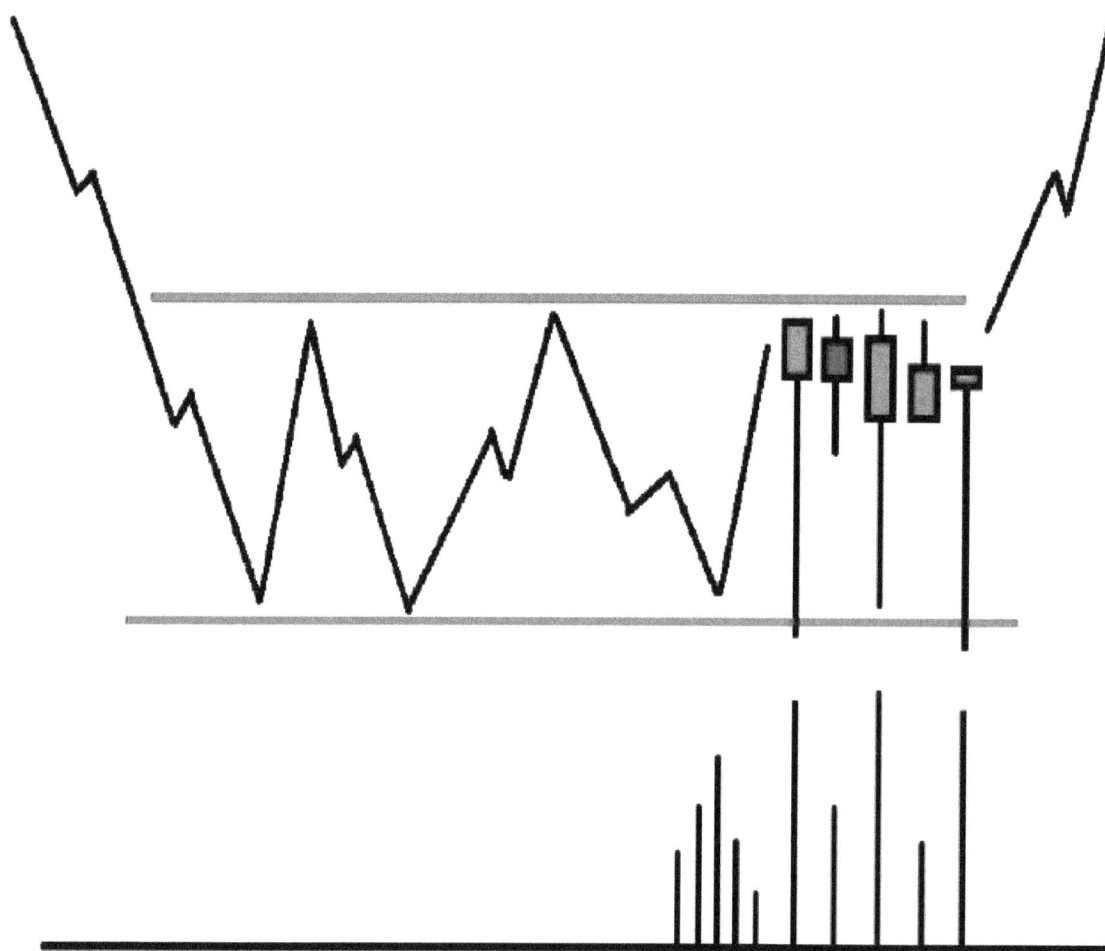

Fig 5.20 Buying Climax

The market is still bearish, and the insiders are forcing the market lower with negative news, and then buying in volume to fill the warehouses which in turn is moving the market higher against them. The action is stopped and the market moves sideways, temporarily.

More bad news is then used to send the market lower, where large volumes are bought once again, with the market rising on the insider buying. This is repeated until the warehouses are full.

In many ways, it doesn't really matter whether we believe the market manipulation aspect of price behaviour or not. What is EXTREMELY important, is that you do believe in the relationship between price and volume in these phases of market behaviour.

The ultra high volumes are showing us, more clearly than anything else, that the market is preparing for a reversal in trend. When we see the price action and high volumes associated with a selling climax, then we know that there is a trend reversal lower in prospect. When we see the price action and high volumes of a buying climax, then we know that we are likely to see a bullish trend starting soon. It's guaranteed.

This is what high volume and the associated price action is telling us. It really couldn't be any clearer.

Chapter Six

Volume Price Analysis – The Next Level

I never argue with the tape.
Jesse Livermore (1877-1940)

In the last few chapters we have gradually started to build our knowledge and understanding of VPA, beginning with a very simple analysis of price and volume at the micro level, the ticker tape level if you like. From there, we moved out to consider some simple concepts of price and volume at the macro level, and finally in the last chapter, the 'global' view and the cycles of behaviour that markets follow with the ebb and flow of volume as the insiders push and pull the price action, this way and that, using the media as their primary vehicle.

However, as I said at the start of this book, there is nothing new in trading, and volume has been around for over 100 years. One thing that has changed since, is the introduction of candlesticks as the 'de facto' standard for analysing price action on the chart. All the original books and articles mentioned so far have one thing in common, namely that the charts use bars to describe the price action. Candlesticks have only been adopted by Western traders since the early 1990's. Again I was fortunate in having been taught the basics by Albert, and I have used candlesticks ever since for a number of reasons.

For me, candles are so much more descriptive than any bar can ever be. VPA with candlesticks is my own methodology. By combining the power of candlesticks with VPA gives us a deeper perspective of market behaviour.

In this chapter I want to move to the next level and explain the various candle and candle patterns that we build into our VPA analysis and education. I must stress, that this chapter is NOT intended as another book on Japanese candlesticks. There are plenty of those already available, and perhaps I may write one myself in the future.

In this chapter I want to explain those candles and candle pattern combinations which are the ones to watch when analysing a chart using VPA.

We're going to look at lots of examples using schematics before moving to actual annotated chart examples in subsequent chapters.

However, before moving forward I would like to explain some broad principles which apply, and which we need to keep in mind in any analysis when using candlesticks.

Principle Number One

The length of any wick, either to the top or bottom of the candle is ALWAYS the first point of focus because it instantly reveals, impending strength, weakness, and indecision, and more importantly, the extent of any associated market sentiment.

Principle Number Two

If no wick is created, then this signals strong market sentiment in the direction of the closing price.

Principle Number Three

A narrow body indicates weak market sentiment. A wide body represents strong market sentiment.

Principle Number Four

A candle of the same type will have a completely different meaning depending on where it appears in a price trend. Always reference the candle to the location within the broader trend, or in the consolidation phase.

Principle Number Five

Volume validates price. Start with the candle, then look for validation or anomalies of the price action by the volume bar.

So, let me start with two of the most important candles, the shooting star and the hammer candle.

The Shooting Star Candle

Price action - weakness.

The shooting star candle is one of our three premier candles in VPA that we watch for in all time frames, and in all instruments and markets.

The price action is revealing weakness, since the price has risen and then fallen to close near the opening price, with the sellers overwhelming the buyers in the session.

Shooting star candles appear in every trend, both bullish and bearish, and at every point within the trend. Their appearance **DOES NOT** signal an immediate reversal. Their appearance signals **POTENTIAL WEAKNESS** at that point in the price action. The candle will **ONLY** gain significance based on the associated volume.

The shooting star price action appears in every up and down trend. It is the classic signal of weakness, and it is only volume which can give a **CLEAR** signal as to the relative strength of this weakness, and consequently the extent of any reversal. The best way to understand these variants is with some examples.

In a bullish up trend any shooting star with below average volume is simply signalling a possible pause in the upwards trend, with a potential short term pull back. Following such a signal, we would then be considering the previous and subsequent price action for confirmation of a continuation of the trend.

As the trend develops further, this initial weakness may be confirmed further with additional shooting star candles, with average volumes. Once we have two candles of similar proportions in a trend, and in the same time frame, we can then compare volume between the two candles. If the first candle was an initial sign of weakness, then the second, with increased volume is confirming this weakness further. After all, if the volume on the second shooting star is higher than the first, so 'weakness' has increased as more selling is coming to the market and forcing prices lower in the session.

This brings me to an important point which I would like to introduce here. It is perhaps an obvious point, but nevertheless one which is worth making.

If we see one shooting star, this can be taken as a sign of weakness. If we see two consecutive shooting stars, or two relatively close to each other, this is increasing the bearish sentiment. If a third appears then this is adding yet more bearish sentiment. In other words, single candles are important, multiple appearances of the same candle, in the same price area, exponentially increase the level of bearish or bullish sentiment. And remember, this is JUST based on price action alone. Add in the volume aspect and this takes our analysis to another level, which is why I find it so strange that PAT traders don't use volume!

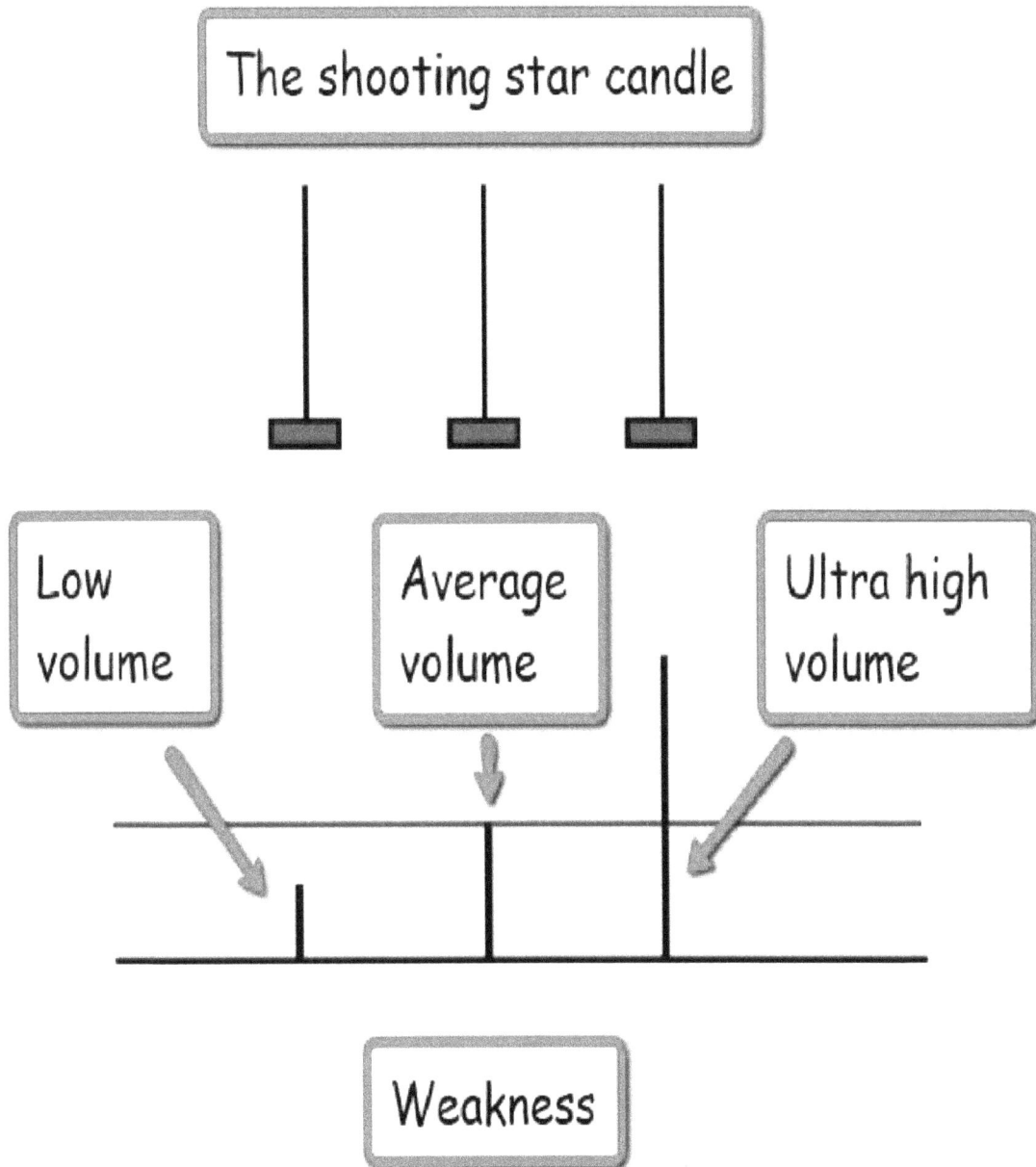

Fig 6.10 Shooting Star Candles And Volume

If we took this price pattern, as shown in Fig 6.10, and imagine that these were in fact three simultaneous candles, each with increasing volume, then based on this combination of candle pattern and volume, do we think the market is likely to rise or fall?

Clearly, the market is going to fall and the reason is very straightforward. First, we have seen three consecutive candles, whose high has failed at exactly the same price level, so there is weakness in this region. Second we have three shooting stars, which we already know are signs of weakness, and finally we have volume. We have rising volume on three identical candles at the same price point on our chart. The market is really struggling at this level, and the last two could certainly be considered part of the selling climax.

Moreover, if these signals were to appear after a period of sideways price action, then this gives the signals even more strength, as we are then validating our VPA analysis with another technique of price analysis, which is support and resistance.

It is very easy with hindsight to look back and identify tops and bottoms. What is far more difficult is to try and identify major turning points in real time so I have created the schematic in Fig 6.11 to explain how this action plays out on a chart. It will also allow me to introduce other broader aspects of this methodology.

Fig 6.11 Typical Price Action And Shooting Star Candles

If we take the left hand side of the schematic first. The market has been trending higher, when a shooting star candle appears on the chart, perhaps it even has above average volume. Does the appearance of this candle signify a major reversal of trend or simply a minor pause and pullback? The answer is, based on this candle, we do not know.

All we can say for sure, is that we have seen a bullish trend develop in the previous sessions, and now we have some weakness. We know that the signal has some validity, as it has appeared after the market has been rising for some time, and this is one of the points I was trying to highlight earlier. We have to consider all these signals in the context of what has gone before.

In this case we had a nice bullish trend developing, when a shooting star candle appeared with above average volume. The chart now has our full attention. What do we do? Do we jump in and take a trade?

Absolutely not. As I mentioned earlier the market does not turn on a dime. It pauses, reflects, then rises, pauses once again and then falls.

We wait for the next candle to form to see if it is confirming this weakness, perhaps some narrow spread up candles, followed by another shooting star. The appearance of the first shooting star is our cue to sit up and take note. It is our cue to check the subsequent candles for confirmation of the initial weakness, and try to deduce with VPA whether this is a sign of longer term weakness or merely a temporary pause. At this point we would also be considering price congestion areas on the chart for clues. After all, if we are in a price region where the market has reversed previously, then this too is a strong signal, and in addition may also give some clues as to the likely depth of any reversal.

In addition, if the price action has only recently broken out from an accumulation phase, then it is unlikely to be the start of any reversal lower, and once again this is a key point. To always consider where we are in the context of the trend and its relation to recent consolidation phases of price action during which the insiders would have been accumulating. After all, it is very unlikely that a new trend would have been started and then promptly reverse, particularly if a successful test had followed. So the context of where the candle comes in relation to the 'bigger picture' is important and helps to answer the question.

The next step is to check the higher and lower time frames for a broader perspective on this signal and for context, as well as applying VPA to these timeframes.

For example, if this price action had appeared on a one hour chart, and on checking the 15 minute chart, we could see two shooting star candles had formed in that time frame, both with above average volume, this gives confirmation that any reversal may be more significant. Furthermore, the 15 min chart may also have significant areas of price congestion which would also contribute to our analysis. All this analysis takes minutes, if not seconds while waiting for the next candle to form.

Using multiple time frames also gives us a view on the longer term trend, and may also help to answer the question of whether the appearance of this shooting start candle is merely a minor reversal or the start of a longer term change in trend. This is one of the many advantages of using multiple time frames for chart analysis. Furthermore, using multiple time frames will give a perspective on how long we are likely to be holding any position.

This makes perfect sense. After all, if the longer term trend is bullish, and we are trading short on a faster time frame chart, then it's likely that we will only be holding this position for a limited period of time, as we are trading against the dominant trend for the session. Once again, this will help to answer the question of whether this is a trend reversal, or simply a minor pause and pull back.

There are a variety of techniques to help us ascertain whether the market is at 'a top' and these will be outlined in detail later in the book. However, I wanted to introduce some of these here. Multiple time frame analysis, VPA analysis, price congestion and candle pattern analysis can all be used to help us answer this question. Furthermore, a rising market with falling volume is also a classic sign of weakness.

The shooting star may have been preceded with a narrow spread up candle on high volume, again classic signs of weakness, but they still do not answer the question of whether this is a minor pull back or a major reversal in trend. To do this we need help, and that help comes from using VPA in other time frames, along with the techniques which you will also discover later.

One such technique is the depth and extent of any price congestion as the longer a market moves sideways at a particular level the more likely a breakout and reversal.

Moreover, VPA is an art and not a science, which is why trading software cannot do this analysis for us. The analysis we carry out on each candle,

candle pattern, associated volumes, and associated price across multiple time frames to assess and determine the dominant trend, is all subjective. Initially it takes time to learn which is why I have written this book in order to short cut the learning curve for you.

The five principles mentioned at the start of this chapter apply to all candles, and all our VPA analysis, but as the shooting star and its opposite number the hammer are so important, I felt it was appropriate to introduce the basic concepts of the next levels of VPA analysis here.

Just to complete this commentary on the shooting star candle, not only do these appear in up trends, but they also appear in down trends, and here they act as confirmation of weakness, particularly if they appear shortly after the start of the move lower. The appearance of a shooting star candle in a downtrend which follows a selling climax could be a test of demand as the market moves lower. Furthermore, if the shooting star is accompanied by low volume, and the market had been in sideways congestion for a period following the selling climax, this also confirms the insiders testing demand as the market moves away from the distribution phase. The shooting star is a sign that the market has been pushed higher, but there is no demand so falls back to close, at or near the open.

Shooting star candles may also appear at minor reversals deeper in the trend, as the downwards pressure pauses and pulls back higher. Here again, if the candle is accompanied with above average volume, it is only telling us one thing, namely the market is still weak, and we have not yet reached the buying climax at the bottom of the trend.

This pattern of price action is the insiders selling back to the market some of the inventory they have collected from panicked sellers who had bailed out earlier. This inventory in the warehouse has to be sold as the market moves lower. After all, the insiders don't like to buy anywhere other than at their target price, in other words, a wholesale price.

Some buyers will come in at these pull backs, thinking the market has bottomed out, and about to turn higher, whilst others continue to sell. This price action occurs all the time in a price waterfall, as the market moves lower and fast. The insiders have to stop the fall, pause, push the market higher using the media and sell into the created demand whilst also dealing with the ongoing selling that is continuing to arrive. The volume will therefore be above average or high, showing further weakness to come.

The Hammer Candle

Price action – strength

The hammer is the second of our three 'premier' candles and another classic candle that we look out for in all markets and time frames. It is the classic candle of strength, for either temporary strength, or as a signal for longer term price reversal.

A hammer is formed when in a session, the price has fallen, only to reverse and recover to close back near the opening price. This is a sign of strength with the selling having been absorbed in sufficient strength for the buyers to overwhelm the sellers, allowing the market to recover. The hammer is so called as it is 'hammering out a bottom', and just like the shooting star, is immensely powerful when combined with VPA.

Once again, the five principles outlined at the beginning of the chapter apply to the hammer candle, and again it is very easy to become over excited as soon as you see this candle. It is so easy to jump into what we think is going to be a change in trend. If the market has been moving lower fast, which they generally do, it is unlikely that a reversal will take effect immediately. What is far more likely, is that the market will pause, mover higher, and then continue lower once again. In other words posting a short squeeze.

As we now know, the insiders have to clear inventory which has been sold in the move lower, and the first signal of a pause is the hammer, as the insiders move in to buy, supporting the market temporarily. They may even push it higher with a shooting star candle. The hammer is signalling 'forced buying' by the insiders, and the shooting star is signalling 'forced selling' by the insiders. Whilst they do move bearish markets fast, there is always selling that has to be absorbed at higher levels, and this inventory has to be cleared before moving lower once again. After all, if this did not happen, the insiders would be left with a significant tranche of inventory bought at high prices, and not at wholesale prices.

A price waterfall will always pause, pull back higher, before continuing lower. As always, volume holds the key, and if the volumes have been rising in the price waterfall lower, then this is a strong signal of further weakness to come. Therefore, a single hammer will simply not be enough to halt the move lower, even if the volume is above average. As always, the price action that follows is key, as is the price and volume in the associated time frames along with any price congestion in the vicinity. This is the same problem as before and the question that we always have to ask, whenever we see a hammer or a shooting star, is whether the price action is signalling a pause in the longer term trend, or a true reversal in trend.

The power of the hammer candle, just like the shooting star, is revealed, once we see a sequence of two or three of these candles accompanied by high or extremely high volume. It is at this point we know, for sure that we are in the realms of a buying climax and only have to be patient and wait for the insiders to complete their task, before they begin to take the market higher.

Furthermore, we also have to remember that once the buying climax is completed, we are likely to see one or more tests using the hammer candle. These candles may be less pronounced than the true hammer, perhaps with relatively shallow wicks, but the principle will be the same. The open and close will be much the same, and there will always be a wick to the lower body.

For a successful test, the volume needs to be low too, and there is also likely to be more than one test in this phase. These tests can appear both in the price congestion area of accumulation as well as in the initial phase of any breakout, as the price action moves back into an old area of heavy selling immediately above.

These are the two candles which are our number one priority in reading of price and volume. As I'm sure you will recall from the introduction to Volume Price Analysis, all we are looking for, on any candle or sequence of candles, is validation or anomaly. Is the volume validating the price action and what signal is this sending to us, or is it an anomaly, and therefore sending us a very different signal.

In a sense, there is never an anomaly with a shooting star candle, since the price action is sending a clear message on it's own. As any price action trader will tell you, this candle is a signal of weakness, in itself. There is no other interpretation. The market has risen and then fallen in the session, therefore the market MUST be weak. What volume does is put this weakness into context, which is why I have shown the schematic with the three volume bars, low, average and high (or even ultra high). A shooting star with low volume is a sign of weakness, but probably not significant, unless it is a test of demand following a selling climax as we start the downwards move lower.

A shooting star with average volume is telling us there is weakness, it is a relatively strong signal, and the pull back may be more significant than in the first example on low volume. Finally, we have the shooting star with high or ultra high volume and this is where the professional money is now selling out. Whether it's the market makers in stocks and indices, or the big operators in futures, or the market makers in forex, or the big operators in bonds, it doesn't matter. The insiders are selling out, and we need to prepare and take note, as a big move is on the way!

The point is this. There is never an anomaly with a shooting star, only ever a validation of the strength of the signal. The volume always confirms the price action with a shooting star, and all we have to do is consider whether it is low, average or high to ultra high, and frame this in terms of the preceding price action across our time frames, and track the subsequent candles as they unfold on the chart.

The same points apply to the hammer candle. Once again, there is NEVER an anomaly with a hammer candle. The price action tells us all we need to know. In the session, for whatever reason, the price has moved lower and then recovered to close near or at the open. It is therefore a sign of strength, and the volume bar then reveals the extent of this strength.

Once again, I have shown three hammer candles with three volume bars, low, average and ultra high as we can see in Fig 6.12.

A hammer with a low volume candle is indicating minor weakness, average volume suggests stronger signs of a possible reversal, whilst ultra high signals the insiders buying heavily, as part of the buying climax. The volume is giving us clues on how far the market is likely to travel. An average volume bar with a hammer candle, may well give us an intra day scalping opportunity. And there is nothing wrong with that. A low volume hammer is simply telling us that any reversal is likely to be minor, as there is clearly little interest to the upside at this price level.

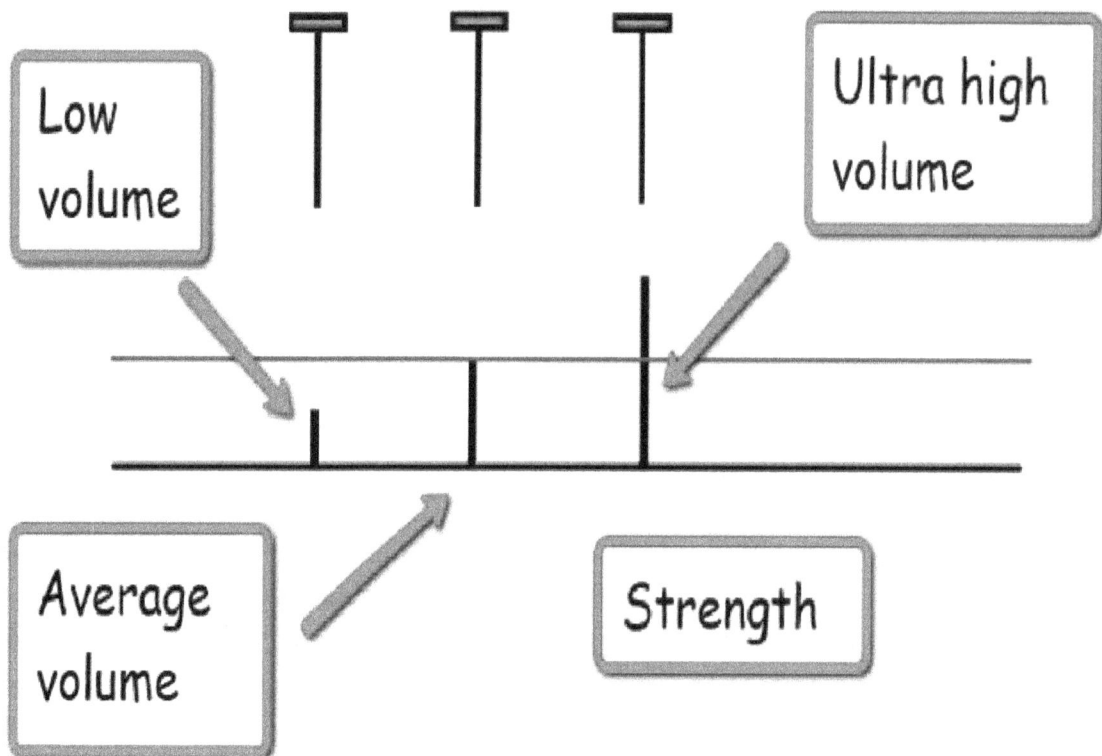

Fig 6.12 Hammer Candles And Volume

This raises another point which I feel I should also mention here.

VPA not only helps us get INTO low risk trading positions, it also helps to KEEP us in those positions, which is often one of the hardest things to do in trading. Holding a position and staying in a trend can be very difficult, and I believe is one of the hardest skills to master. It is also a primary reason why so many traders fail. After all, it is staying in a trend where we maximise any profit, and a trend can be from a few minutes or hours, to several days and weeks.

We all know as traders, that the market only goes up in steps and down in steps, never in a straight line, and we have to stay in positions through these minor pull backs and reversals. This is one of the many great powers of VPA as it will help to keep you in an existing position, and give you the confidence using your own analysis, to truly see inside the market.

For example, the market may be moving lower, we are short the market, and we see a hammer formed. Is this a reversal in trend and time to exit, or merely a short term reversal in a longer term trend lower? If the volume is low, then clearly the insiders are not buying at this level. Perhaps the hammer is followed by a shooting star on average to high volume, a sign of weakness in the down trend, and confirming the analysis of the hammer candle. The market is weak and our analysis using VPA has given us the confidence to hold the position in the market through this pullback. Without volume, we would have little idea of the strength or weakness of this price activity. With volume, it is all revealed, and we can base our decisions accordingly.

This is the power of VPA. Not only does it get us into trades, but it helps keep us in, and finally gets us out.

Taking the above example again in Fig 6.12, and the hammer which arrives with high or ultra high volume. This is an early warning signal of a potential reversal. The big money is moving in, and as a short seller it is potentially time to exit the market, take some or all of our profits off the table, and prepare for a long position when the break out occurs.

Getting into a trade is the easy part, staying in and then getting out at the right time is very difficult. And this is where VPA is such a powerful technique in giving us the insight we need into market behaviour. Once you begin to interpret and understand what the price and volume relationship is signalling, then you have arrived at trading Nirvana.

Now finally, if we do see the hammer candle at the top of a bullish trend, it has a different name, and a completely different interpretation. This will be covered later in this chapter when we consider other candles and candle patterns, as we continue to build on our knowledge.

This is what I meant by Principle 4 – a candle can have a very different meaning depending on where it appears in the overall trend. At the top of a trend the hammer is called a 'hanging man' and when it appears in a candle pattern with a shooting star is signalling weakness.

The final candle in our trio of premier candles is the doji, but not just any doji candle, it is the long legged doji.

The Long Legged Doji Candle

Price action – indecision

There are many variants of the doji candle, and you will see them continuously in every chart. They are all characterised in the same way with the open and close being the same or very close, and with a wick to the upper and lower body.

This is the price action which creates the unique pattern of the doji candle, or doji cross. Whilst there are many different sizes and types of doji candle, there is only ONE which I believe is significant in the context of VPA, and that is the long legged doji.

In itself the doji candle signifies indecision. The market is reaching a point at which bullish and bearish sentiment is equally balanced. In the context of what actually take place in the session, it is something like this. The market opens, and sentiment takes the price action in one direction. This is promptly reversed and taken in the opposite direction, before the opening market sentiment regains control and brings the market back to the opening price once more. In other words, there have been some wild swings in price action within the session, but the fulcrum of price has remained in the middle.

The key point about this type of doji candle, is that both the upper and lower wicks are long in comparison to the body, and should resemble what I used to call, a 'daddy long legs' – a small flying insect with very long legs!

The power of the candle lies in it's predictive power as a potential signal of a reversal in trend. Just like the hammer and the shooting star, the price action alone gives us a firm signal, but when combined with volume, it becomes immensely powerful. The price action in the candle is sufficient, in itself, to tell us visually that there is indecision. After all, if this were not the case, then the candle would be very different in construction.

Once again, the price action reveals the sentiment, which in this case is indecision and therefore a possible reversal. The long legged doji can signal a reversal from bearish to bullish, or bullish to bearish, and the change in direction depends on the preceding price action. If we have been in an up trend for some time, and the long legged doji appears, then this may be the first sign of a reversal in trend to bearish. Conversely, if we see this candle after the market has been falling for some time, then this may be signalling a reversal to bullish.

However, unlike the shooting star and the hammer candle, with the long legged doji candle we CAN have an anomaly in volume. Once again as we can see in Fig 6.13 I have shown the candle with three volume bars beneath, and the one which is an anomaly is the first one on low volume.

Let me explain why this is an anomaly, and also introduce another concept here which fits neatly into this section.

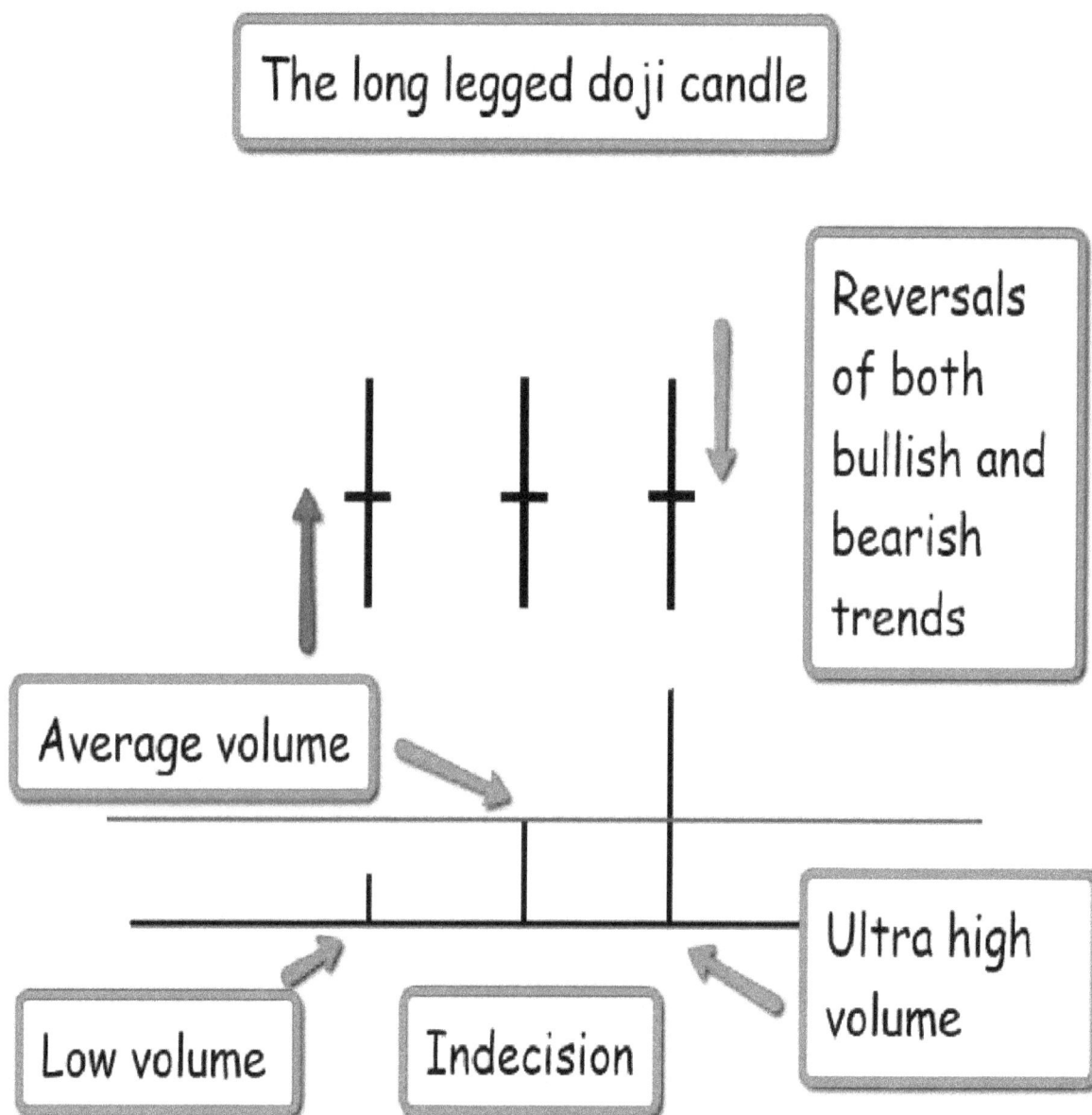

Fig 6.13 The Long Legged Doji

Why is low volume on such a candle an anomaly? Well, let's think about this logically. The market has moved sharply in both directions and finally closed back or near the opening price. This price action is a sign of volatility in the market, as the market has swung back and forth in the session. If the market were not volatile, then we would see a very different type of candle. Therefore, if the market is volatile, why is there low volume.

Volatile markets require effort and as we know effort and result go hand in hand. However, in this instance we have no effort (low volume) and a big result (wide price action). Clearly this is an anomaly, and the only logical answer is that the price is being moved by the insiders, who are simply not joining in at the moment. The most common reason for this is stop hunting, where the market makers and insiders are moving prices violently, first one way and then the other, to shake traders out, and to take out stop and limit orders in the process. They are not buying or selling themselves, but simply 'racking' the price around, generally using a news release as the catalyst, and this brings me to an important point in the VPA story.

The long legged doji is seen most often during a fundamental news release, and the classic one for the US markets is the monthly Non Farm Payroll data, released on the first Friday of every month. On the release, price behaviour becomes extremely volatile, where this candle is created repeatedly when economic data such as this is released. The market swings violently one way, then the other, and then perhaps back again. It is the ideal opportunity for the insiders to whipsaw traders in and out of positions fast, taking out stops and other orders in the market at the same time.

And the reason we know this is happening is volume, or rather the lack of it. If the volume is low, then this is NOT a genuine move, but an ANOMALY. For the price to behave in this way takes effort, and we are seeing this with no effort, as shown with low volume. The insiders are simply manipulating prices, and in this case, the long legged doji is NOT signalling a reversal, but something very different. Insider manipulation on a grand scale at this price level. It may well be that the market does reverse later, but at this stage, we stay out, and wait for further candles to unfold.

The next point which leads on from this is the interaction between volume and the news. Whenever we have an economic release, a statement, a rate decision, or any other item of fundamental news, then the associated volume reaction will instantly tell us whether the market is validating the news or ignoring it. In other words, here too volume validates the news release, and tells us immediately whether the market insiders are joining in any subsequent price action or waiting on the sidelines and staying out.

If the insiders are joining in, then we can too, and if not, then we stay out, just like them.

For example, when a 'big number' is released, say NFP, which is seen as positive for risk assets such as equities, commodities and risk currencies, and perhaps we are trading a currency. Then we should see these assets rise strongly on the news, supported by strong and rising volume. If this is the case, then we know the markets have validated the news and the insiders and big money are joining in. We might see a wide spread up candle, with high volume. The news has been validated and confirmed by the price action and associated volume.

I would urge you to study volume whenever news is released, as it is one of the quickest ways to learn the basics of VPA. Here you will see it at work. Surges in volume accompanying large price moves, large price moves on low volume, and trap moves, such as low volume on a long legged doji. It will all be there for you. However, the key point is this. When news is released, it is often the first place where we see volume surges in the market, and they are excellent places to start our analysis. If the volume surge has validated the price move, then we can be sure that the insiders are joining in the move higher or lower. If the price action has moved on the news, but has NOT been validated by supportive volumes, then it is an anomaly and other forces are at work. This is telling us to be cautious.

Volume and the news should go hand in hand. After all, the markets generally react to the major news releases which occur throughout the trading day, and this is the easiest, quickest and simplest way, to begin to read the market, and also gain a perspective on what is low, medium, high or ultra high volume, for all the various instruments and markets you may be trading.

A long legged doji candle, should always be validated by a minimum of average volume, and preferably high or ultra high. If it is low, then it is an anomaly and therefore a trap set by the insiders.

Those then are our trio of 'premier candles' that we watch for in all time frames. They are our cue to pay attention and start our VPA analysis. If we are not in a position, we are looking for confirmation of an entry, and if we are already in the market, we are looking for signals either to stay in, or exit.

Now let's move on to some of the other key individual candles, and then on to consider some candle patterns.

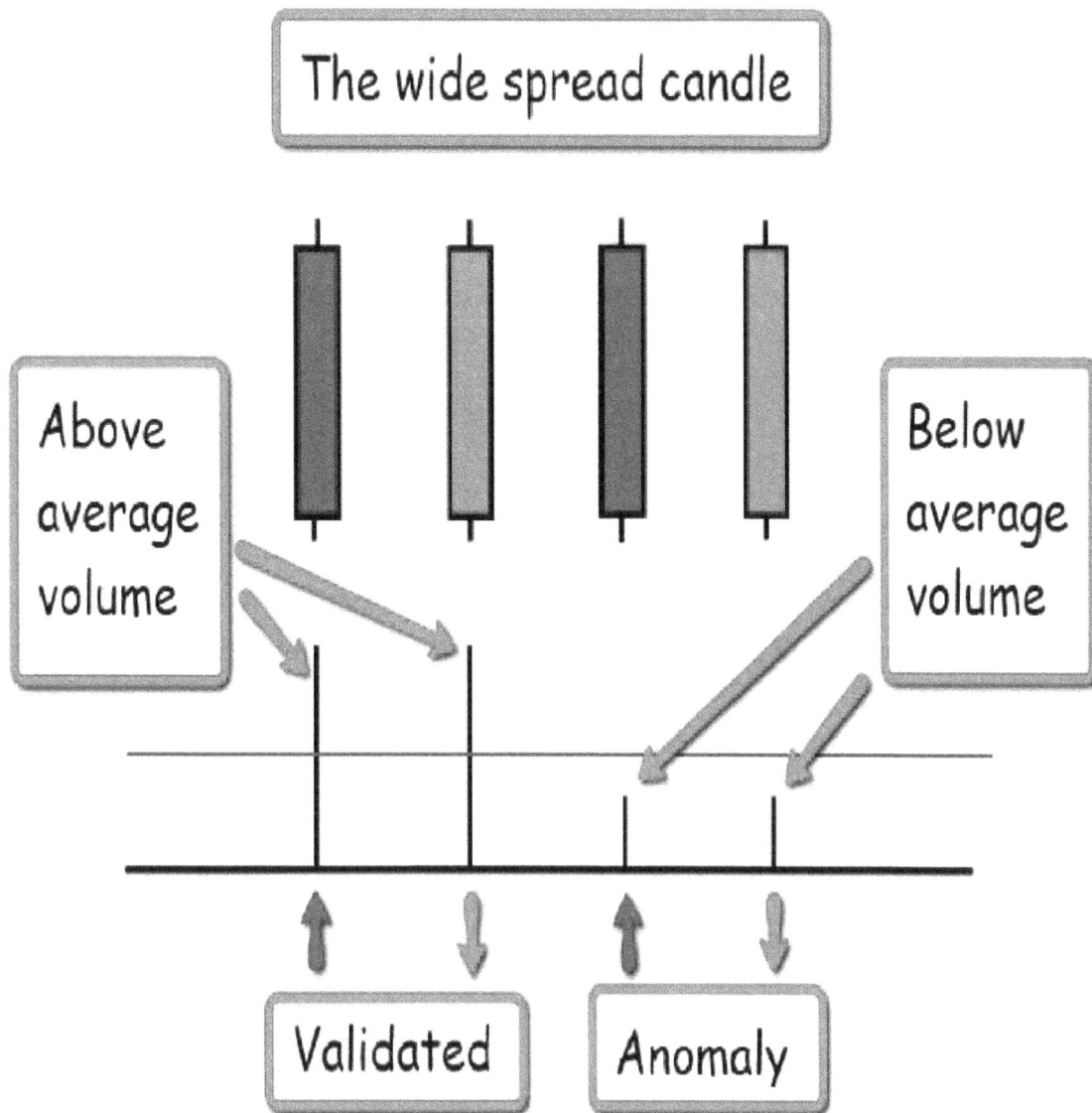

Fig 6.14 Wide Spread Candle

Price action – strong market sentiment

The price action of the wide spread candle is sending a clear signal with only ONE message. Sentiment for the session is strong. It is either strongly bullish or strongly bearish, but the word is STRONG. The price action has risen sharply higher or lower in the session and closed at or near the high of an up candle, or at or near the low of a down candle. The associated volume should therefore reflect this strong sentiment with 'strong' volume.

As we can see in the example in Fig 6.14, if the volume is above average, then this is what we should expect to see as it validates the price. The insiders are joining the move higher and everything is as it should be.

If the volume is below average or low, this is a warning signal. The price is being marked higher, but with little effort. The warning bells are now ringing. Many retail traders will be rushing to join the move higher or lower thinking this is a valid move by the market. But the volume reveals a very different story. If we are in a position, we look to exit. If we are not in a position we stay out, and wait for the next signal to see when and where the insiders are now taking this market.

Narrow Spread Candles

Price action – weak market sentiment

You may be wondering why we should be interested in a narrow spread candle, which tells us when market sentiment is weak. After all, shouldn't we simply be interested when the insiders are in the market, to which the answer is, yes, of course. Narrow spread candles can be found everywhere and in quantity. But the reason we need to consider them is that, in general markets move higher slowly. Markets pause, consolidate and reverse, often on narrow spread candles. Therefore, the interesting ones are NOT those validated by volume, but the anomalies.

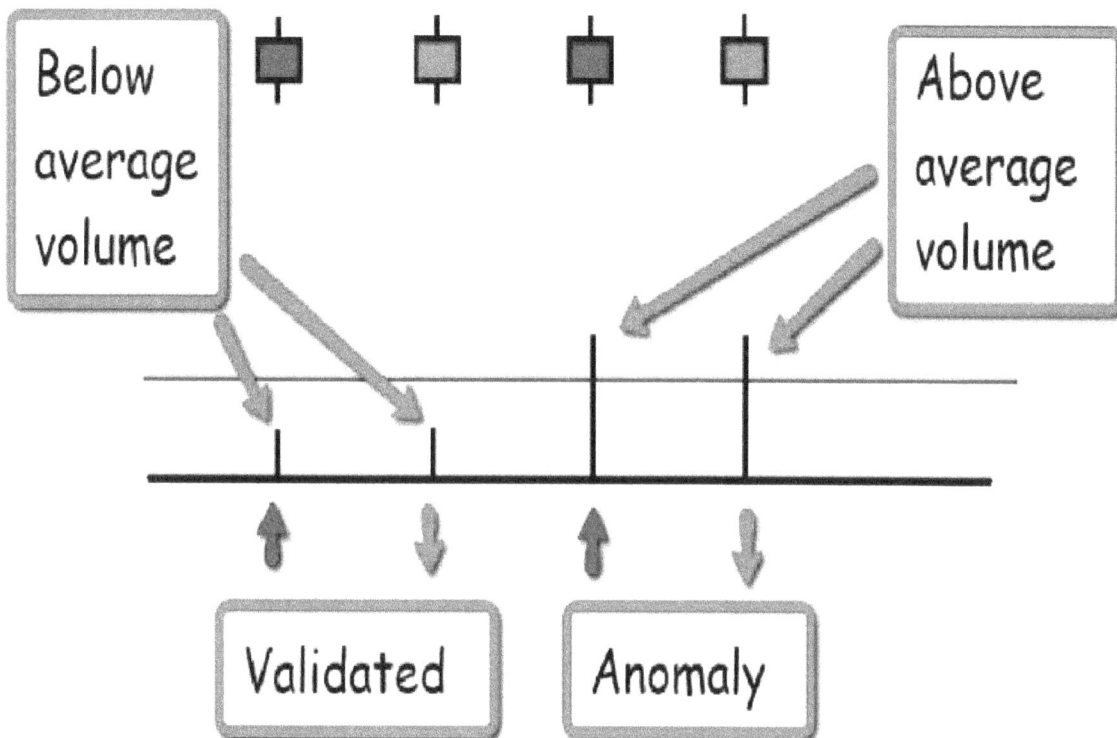

Fig 6.15 Narrow Spread Candles

A narrow spread candle should have low volume – again effort vs result. These are of little interest to us. However, the ones that are of great interest are the anomalies, where we see above average, or high volume, on a narrow spread candle. This should instantly alert us, and we should ask ourselves why.

The reason is very simple and can be seen in Fig 6.15. If we have an up candle with a narrow spread and relatively high volume, then the market is showing some signs of weakness. As we know high volume should result in a wide spread candle, not a narrow spread. Effort vs result again. The insiders are starting to struggle at this price level. The market is resistant to higher prices, and although it has moved a little way higher, is now proving resistant to any further progress, and the next candle could be a shooting star, which would then confirm this weakness further.

Equally, if we see high volume on a down candle then the reverse applies. Here the insiders are starting to see signs of bullish sentiment enter the market. The price is narrow, with buyers (insiders) coming in, and supporting the market at this level. Again, this is the first sign of a potential reversal from bearish to bullish. Subsequent candles may confirm this and we would now be waiting for a hammer, or possibly a long legged doji to add further weight to the analysis.

The Hanging Man Candle

Price action – potential weakness after bullish trend

When I first started using VPA and candles, I always used to assume that a hanging man appearing in a bullish trend was a sign of strength, and continuation of the trend, since to me this was the same action as the hammer candle. It isn't. It is in fact the opposite, and is a sign of weakness, provided it is associated with above average volume as shown in Fig 6.16.

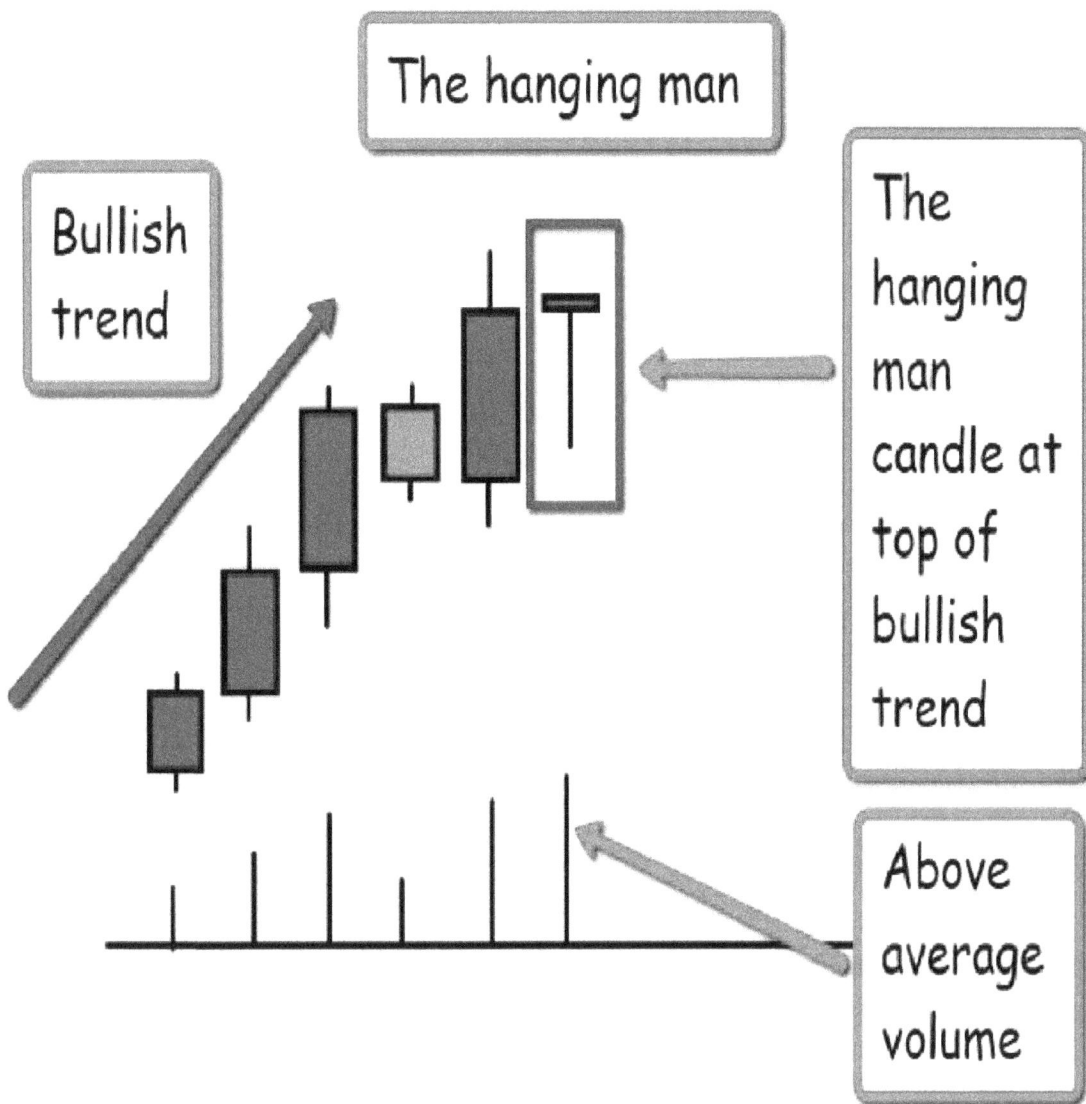

Fig 6.16 Hanging Man

And the question is, why is it a sign of weakness? The answer is very simple. The market has been rising steadily on rising volume, when at some point in the bullish trend, the market sells off sharply, with the price moving lower in the session, only to recover and close at, or near the high of the session, creating the familiar 'hammer candle price action'. Except here we now refer to this candle as the hanging man candle, as it is now at the top of a bullish trend.

The reason this candle is considered to be bearish is that this is the first sign of selling pressure in the market. The insiders have been tested, and the buyers have supported the market, but this candle is sending a signal that the market is moving towards an over sold area. The body of the candle can be either red or blue, but the price needs to close at, or near the open.

The price action is confirming the appearance of sustained selling pressure, which on this occasion has been supported by the buyers, but it is an early warning of a possible change. It is an early warning signal, and now we need to watch our charts for confirming signals.

The insiders will have seen this weakness appearing too, and be starting to plan their next move.

The hanging man is validated if it is followed by the appearance of a shooting star in the next few candles, particularly if associated with above average or high volume. The key here is validation. On its own it is not a strong signal, but merely gives us early warning of a possible change.

For this candle to be validated and confirmed we need to see further signs of weakness at this level, or close to this level, which would then increase the significance of the candle. For example, a hanging man, immediately followed by a shooting star is an excellent combination and adds considerably to the strength of the initial signal. Even if the shooting star appears later in the candle sequence, this is still a strong confirming signal, provided it is associated with high volume.

Stopping Volume

Price action - strength

This is what the price action looks like as the brakes are applied by the insiders, and is generally referred to as stopping volume. As I have said many times before, the market is like an oil tanker. It never reverses on a dime for many reasons, not least because just like a supertanker it has momentum, and therefore takes time to respond, once the brakes are applied.

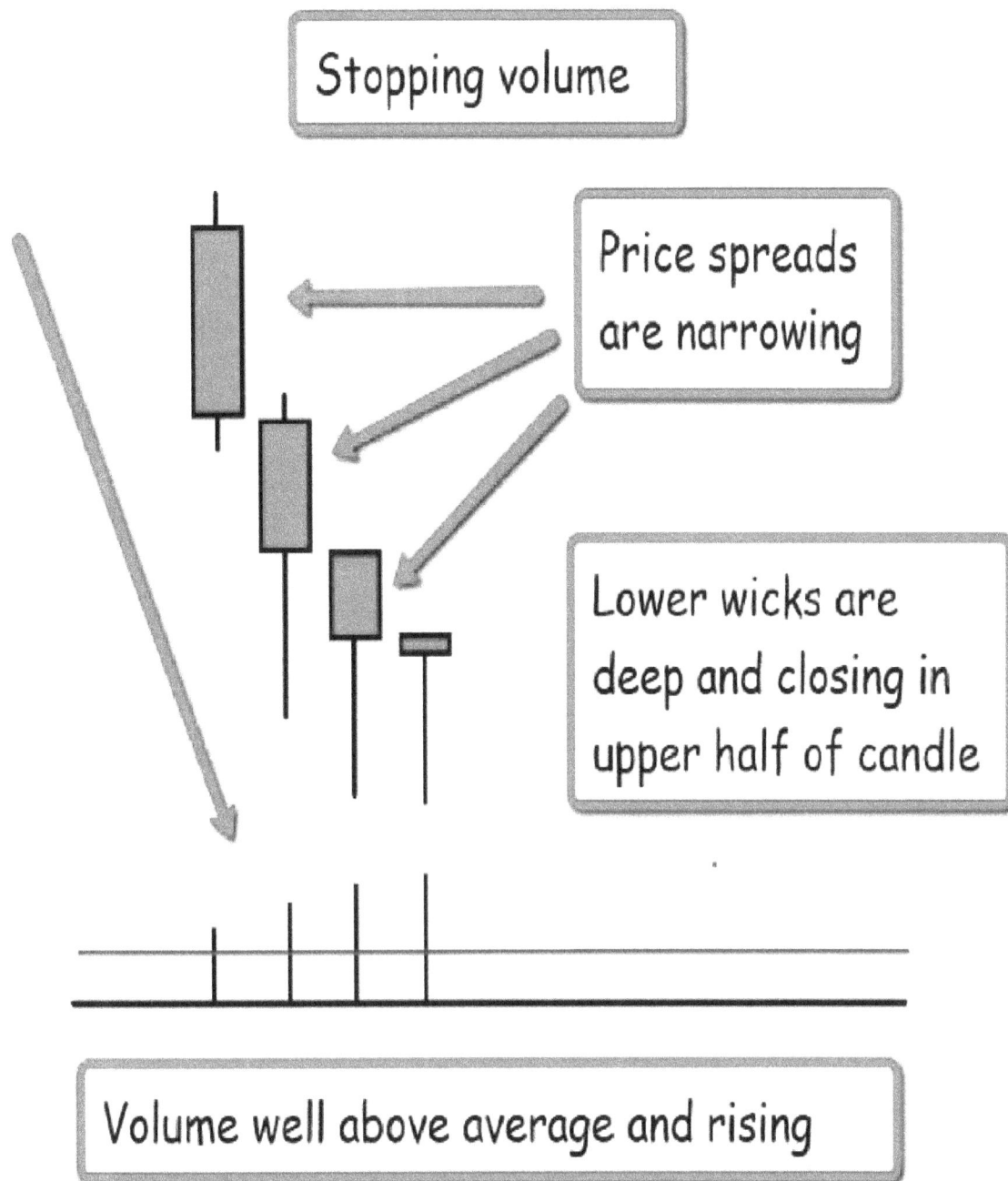

Stopping volume

Price spreads are narrowing

Lower wicks are deep and closing in upper half of candle

Volume well above average and rising

Fig 6.17 Stopping Volume

In Fig 6.17 we are in a strong down trend, the price waterfall has been in action and the market has been moving lower fast. However, the insiders now want to start slowing the rate of descent, so start to move in and begin the buying process. This buying is then seen in subsequent candles with deep lower wicks, but generally with relatively deep bodies. However, for additional strength in the signal, the close of the candle should be in the upper half of the open and close price. This is not a hard and fast rule, but generally describes the candles as shown in Fig 6.17.

What is happening, is that the weight of the selling pressure has become so great at this point, that even the insiders moving into the market have insufficient muscle to stop the market falling in one session. It takes two or three sessions for the brakes to be applied and is like our tanker. Switch off the engines and the ship will continue for several miles. It's the same with the markets, particularly when you remember that markets fall faster than they rise. In a market that is being driven by panic selling, the pressure is enormous.

The insiders move in and manage to absorb some of this pressure with prices recovering in the session, to close well off the lows of session thereby creating the deep lower wick. The selling then continues into the next session, and the insiders come in again with higher volumes, driving the price back higher off the lows, and perhaps with a narrower body on the candle, signalling that the buying is now starting to absorb the selling to a greater extent. Next, we see another candle with a narrower body and a deep wick. Finally, we see our first hammer candle.

The sequence of candles in Fig 6.17 is an almost perfect example, and if we do see this combination following a sharp move lower, then we would be on full alert for the forthcoming move higher.

Stopping volume is exactly that. It is the volume of the insiders and professional money coming into the market and stopping it falling further. It is a great signal of impending strength, and a potential reversal in the bearish trend to a bullish trend. It is the precursor to the buying climax which should follow as the last remnants of selling pressure are mopped up, the warehouses are filled to over flowing, and the insiders are ready to go. You should be to!!

Topping Out Volume

Price action - weakness

The clue is in the name! Just as stopping volume was stopping the market from falling further, so topping out volume is the market topping out after a bullish run higher.

Once again, the market does not simply stop and reverse, it has momentum, both in up trends and in down trends. The down trend pressure is certainly more intense as the market is generally moving faster. Nevertheless, in an up trend we still have momentum generated by the insiders driving demand. Traders and investors are jumping into the market, driven by greed and fear of missing out on easy profits. The volumes are high and rising, and the insiders are now selling into this demand, driving the market higher into this selling pressure, which is building. This is the price action we are seeing reflected in the deep upper wicks to each subsequent candle.

At this point it is becoming increasingly difficult for the insiders to keep the market momentum going, as they continue to sell at this level, with the candles creating the 'arcing pattern' as the spreads narrow and the price rise slows. Volumes are well above average and probably high or ultra high.

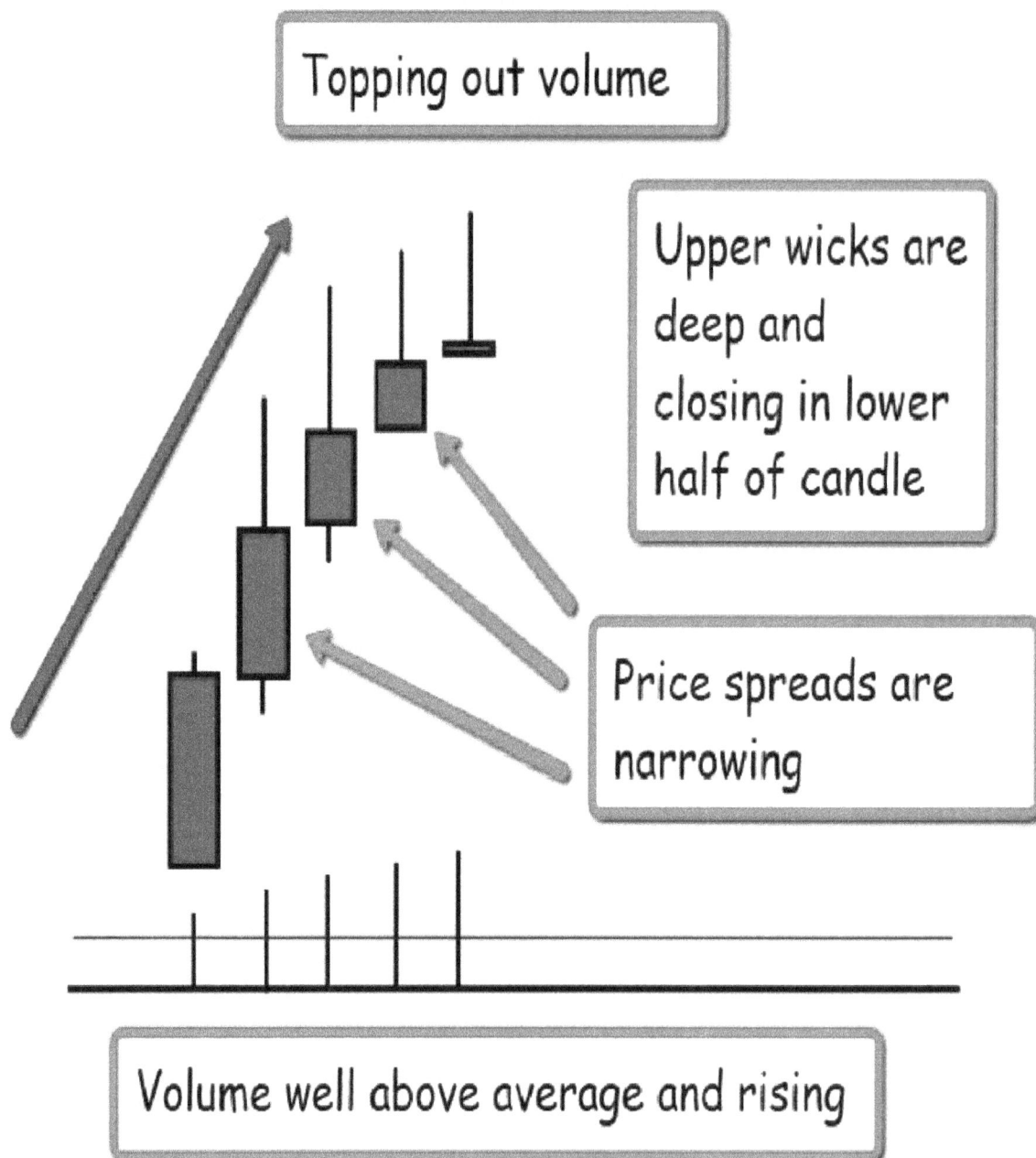

Fig 6.18 Topping Out Volume

In Fig 6.18 the last candle in this 'perfect' schematic is our old friend, the shooting star. We are now looking at the distribution phase which then culminates in the selling climax, before moving off to the next phase of the market cycle.

These then are the candles, candle patterns and associated volume, you will be looking for in all markets, in all instruments and all time frames. They are the MAJOR signals which are the wake up call to you as a VPA trader. They may be on a tick chart, they may be on a time chart. It makes no difference. The analysis of volume and price makes no distinction. Once you have practised using the basic principles that we have covered in the last few chapters, and further techniques you will learn in the following chapters, you will be ready to apply your new found knowledge and skills to any market. VPA is simple, powerful and it works, and once learnt is never forgotten.

There are many other candles and candle patterns in candlestick analysis, but as I said earlier, this is not a book about Japanese candlesticks. The ones I have illustrated here, are those that I look for all the time. They are the 'king pins' around which VPA revolves. Understand and recognise these instantly, and you will be amazed how quickly you will become confident and assured in your trading decisions. More importantly, if you have a position in the market you will have the confidence to stay in that position, and exit when your VPA analysis signals tell you to close out.

In the next few chapters we are going to build on our knowledge, and add further techniques, before finally putting it all together with annotated examples from live charts.

Chapter Seven

Support And Resistance Explained

Money and markets may never forget, but surely people do. And that will not be different this time, next time, or any time in your life.
Kenneth L Fisher (1950-)

So far in this book on Volume Price Analysis we have focused on the 'pure' relationship between volume and price.

In this chapter I am going to introduce the first of our analytical techniques, which helps to give us our 'perspective' on where we are in terms of the price behaviour on the chart. More importantly, when combined with VPA, this technique also reveals when trends are about to start or end, and equally when markets are moving into congestion phases.

To use a building analogy for a moment. If volume and price can be considered the foundations, then the analytical techniques I explain in the next few chapters are the walls, floors, ceilings and the roof. In other words, they provide the framework for volume and price. VPA on it's own is extremely powerful. However, what these additional techniques will add are the markers, the signposts if you like, as to where the market is in its longer term journey on the chart.

Perhaps one of the most difficult aspects of trading is managing and exiting any position. As I said earlier, getting in is the easy part, getting out is hard, and this is where these techniques will help in 'mapping' the price action. They are milestones if you like, and understanding these milestones and the messages they convey will then help you to understand not only when a market is about to trend, but also, and perhaps more importantly, when it is coming to an end.

Let me begin with the first of these techniques which is known as support and resistance. Once again, this is a powerful concept which can be applied to any market, any instrument and in any time frame, so whether you are using VPA as a scalping intra day trader, or as a longer term investor, support and resistance is one of the key principles of price behaviour on a chart.

However, the irony of support and resistance is that it is in sharp contrast to VPA itself. Volume Price Analysis focuses on the 'leading' aspects of price behaviour and tries to analyse where the market is heading next. Support and resistance does this in a different way entirely, by focusing on what has gone before. The history of price behaviour, the 'lagging' aspects of price behaviour.

Despite this irony, it is the combination of the two which gives us a perspective on where the market is in terms of its overall journey. It tells us where the market might pause, breakout, or reverse, both now and in the future, all important markers for the entry, management and exit of trading positions.

Therefore, let me recap the basics of price behaviour. In broad terms a market can only move in one of three ways, up, down or sideways. In other words, a market can only trend higher, trend lower or move sideways in a consolidating phase of price action. Of these three states, markets spend considerably more time moving sideways, than they do trending either higher or lower. As a rough rule of thumb this is generally considered to be around 70% of the time, whilst only trending for 30% of the time. Markets move sideways for all sorts of reasons, but primarily there are three.

First, is the pending release of an item of fundamental news. To see this in action simply watch the price action ahead of the monthly Non Farm Payroll for example. Prices are likely to trade in a narrow range for several hours ahead of this key release.

Second, markets move sideways in both the selling climax and the buying climax phases, when warehouses are either being filled or emptied by the insiders.

Third and finally, markets move sideways when they run into old areas of price, where traders have been locked into weak positions in previous moves. As the market approaches these areas, speculators and investors grab the chance to exit the market, usually grateful to be able to close out with a small loss.

Whatever the reason, areas of support and resistance will look something like Fig 7.10. This price behaviour appears on all charts, with clearly defined areas where the market has moved sideways for an extended period.

Support And Resistance

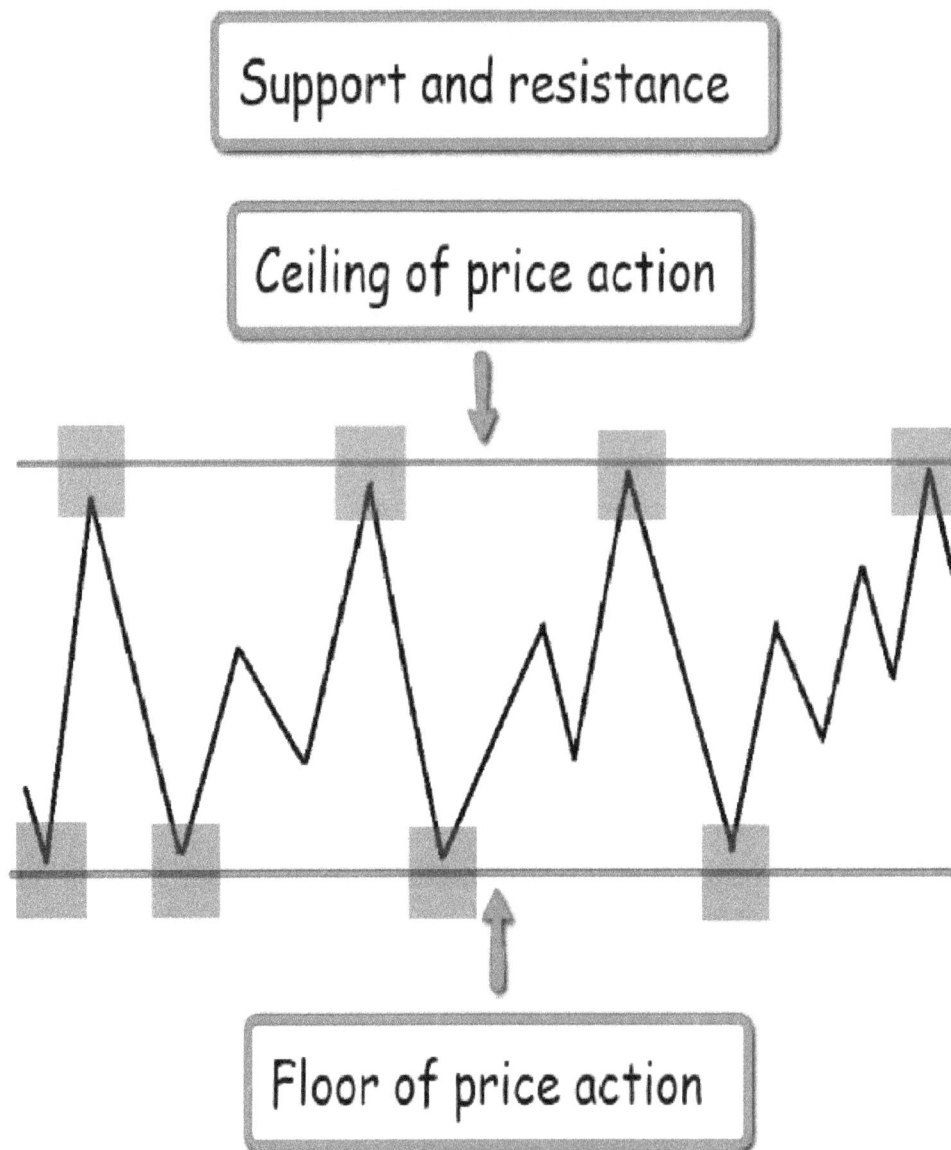

Fig 7.10 Support & Resistance

The analogy that I always use to explain this type of price action is that of a house, with floors and ceilings, which I hope will help to fix this more vividly in your mind's eye. What is happening in the schematic in Fig 7.10?

To begin with the price has fallen, before reversing higher, only to fall back again, before reversing higher again. This zig zag price action is repeated over and over again, and as a result, has created the 'channel' of price action with peaks and troughs as shown on the schematic. This oscillating price action creates what we call the floor of support and the ceiling of resistance. Each time the price action comes down to the floor, it is supported by what appears to be an invisible cushion. Not only does this help to prevent the market from falling further, but also helps the price to bounce higher.

Once the price has bounced off the floor of support, it heads back towards the ceiling of resistance, where an invisible barrier appears again, this time preventing the price moving higher and pushing it back lower again. For any of you who remember the very first computer games such as ping pong with the two paddles, it is very similar, with the ball, or the market in this case, bouncing endlessly back and forth between the two price levels. At some point the price will break out from this region.

However, before moving on there are several points I would like to examine and the first, and perhaps most obvious is, why is this price action so important. Therefore let me try to address this issue here.

Suppose for a moment that the price action in Fig 7.10 is taking place following a long bullish trend higher, but that this is NOT a selling climax. What is actually happening in this scenario?

First the market has moved higher, buyers are still buying into the trend, but then the price reverses, and moves lower. The buyers are trapped at this higher level, and are now regretting their decision. They are trapped in a weak position. The market moves lower, but then starts to move higher again, as buyers come in at this lower level, fearful they may miss out on another leg higher in the trend. As the market approaches the first reversal point, those buyers in a weak position, sell, glad to exit with a small loss or at break-even. This selling pressure sends the market lower, away from the ceiling level, but with a second wave of buyers now trapped in weak positions at this higher level.

The market then approaches the floor again, where buyers enter, seeing an opportunity to join the bullish trend, and take the market back to the ceiling again, where the second wave of weak traders sell out, and exit with either a small loss or marginal profits. This oscillating price action is then repeated.

At the top of each wave, buyers are left in weak positions, and then sell out on the next wave, to be replaced by more buyers at the top of the wave, who then sell out at the top of the subsequent wave. It is this constant buying and then selling at similar price levels, which creates the 'invisible' bands, which are made visible by joining the highs and lows on the price chart.

The buyers who bought at the floor of the price action, are happy to hold on, expecting higher prices. They have bought at the lower level as the market has pulled back, seen the market rise, and then reverse back to the original entry level. Unlike those buyers who bought at the ceiling level, their positions have never been in loss. So far, all that has happened, is that a potential profit has been reduced back to zero, or close to zero, so these buyers are still hopeful of making a profit from their position. Fear is not yet driving their decision making.

In fact, there is nothing magical about these price levels of the floor and the ceiling. They simply represent the 'extreme' psychological levels of fear and greed in that particular price region and time. We must always remember, price action is fuelled by these two basic emotions, and it is in the price congestion phase of market behaviour, that we see these emotions in their most basic form. At the top of the first wave, greed is the over riding emotion. By the time the market returns on the second wave, fear and relief are the over riding emotion for these traders.

Fear And Greed Riding The Wave – Top Of Bull Trend

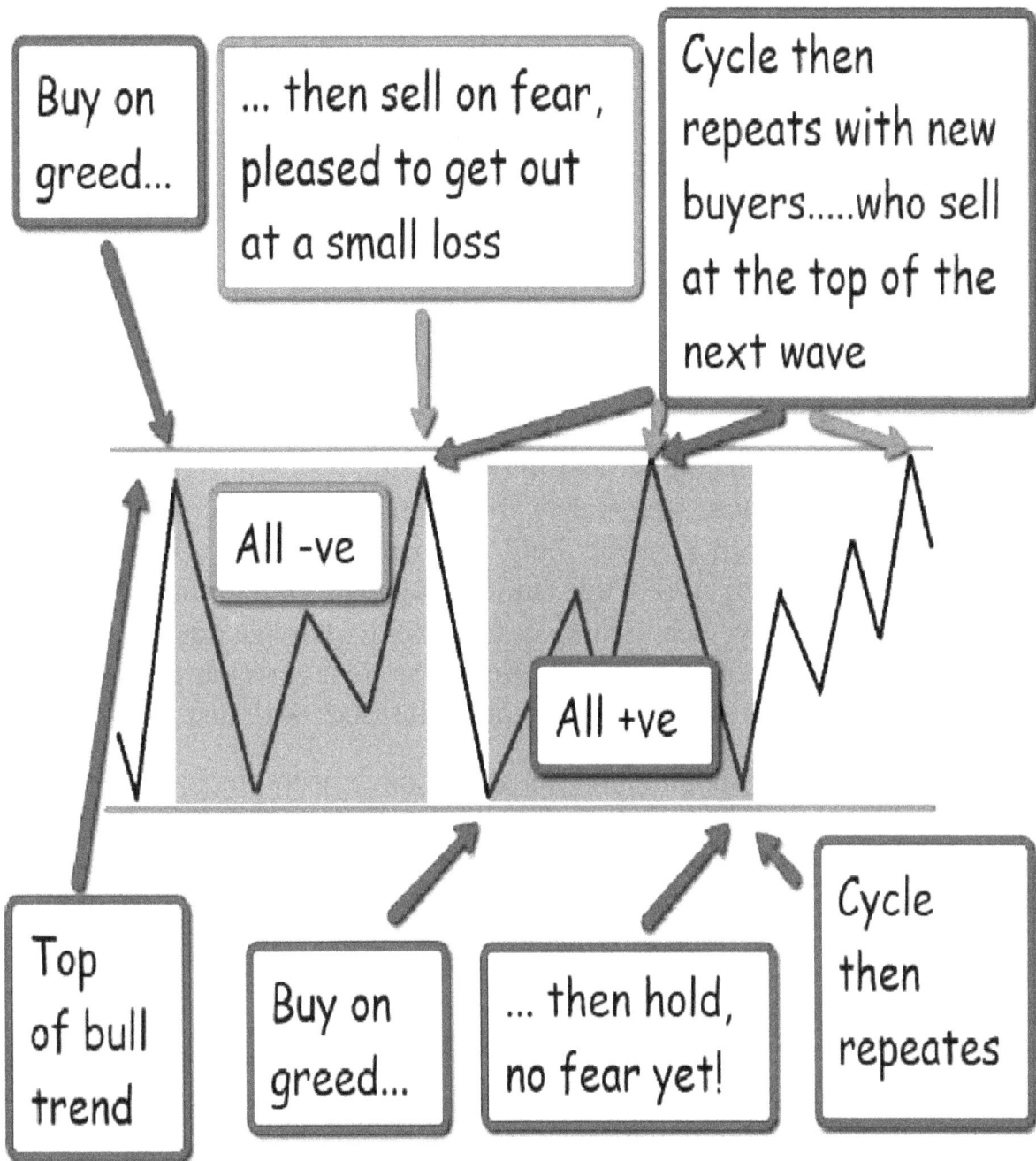

Fig 7.11 Fear & Greed : Bull Trend

As we can see in the schematic in Fig 7.11 it is all very logical once we begin to think of it in terms of emotional buying and selling. The over riding emotion as the market hits the top of the first wave is greed, combined with the emotion of fear – the fear of missing out on a good trading opportunity. Remember, these traders are weak anyway. Why? Because they have been waiting and waiting, watching the market continue higher, frightened to get in, as they are nervous and emotional traders, but at the same time, frightened of missing a 'golden opportunity' to make some money. After all they have seen the market rise and are now wishing they had entered earlier. They eventually buy at the top of the first wave.

The market then promptly reverses, and they immediately become fearful of a loss. The market moves lower then bounces. At the bottom of the first wave, buyers come in, entering on the pull back and pleased to be getting into the market at a 'good price'. The market moves back higher towards the top of the first wave.

The buyers at this level cannot wait to exit, as the fear drains away and they get out with a small loss. Remember, throughout this phase of price action, they have NEVER seen a profit, only an increasing loss, which has then reduced back to close to zero. Their emotional level of fear, a fear indicator if we had one, would have been rising steadily on the downwards leg, and then falling on the upwards leg, but at no time was their position in any sort of 'potential profit' so this group is simply pleased to exit with just a small loss.

After all, at one point the potential loss could have been much worse, so this group considers it has done well in closing with just a small loss. Remember also, that this group always trades on emotion anyway, so is almost always in a weak position when they open any trade, and therefore very easy to manipulate using emotional price swings.

The group that has bought at the bottom of the first wave lower are a completely different proposition. They have been prepared to wait, and buy on a pullback in price, they are not chasing the market, and are prepared to be patient. In general, they are more experienced.

As the market moves higher to the top of the third wave, their position has a potential profit, before it reverses lower, back to the level at which they entered the market. However, at no point during this journey have they suffered the emotion of a potential loss. They may be regretting the decision not to close at the top of the wave, but are likely to continue to hold on the expectation of a bounce back higher.

Their emotional response is therefore very different. Unlike the weak group at the top of each wave, this group has less emotional stress pressure to deal with on each wave. All they have to deal with is the emotional pressure of seeing a potential profit drain away, not the emotional pressure of recovering from a potential loss. The buyers at the top of each wave can be considered to be weak, but the buyers at the bottom of each wave can be considered to be strong. Naturally I accept this is a very simplistic way of looking at market price action in these regions, nevertheless it is typical of what happens when markets consolidate.

It is this constant flow of buyers and sellers entering the market in these contained areas, that creates the invisible barriers of price, which then become barriers and platforms in the future, since within these price regions we have dense populations of buyers and sellers, both weak and strong.

So do we see the same at the bottom of a trend lower? And the answer is, yes. We have exactly the same principles at work here.

Fear And Greed Riding The Wave – Bottom Of Bear Trend

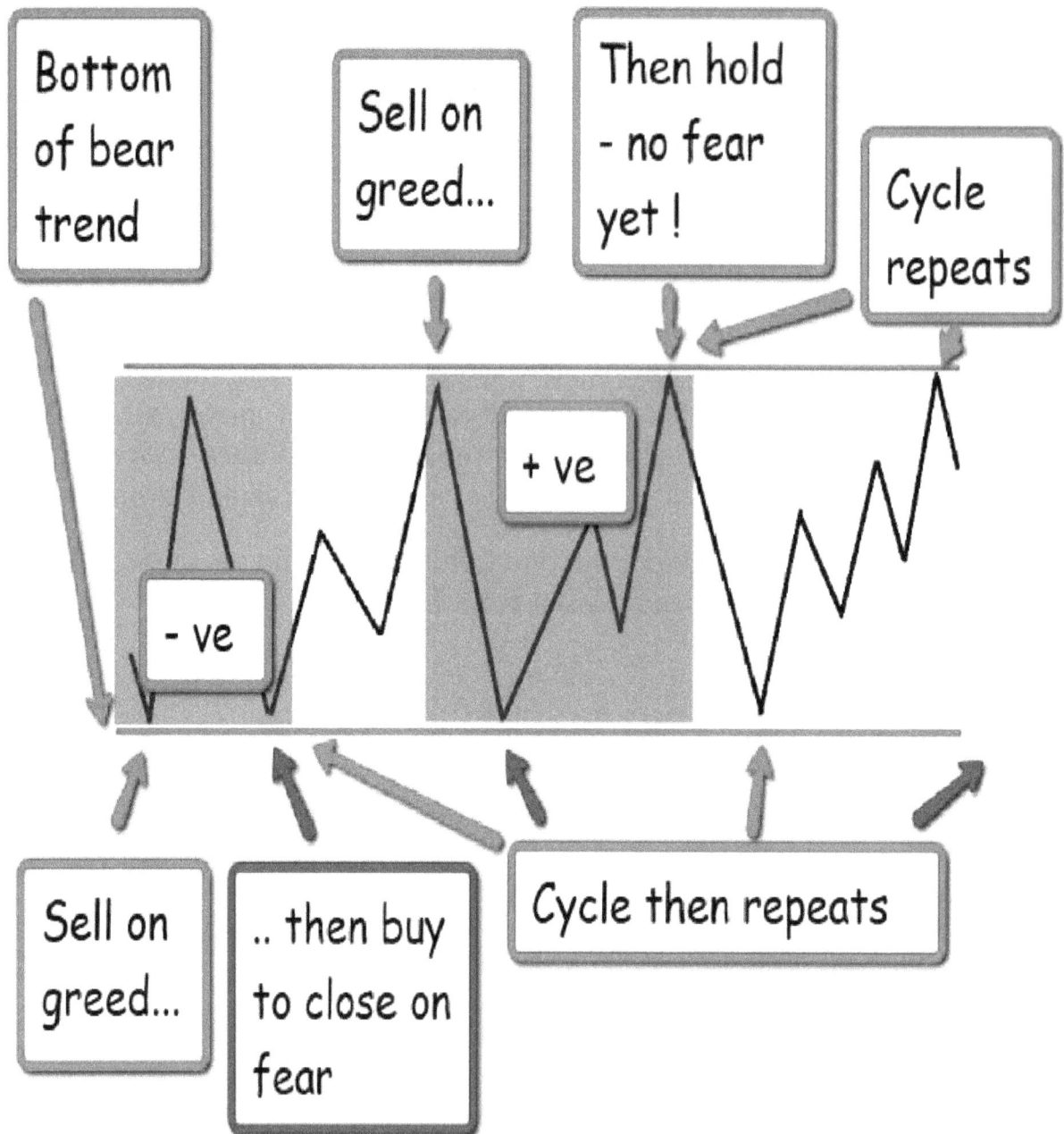

Fig 7.12 : Fear & Greed Bear Trend

The principles here are exactly the same as for the bullish trend that we looked at earlier. As we can in our schematic in Fig 7.12 the market has been in a down trend for some time, and once again, the weak emotional traders are drawn into the market, just as it is about to reverse. They have seen other traders making nice profits from the move lower, and finally overcome their fear of trading, and make an emotional decision to join the market.

The market immediately reverses against them and bounces higher locking them instantly into a losing position, which then worsens. Fear mounts as the losses increase.

Finally the market reverses back to where they first entered their position, and they exit, relieved to have been able to close out with just a small loss.

The strong traders are selling into the market at the tops of the waves, and their positions are generally positive throughout as the market moves back and forth in the trading range.

Once again, the price consolidation creates the invisible barriers which are then densely populated with both weak and strong groups of traders, and which then become platforms either of support or resistance during future market activity.

I hope the above explanation has at least given you an insight into why these levels are important. What this constant price action creates is invisible barriers and platforms all over our charts, which we then 'see' by joining up the price action at the top and bottom of each wave with horizontal lines. These give us the visual perspective on where these regions are on the charts. Each time future price action approaches these regions, because of the dense population of buyers and sellers marooned in these zones, we can expect the market to at least pause and 'test' these areas in the manner I will be covering shortly.

Of equal importance is when the market pauses in one of these areas, but then continues on its journey in the same direction as the original trend. Both of these have important consequences and send us key signals, all validated with volume, which we will look at shortly. But first, let me set out some general principles when using this analytical technique.

First Principle

The lines we draw on our charts to define the ceiling and the floor of these price regions are NOT rods of steel. Consider them more as rubber, flexible bands. Remember, technical analysis and VPA is an art, and NOT a science. Whilst these levels do constitute barriers and platforms, they are not solid walls, and on occasion you will see them broken, only for the market to then move back into the channel once again. Consider them to be 'elastic' with a little bit of 'give'.

Second Principle

Always remember Wyckoff's second law, the law of cause and effect. If the cause is large, then this will be reflected in the effect, which applies to support and resistance. The longer a market consolidates in a narrow range, then the more dramatic the resulting price action once the market moves away from this region. Naturally this is all relative, not least because a market that has been consolidating on a daily chart for several weeks is likely to trend for a similar period, whilst any breakout from a consolidation phase on a 5 minute chart may only be for an hour or so – it is all relative.

Third Principle

The third principle is perhaps the one which perplexes most new traders and it is this – how do I know when the market is in congestion? After all, it's easy to look back in hindsight and see where the price action has been consolidating for some time, but when the market action is live, it is only 'after the event' that any consolidation phase becomes self evident.

This is where the concept of an isolated pivot high and an isolated pivot low become key signals, and whilst there are indicators available to create these automatically, they are simple to spot visually.

Isolated Pivots

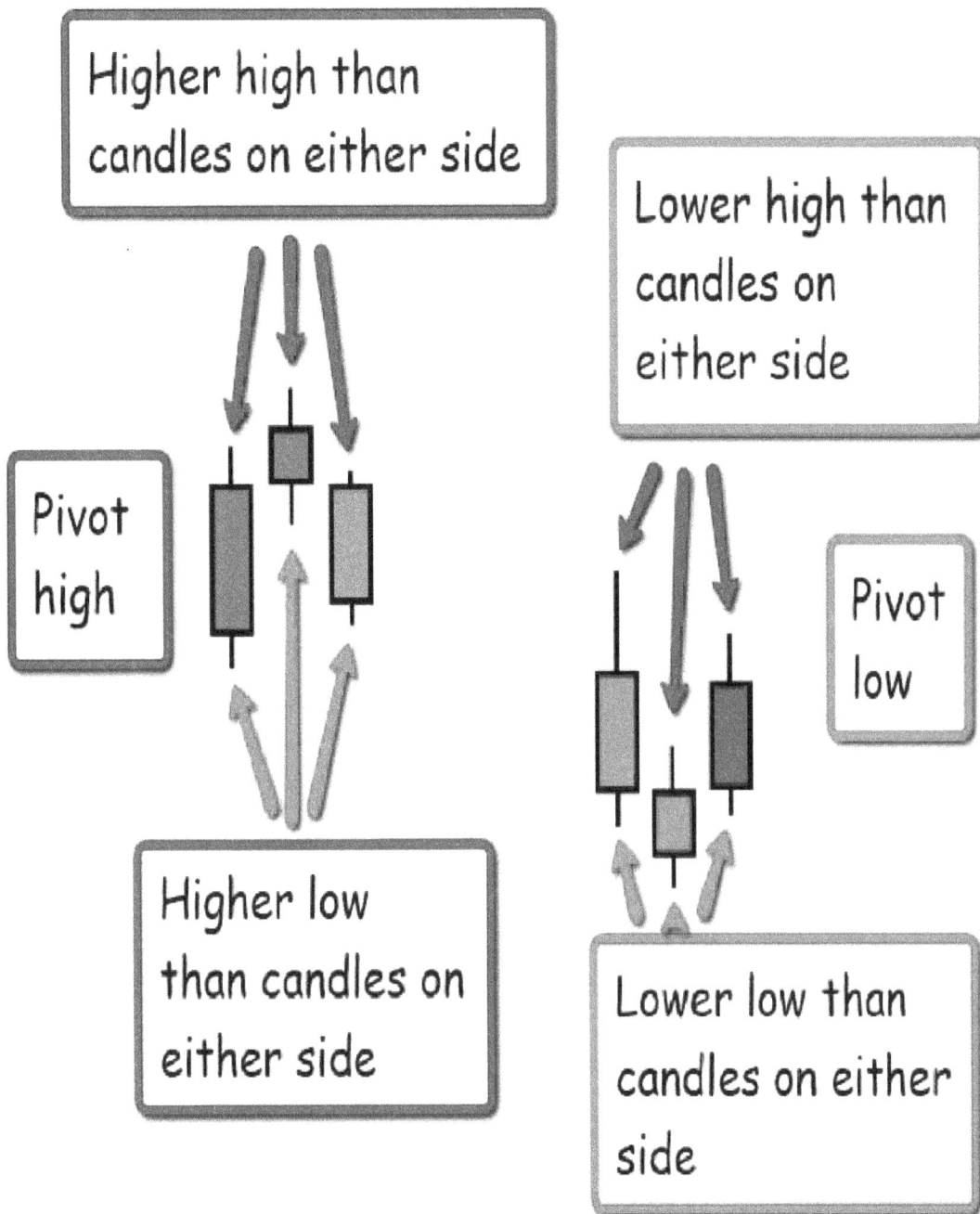

Fig 7.13 Isolated Pivots

These are the defining points for the start of any congestion phase. And the easiest way to understand pivots is to suppose the market is moving higher in an up trend, and we see an isolated pivot high formed on the chart. We have now seen the first sign of possible weakness in the market. These pivots are created by a three bar/candle reversal and as shown in Fig 7.13 above. To qualify as a three bar/candle reversal the candle in the centre has to post a higher high and a higher low, creating the pivot high pattern. The appearance of one pivot does not mean we are moving into a congestion phase at this point. All we can say at this stage is that we have a possible short term reversal in prospect.

Now we are waiting for our equivalent isolated pivot low to be created. This occurs when we have a three bar/candle pattern where the centre candle has a lower low and a lower high than those on either side. Again we have an example in Fig 7.13.

Once this candle pattern appears on our chart, we can now draw the first two lines to define the ceiling and the floor of our congestion zone. The pivot high is the ceiling and the pivot low is the floor. These simple candle patterns not only define the start of any congestion phase, they also define the upper and lower levels as the market moves into a period of sideways price action. This is referred to as congestion entrance as we can see in Fig 7.14.

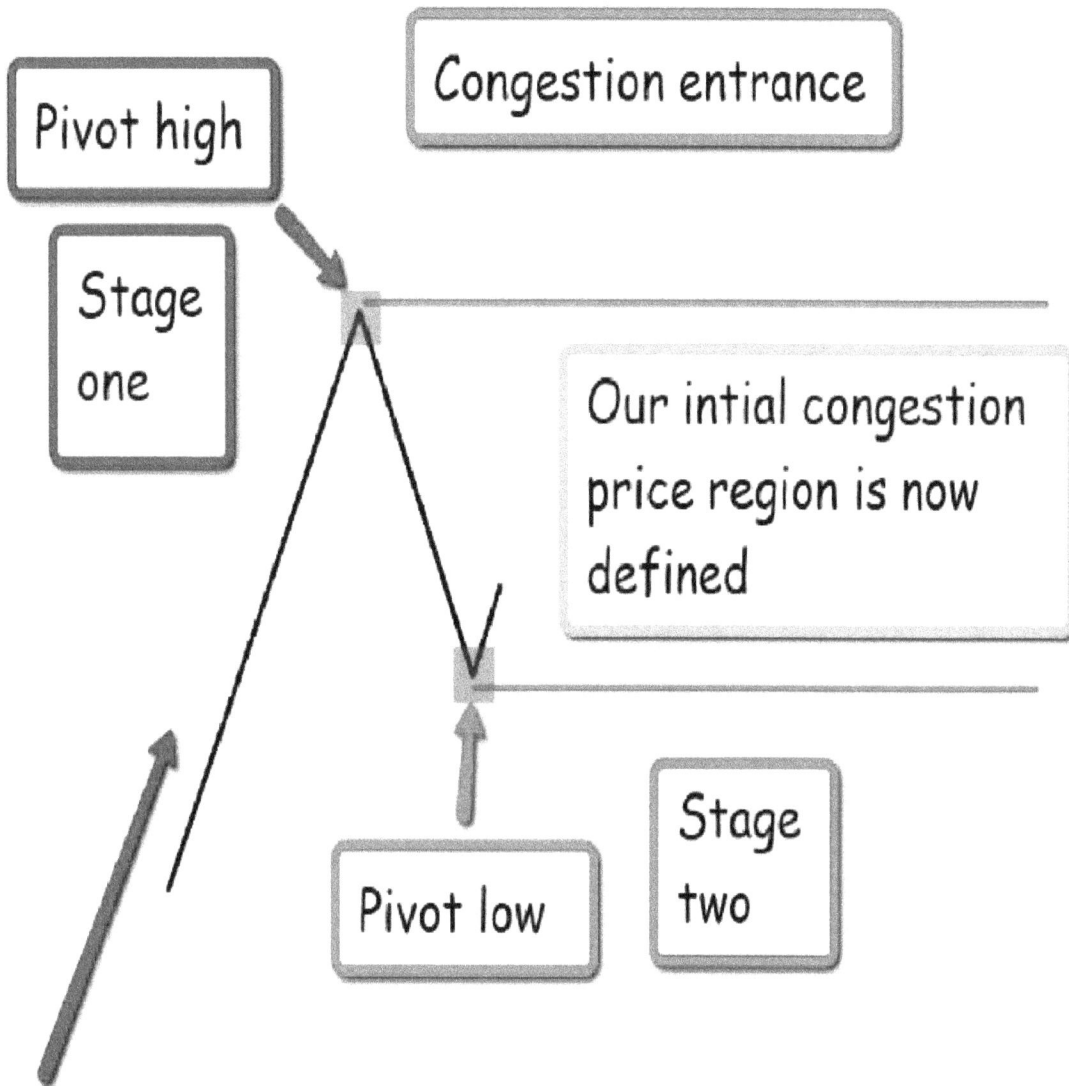

Fig 7.14 Congestion Entrance - Bullish Trend

The same applies when a market has been falling and enters a congestion phase. Here we are looking for the reverse, with an initial pivot low, followed by a pivot high which we can see in Fig 7.15.

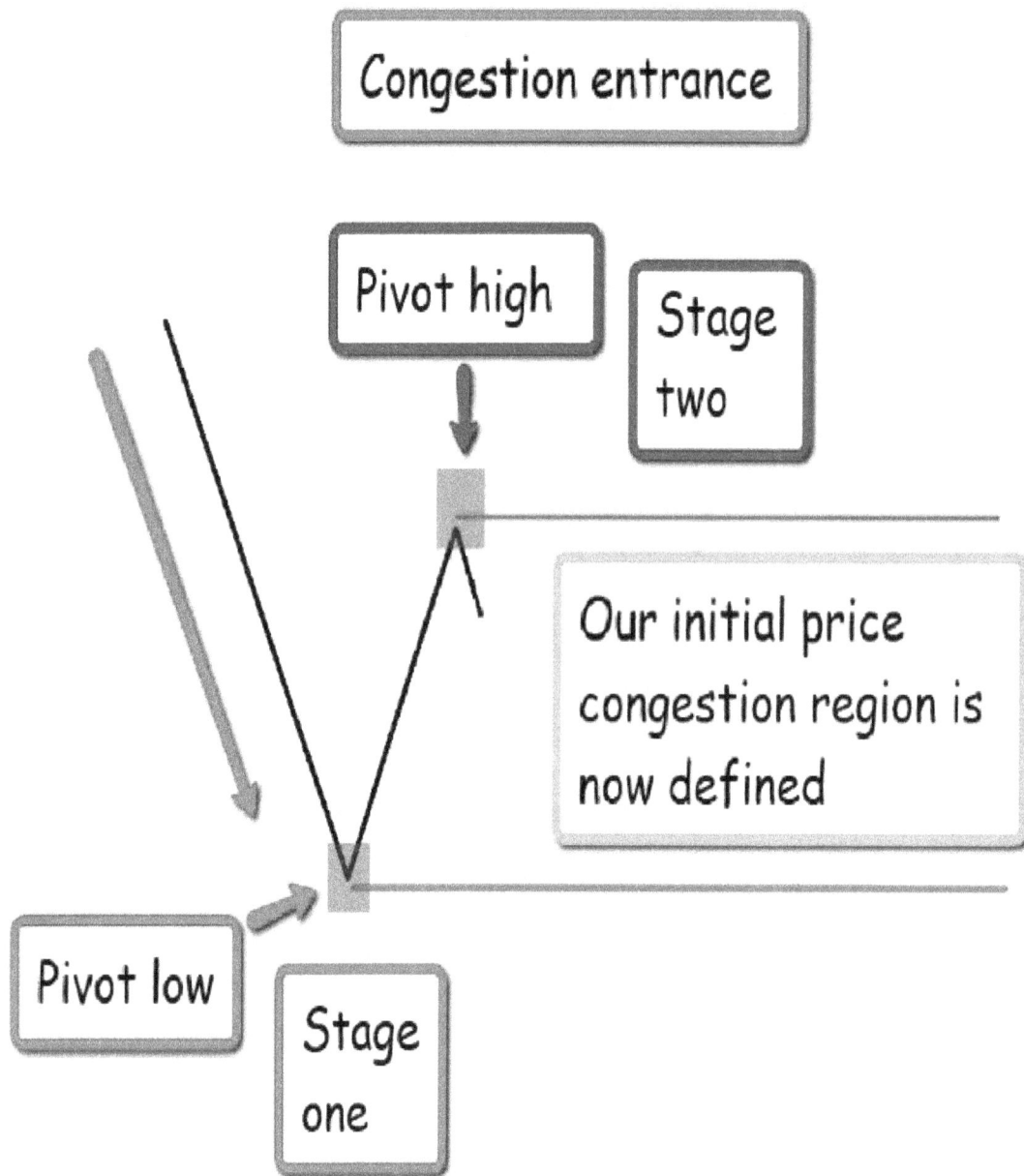

Fig 7.15 Congestion Entrance - Bearish Trend

At this point we now have our ceilings and floors clearly defined, and as the market moves further into congestion, we see further pivot points to the upper and lower price levels, which adds further reinforcement to these areas. What happens next?

At some point of course, the market finally breaks out from these regions, and this is the trigger that we have been waiting for, either to confirm the continuation of a current trend, or to signal a reversal.

However, throughout the price congestion phase we are constantly looking for clues and signals using our VPA knowledge to confirm weakness or strength as the market moves sideways. Moreover, if the congestion phase has been created as a result of a buying or selling climax, then the signals will be very clear.

But, the signal we are constantly watching for now, once we are in a congestion phase, is the volume associated with any breakout and consequent strong move away from this region. As we have already seen, congestion areas, are densely populated areas, with traders locked in a variety of weak positions, and therefore any break away from these areas requires volume, and generally lots of it. A break out from such a price area on low volume, is a classic trap move by the insiders, and is often referred to as a 'fake out'.

The insiders are trying to trap traders on the wrong side of the market once again, and a break out from recent congestion is another classic strategy. Only VPA traders will be aware of such a false move, since the volume associated with any move higher or lower will be clearly visible. This is why these price regions are so important and they are important for three reasons :

First, if we have a current position in the market, and we see a breakout validated in our direction, then this is a VERY clear signal of a continuation of the move, and therefore gives us confidence to hold the position.

Second, if we do NOT have a current position, then this gives us an excellent entry signal, once the move away has been validated with volume.

Third, if we have an existing position and the trend reverses against us, then we have been given a clear signal to exit.

Finally, once the market has broken away from these regions, we then have clearly defined platforms of future price regions, which then come into play as both support and resistance. These are immensely powerful and helpful in giving us simple targets for managing and exiting positions, based on the price action on our charts. If you remember back to something I wrote earlier; getting in is easy, it's getting out that is always the hardest part, and this is where these areas can help, in providing a visual map of likely places where the market may struggle, reverse or find support. This helps us as traders to manage our positions more effectively.

Let's start with breakouts and volume and what we should expect to see as the market pulls away from these congestion zones.

Fig 7.16 is an ideal schematic of what we should expect to see, and in this case we are seeing a bullish breakout. This could either be a continuation of a recent bullish trend higher, where the market has paused, before moving on once more, or this could be a reversal in trend. It doesn't really matter. The key points are the same, and are these.

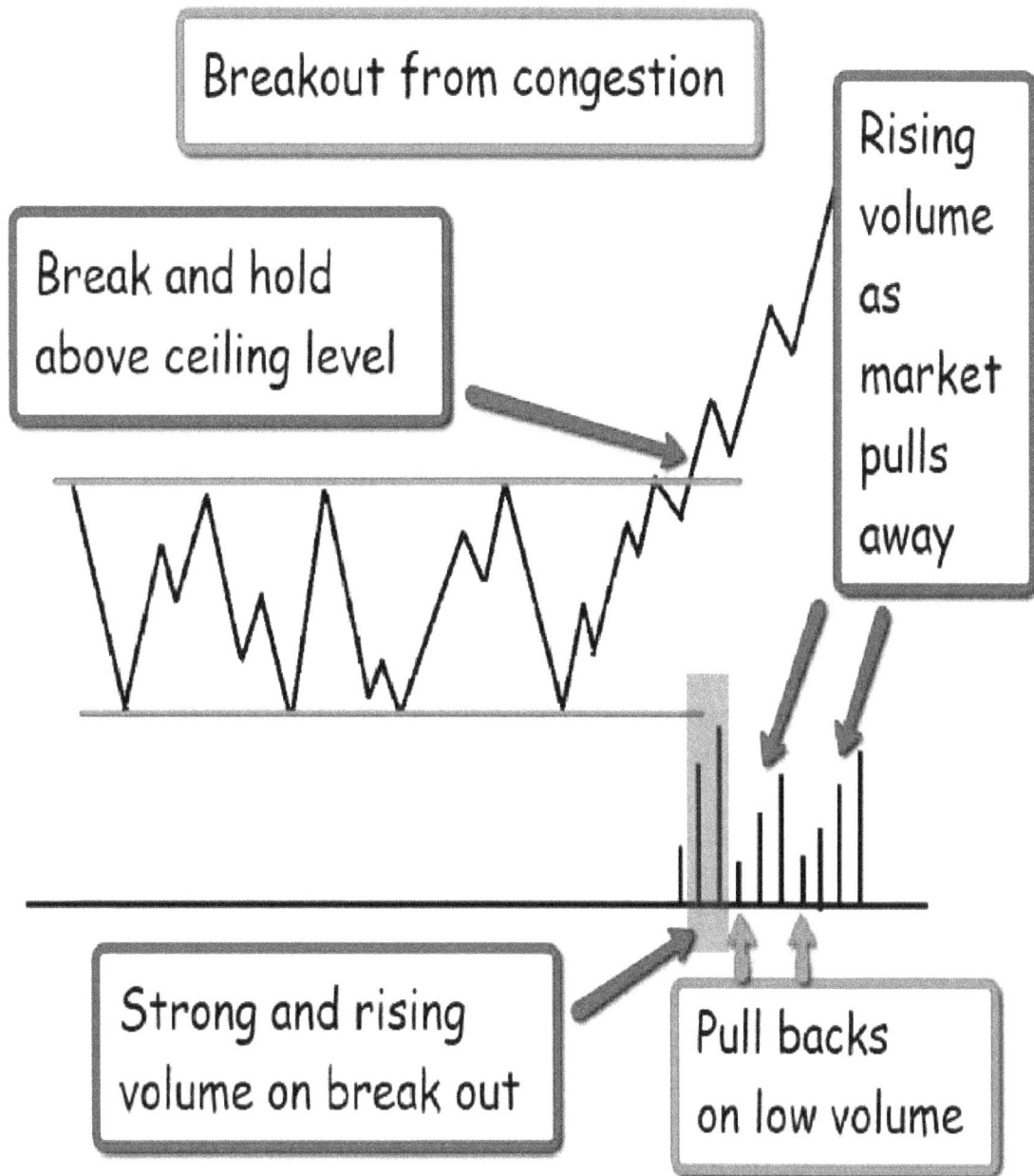

Fig 7.16 Breakout From Congestion : Bullish Trend

First, for any break and hold out of congestion to be valid we need to see 'clear water' above the ceiling of price action. Remember what I said earlier. These lines are NOT rods of steel, they are pliable, rubber bands and we have to treat then as such, so if the market ticks a few points above or below, this is NOT in itself a signal of a breakout. We need to see a clearly defined close above the ceiling. And one question I am always asked is how much is 'clear water'. Unfortunately, there is no hard and fast rule. It all comes down to judgement, experience, and the market or instrument as each will have its own unique price behaviour and risk profile. But there needs to be a 'clearly visible' gap in terms of the closing price of the candle which finally breaches the ceiling level. This is the first signal that a breakout is in progress. The second is volume.

As we can see in Fig 7.16 the initial move higher up and through the ceiling level, has to be accompanied by strong and rising volume. It takes effort for the market to move away, rather like dragging someone out of quicksand or a bog. The same applies here, and you should see this reflected in the associated volume of the next few bars. If you DON'T see this, then you know it is either a trap up move by the insiders, or there is simply no interest from market participants to take the market higher at this stage.

If it is a valid move, then the volumes on the initial break will be well above average and rising, as the market finally throws off the shackles and starts to build a trend. At this stage, do not be surprised to see the market pull back to test the ceiling as it moves higher, but this should be accompanied with low or falling volume, since we are now developing a bullish trend higher and expect to see a rising market with rising volume, if this is a true move higher. Once clear, VPA then takes over and we are back to a candle by candle analysis of the price action as the trend unfolds.

Exactly the same principles apply when the breakout is into a bearish trend (See Fig 7.17). Once again, it makes no difference whether this is a continuation of a bearish trend, or a reversal from bullish to bearish. The only difference is that this time we are breaking through the floor of price congestion, and not the ceiling.

As before, this breakout should be clean and well developed, and accompanied by well above average volume to reflect the effort required to break away. Again, do not be surprised to see the market move back higher to test the floor area, but this should be on low volume, and as the market pulls away rising volume should reflect the downwards move. Remember, falling markets should ALSO see rising volume reflecting a genuine move lower.

Breakout from congestion

Break and hold below floor level

Strong volume on break out

Rising volume as market pulls away

Pull backs on low volume

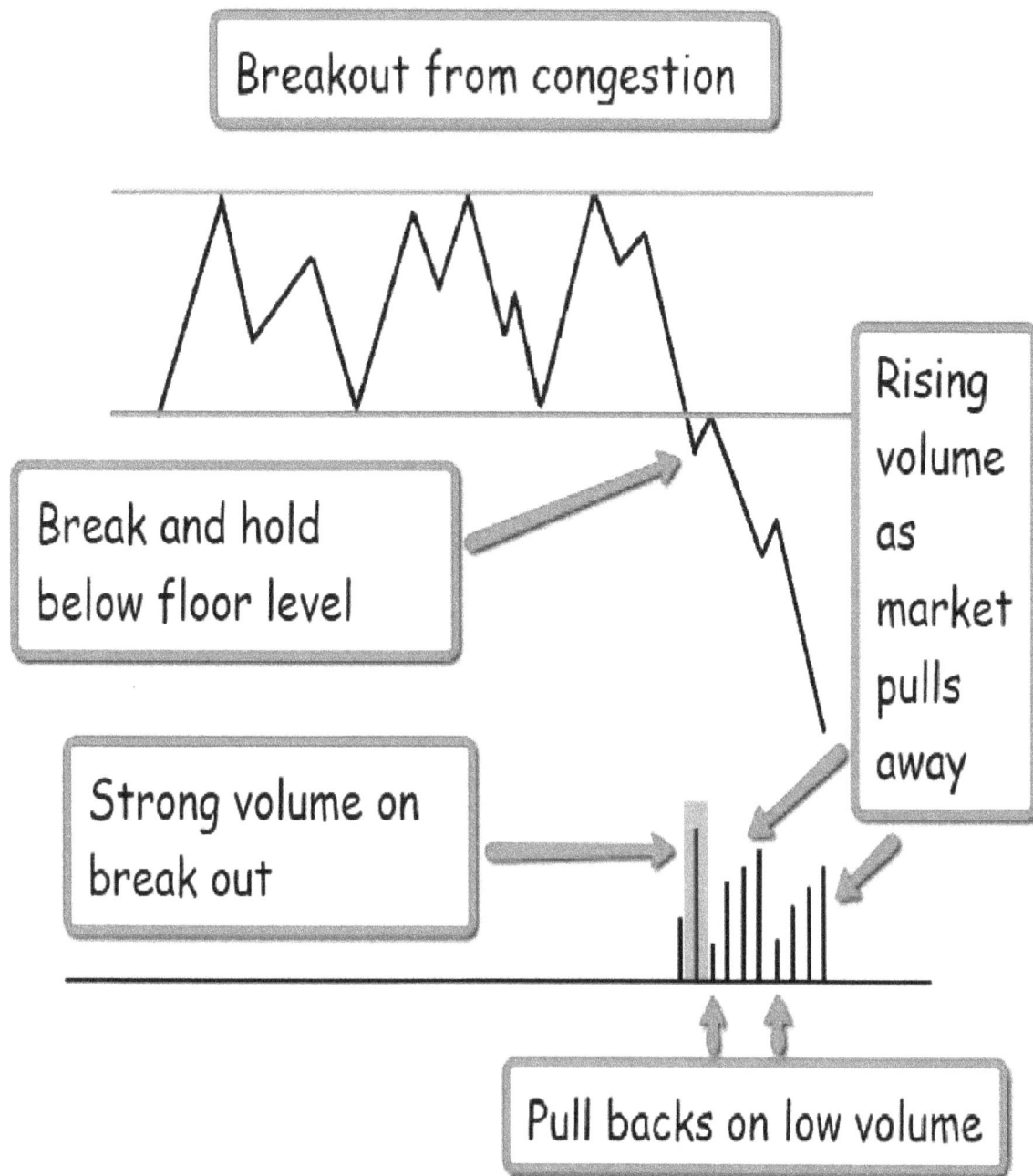

Fig 7.17 Breakout From Congestion : Bearish Trend

I cannot stress too strongly the importance of price congestion regions. They are one of the foundations stones of price action, as they reveal so much, and give us so many trading opportunities. There are many traders around the world who only trade on breakouts, and nothing else.

We can trade breakouts by defining congestion zones using pivots, then charting the price action using VPA, and finally when the breakout is validated by volume, enter any positions.

At this point I cannot reiterate too strongly support and resistance is one of the foundation stones of price analysis. Every full time trader I have ever spoken to, uses this concept in one way or another, and as you will see, now that we understand price congestion, it is a powerful and simple concept which can be applied in several ways.

It can be used to identify entry positions; it can be used in managing positions, and finally it can also be used as a target for closing out positions. In simple terms, it is one of the most powerful techniques you can apply, and when combined with an understanding of VPA, will give you an insight into market behaviour that few traders ever achieve. It is also the phase of price action where trends are borne. Many traders become frustrated when markets move into a congestion phase, but in reality this is one of the most exciting phases of market behaviour, as it is just a question of being patient and waiting. When the market is ready, it will break out, and a new trend will then be established. And the extent of any trend will be dictated by the cause and effect rule!

To round off this chapter, let me summarise the concept of support and resistance which builds on the knowledge we already have of price congestion, and the analogy I always use here, is that of a house! Which is why I have used the terms floor and ceiling to describe the upper and lower levels of price congestion.

Support And Resistance – The House!

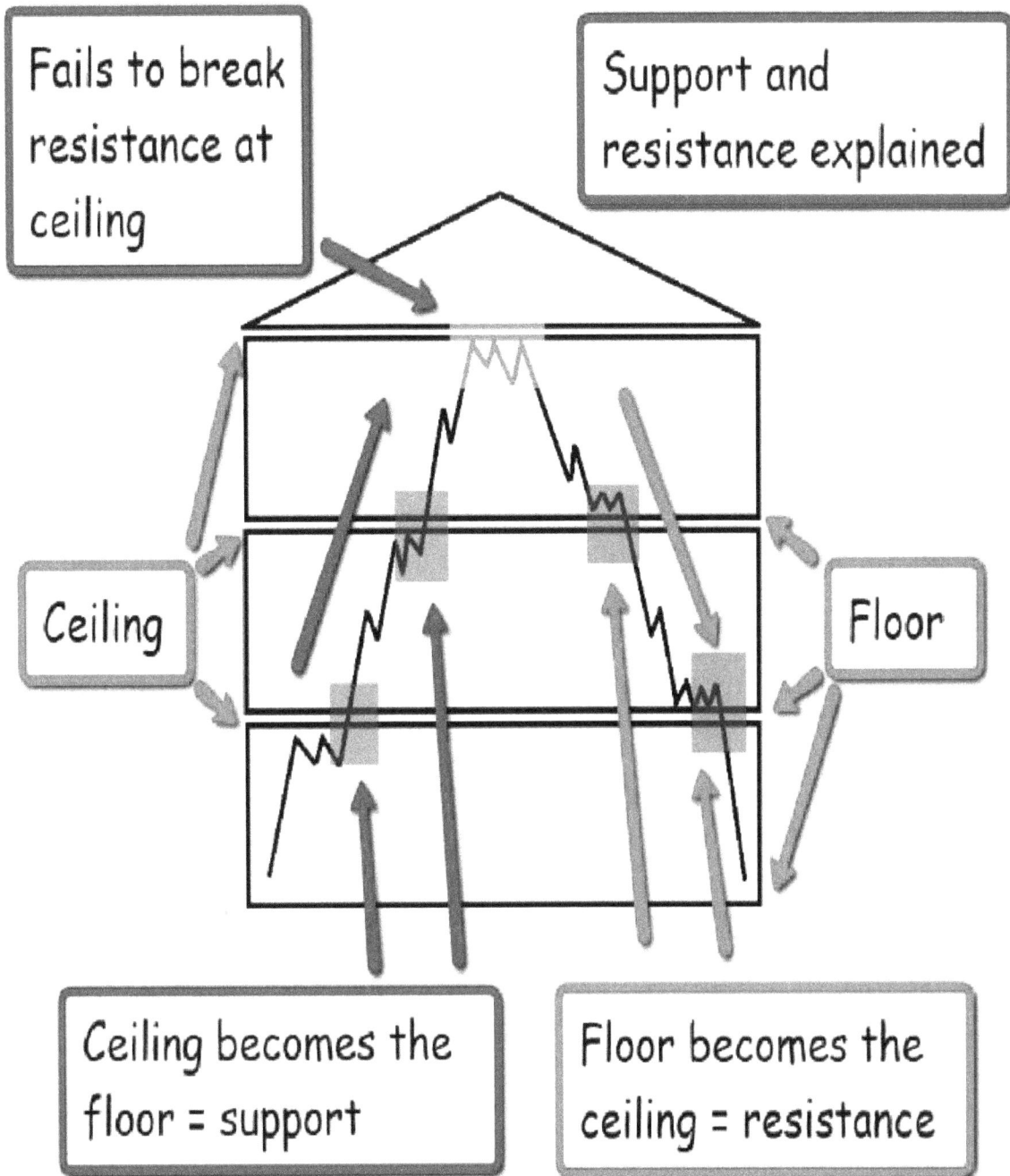

Fig 7.18 Support & Resistance : The House

Imagine that you are looking at a vertical cross section of a house which is shown in the schematic in Fig 7.18. In other words, what we are looking at here is a house with the whole of the front removed, rather like an old fashioned dolls house with the door open. Now you can see all the floors and ceilings in the house, and as you can see here we have a ground floor, first floor, second floor and roof.

The black line is the market which has moved from the ground floor to the roof and back again. Let me explain the price action on the schematic as it moves through the house, to better visualise the concept of support and resistance.

The market moves higher from the ground floor, and eventually reaches the ceiling, where it moves into sideways price congestion. At this point, the ceiling is providing an area of price resistance to any further move higher for the market. However, at some point the ceiling is breached and the market climbs through to the first floor level. Now at this point, what was the ceiling of the ground floor, has now become the floor of the first floor. In other words, what was an area of price resistance, has now become an area of price support.

Once again, the market continues higher until it reaches the ceiling of the first floor, where once again the price moves into a consolidation phase. Finally it breaks out into the second floor level. Now what was price resistance, as represented by the ceiling of the first floor, is now support as represented by the floor of the second floor.

Finally the market continues higher in our house until it reaches the ceiling of the second floor, where the price resistance proves to be too strong, and the market reverses at this level. The ceiling has remained firm and the barrier of price activity has prevented the market continuing any further.

The market then moves lower, having reversed, back to the floor, where it consolidates, before breaking through and back down through the floor and past the ceiling of the first floor level. Here we see the reverse in action. What was price support in terms of the floor, has now become price resistance in terms of the ceiling.

This is repeated once again at the first floor level, before the market finally breaks lower once more, with the floor of price support now becoming price resistance in the ceiling, and we are then back to square one again.

But, why is this concept so important?

The concept of support and resistance is important for a number of reasons. First, as we have already seen, a breakout from a consolidation phase can be validated with volume, and if confirmed, provides excellent trading opportunities. The so called breakout trades.

Second, and perhaps just as important, the reason that this trading approach is so popular is that it embraces in its strategy, the whole concept of support and resistance which is this – that in creating these regions, and using them as part of the trading strategy, you are in effect, using the markets own price behaviour to provide you with protection on your positions. By this I mean that in trading using a breakout, the market has put in place its own natural barriers to protect you against any sudden changes in market direction as the trend develops.

Returning to the price action in our 'house'. As we approach the ceiling of the first floor we move into price congestion, pause, and then break through into the first floor room above. We now have a 'natural floor' of price support in place, which is giving us protection in the event that the market pauses and perhaps moves back to test the price in this area. This floor is our natural protection, defined by the market for us. After all, we know from our VPA studies that to move back and through this area would take effort and volume, so we therefore have a natural area of support now working in our favour. Not only does the floor offer us protection should the market pull back, it also offers the market support to the continued move higher.

It is a WIN/WIN. You have the comfort of knowing that once the market has broken through a ceiling of price resistance, not only does this become a floor of price support, it has also become a barrier of price protection in the event of any short term re-test of this area. Any stop loss for example could then be placed in the lower regions of the price congestion. This is why breakout trading is so popular, and when backed with VPA validation becomes even more powerful.

The same principles apply when markets are moving lower. In our 'house' example we were in an up trend, but if we take the down trend example, then this works in identical fashion.

Picking up the price action where the market has reversed at the roof level, we are approaching the second floor, floor level. The market moves into congestion and then breaks through the ceiling of the first floor room below. What was the floor of price support has now become the ceiling of price resistance, and once again offers two things. Price resistance to any short term reversal, adding pressure to any downwards move lower, and secondly, a natural barrier of price protection in the event of any short term pullback.

Once again, it is a WIN/WIN situation for the breakout trader, this time to the short side of the market.

This is using this concept in taking trading positions as the market action develops, but its power also lies in the price action and history that the market leaves behind. The market leaves its own DNA, buried in the charts. These areas of price congestion remain on the charts forever. The price moves on, but these areas remain, and at some point in the future, price behaviour moves back into these regions, and at this stage these areas, often dormant for long periods, then become powerful once again, and begs the question as to whether the market has a memory.

Or is it because, as traders we are all looking at the same charts, and therefore these areas of price become self fulfilling prophecies? Perhaps it's because these areas are densely populated with weak traders, still holding on and waiting for a reversal so they can exit with small losses or small profits?

It may well be a combination of all of these. Whatever the reasons these areas can and do play a significant role in price behaviour as they are visited by the market repeatedly. Once again, where there are extensive areas of congestion, then the more significant will be their impact.

Let's go back to our house schematic again, and in particular the failure to break the ceiling of resistance on the second floor. The reason for this failure on the price chart, may well have been as a result of sustained areas of old price congestion in the same region, and failures at this level in the past. If the market has failed at this level previously, which as a trader you will see on your price chart with areas of price congestion on the longer time frames, then there is every chance that it will fail at this level again. After all, there was a reason. This could have been a selling climax, occurring years previously and what was once considered overbought at this level is now considered fair value.

Nevertheless, as traders, this is a key level, and volume will give us all the clues we need to validate the subsequent price action. If this is in fact an old area of price congestion, at which level the market failed and reversed previously, then if it does succeed in breaching the ceiling on this occasion, then this adds greater significance to the move higher, and a strong platform of support would then be in place. Equally a failure would suggest an extremely weak market, and something we will look at when considering key price patterns.

This is the power of support and resistance. It is the market signalling all those areas of price congestion which come into play constantly. They are the DNA of the market. Its history and life story rolled into one, and as you would expect works exactly the same way regardless of whether markets are falling or rising. In this example the market reversed from resistance, but equally powerful is the concept of old support regions when a market is falling. These areas then provide natural platforms of support, to stop any further decline in the market, and just as in a rising market, if these areas are deep and wide, then they take on increased significance, which is further enhanced if there has been any major reversal at this level in the past.

Naturally, price congestion areas come in all shapes and sizes, and in all time frames. A stock index may trade in a narrow range for days or even weeks. A currency pair may move sideways for months. Bonds often trade in very narrow ranges, particularly in the current financial crisis. Stocks may remain waterlogged for months.

Conversely, areas of price congestion may last for a few minutes or a few hours. The underlying concepts remain the same, because as VPA traders all we have to remember is that cause and effect go hand in hand. An area of price congestion on a 5 minute chart will still offer support and resistance to the intra day trader, along with any breakout trading opportunities, but in the context of the longer term will have little effect. However, move to the same instrument on the daily chart, and if we see a deep area of price congestion, then any move through the ceiling or floor will be significant.

This is yet another reason for trading using multiple charts and time frames. Price congestion on a 5 minute chart will have less significance than on a 15 minute, than an hourly chart. In other words the longer the time frame then the greater the significance, all other things being equal.

Support and resistance is a powerful concept in its own right. Match it with VPA, and it will become another of the cornerstones of your trading methodology, based on volume and price.

Chapter Eight

Dynamic Trends And Trend Lines

The loss was not bad luck. It was bad analysis.
David Einhorn (1968-)

In this chapter I want to explore the concept of trends and trend lines. And no doubt you will have heard the oft quoted term 'let the trend be your friend', which in my humble opinion is more or less meaningless mumbo jumbo.

It is the one mantra that people who profess to be mentors and coaches parrot to their students in an effort to impress. However, just like price congestion where, with hindsight any fool can see when the market has been trading sideways, so it is with trends. And anyone who quotes this axiom has clearly little, live trading experience, in my view. Generally they will show you a lovely trend with several lines on, and sagely advise that this was the place to enter and then hold for the duration of the trend, before finally exiting at the end of the trend run higher or lower. All easy stuff when you are considering an historic chart.

Let me start with some basic thoughts on trends, as I want to dispel some of the nonsense that has been written on the subject. And the first, and most important question is this - how do we know when a trend has started?

Just as with support and resistance, the short answer is that we won't, until it's over. It's that simple. It was the same with our congestion phase. We have to have some parameters to give us the clues as to whether a trend is beginning to develop in whatever time frame we are considering. As a trader, it is pointless to look back over an extended period, draw some lines on the chart, and then decide that this is a trend. By then you will have missed most, if not all of the trend, and are probably just getting in, when the insiders are getting out.

This is why VPA is so powerful. It validates the price action for us, and reveals where we are in the longer term trend. After all, if we see a selling climax or a buying climax, then we KNOW that a new trend is about to begin. We are in at the start, which is where we want to be, NOT at the end, which is where trend lines inevitably point to, particularly if you only rely on this technique. I must stress that I am not saying trend lines are not useful, they are, but only when used in the correct way which is what I am going to teach you in this chapter.

Let's start with Charles Dow who really laid down the foundations of trend analysis. His core beliefs in this aspect of price behaviour were founded on one simple principle which was this – that the trend in an index, was far more revealing and valuable than the trend in an individual stock. His view was very simple. An individual stock could be influenced by any number of factors, from earnings reports, broker recommendations, and analysts views, all of which would affect the price. An index, on the other hand, was far more representative of the broader sentiment in the market and therefore far more likely to be of use in identifying market trends. One of his many axioms, that have since been absorbed into modern day technical analysis, is the concept of systematic and unsystematic market risks.

Systematic risks affect all stocks in an index, whilst unsystematic risks may affect only one or a group of stocks in one particular market. Dow's own work centred around the creation of indices, which now form the cornerstones of the financial markets, with the S&P 500, the Dow Jones (DJIA), the Nasdaq (NQ100) and many more around the world. In addition, the concept of an index has been adopted by virtually every other market and instrument and led to the creation of volatility indices, such as the VIX, sector indices for stocks, currency indices such as the Dollar Index (DXY) and commodity indices such as the CRB, with hundreds of others in between. In some markets, indices are now considered more attractive to trade than the underlying assets from which they are derived.

Another of Dow's guiding principles was the concept that trends were classified into three broad time related phases, which he referred to as primary, secondary and minor trends. Now in his world, of course, the ticker tape was still the main source of data, and for Charles Dow and the other iconic traders of his day and later, the time frames were very different to those of today. A minor trend for example would be one lasting for 2 to 3 days, whilst a secondary trend might be 2 to 3 weeks and a primary trend for 2 to 3 months. For our purposes, with electronic charts, our time horizons are much shorter. For intra day traders, a minor trend might last 2 to 3 hours, whilst a secondary trend may last 2 to 3 days and a primary trend 2 to 3 weeks. These are much more realistic, and indeed for many markets, the days of extended trends which last for months or longer are almost a thing of the past. The markets have changed beyond all recognition. High frequency trading, market manipulation and the move to electronic trading have all seen to that.

Nevertheless, Dow's original and pioneering work gives us a hook on which to hang our hat. What is also interesting is that in developing his ideas of trend, he also introduced the concept of the three stages of a trend as follows :

1. The accumulation phase

2. The technical trend following stage

3. The distribution stage

If this sounds familiar, then it should because this is the cycle the insiders follow in the constant round of first filling, and then emptying their warehouses, as developed and expanded by Richard Wyckoff. Charles Dow referred to the insiders as the 'smart money' with the distribution phase of the trend where the 'smart money' is taking its profits and heading for the sign marked 'Exit'.

Now at this point we are going to diverge from standard trend analysis and look at it in slightly different terms, which I hope you will find marginally more useful when trading live, rather than the theoretical nonsense that appears in most books. The above introduction has given us the framework to move on, but at this stage most trend analysis would then present you with the schematic in Fig 8.10

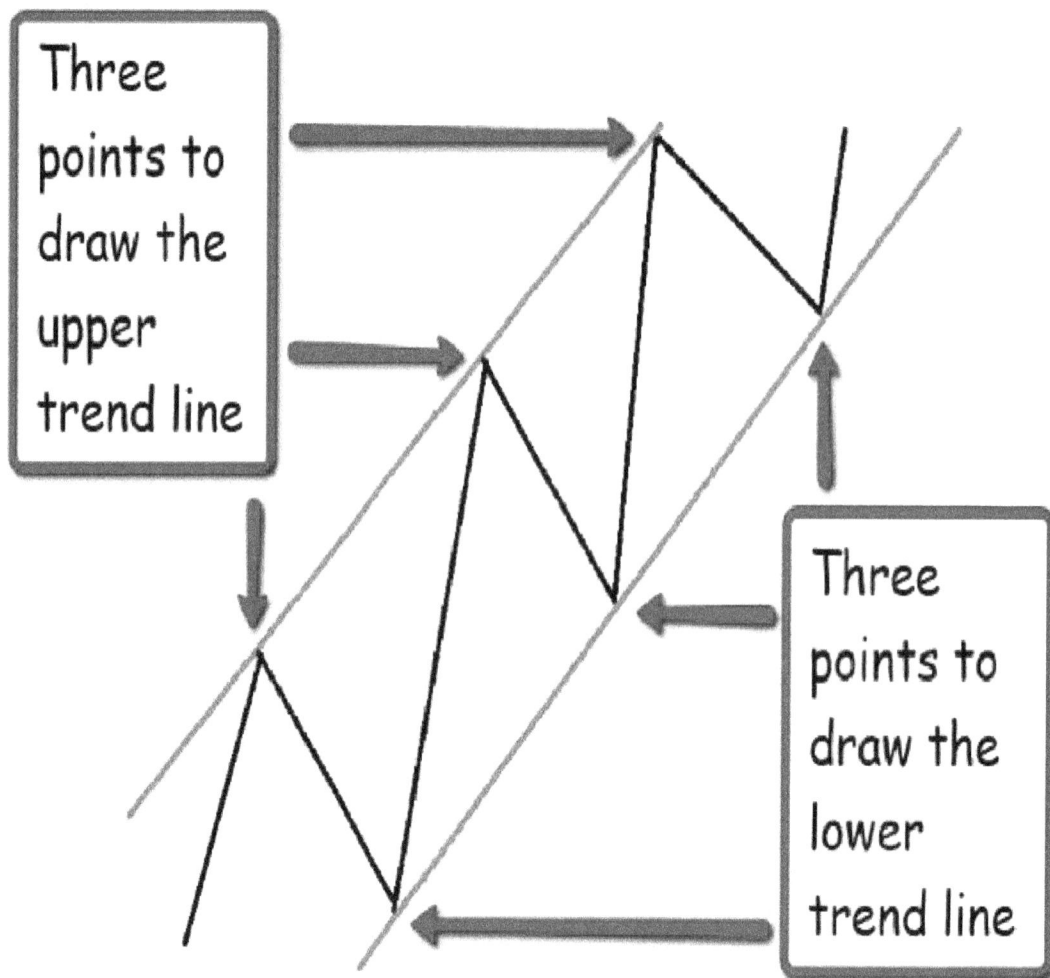

Fig 8.10 A Bullish Trend Higher – Surely Not!

Here we have the traditional picture of a trend. The market has moved higher in a series of steps, and once we have three steps in place, we can draw our upper and lower trend lines, which define the channel clearly. Most text books will tell you that it is impossible to define a trend using two points, since the possibilities for interpretation are endless and ultimately meaningless, which is why we have to wait for three points, before joining them up to create the trend lines themselves.

These are the higher highs and higher lows which define the peaks and troughs as the market moves higher, and lower highs and lower lows as the market falls.

Now we have a clear picture that a trend has been established, we are ready to enter the market, and wait for this trend to develop further. That is the theory, but unfortunately, by the time we have waited for our three higher highs and higher lows, the trend is already reaching a climax. We have already been through the technical trend following stage and we are about to buy, at the start of a distribution phase.

But how do we know this? Because most likely you have been reading too many text books written by people who have never traded or invested in their lives. This is all theoretical and, as I said earlier, very easy to see in hindsight, and once the trend is this well developed, it is not of much use.

What is the answer? And for this we need to return to support and resistance which holds the key, and which is why I covered it in such detail in the previous chapter.

Support and resistance is where trends are created, born and then propelled on their way. This is where trends reverse and change direction. This is where accumulation and distribution phases occur, along with selling and buying climaxes. It is the most important area of price behaviour on any chart. These areas are like the spawning grounds at the head of a great river, to which the salmon ultimately return to spawn.

This is where we start to answer the question that ALL traders, investors and speculators have at the forefront of their minds at all times. Is this the start of a trend, and if so, what is the strength of the trend and how far is it likely to run? These questions can only be answered by understanding support and resistance in the context of Volume Price Analysis.

To attempt to do so in any other way is doomed to failure, and drawing a few lines on a chart, is a pointless and meaningless exercise. In my humble opinion. I do accept they may help to clarify the trend a little and may even be of limited use once the trend has started, but in terms of getting you into a strong position, they are of no value whatsoever.

However, let's return to basics and revisit our congestion phase, where the market is moving sideways and creating the floors and ceilings of price support. The market is preparing to breakout, and all we need to do as traders, investors or speculators is to wait, be patient and then to validate the breakout using volume. How do we know the extent of the trend at this stage? The short answer is we don't, but we do have several clues which will allow us to make an educated guess at this stage.

First, is the extent of the price congestion phase. Again we must recall Wyckoff's cause and effect as this will dictate whether we can expect to see a primary, a secondary trend or a minor trend develop. For an intraday scalper, the trend will almost certainly be a minor trend, but this may well sit within the context of a longer term trend in a slower time frame. In this context our scalper would then be trading, with the dominant trend in a higher time frame. In other words the minor trend being traded, is in the same direction as the longer term trend, which for an intra day trader may be the hourly chart.

This is one of the many reasons why trading using multiple charts is so powerful. It helps to frame the trend that we are trading. However, there is nothing wrong with taking a trade against the dominant trend in whatever time frame that may be. For example, the dominant trend in a stock market may be bullish on the index, but there may be a bearish opportunity in a stock. This is fine, as long as we recognise that we are trading against the 'dominant trend'. This type of trading is often referred to as 'counter trend trading', and there are two points that define this type of position.

First, it is a higher risk position as we are trading 'against the market flow' – swimming against the tide if you like. Second, and following on from the first point, we are only likely to be holding such a position for a short period of time, since by definition we are trading against the longer term dominant trend.

Next, in any congestion phase as VPA traders we are always analysing the volume from two standpoints. First the volume associated with the sideways price action to determine whether this is a major reversal evidenced by volume, as either a selling or a buying climax. Secondly, the volume and price action following any associated breakout, which will then provide us with additional clues as to the likely extent of the trend. In turn this will also be validated by considering the associated volume and price action on slower time frames along with analysing potential support and resistance areas ahead, which might create pause points in any longer term trend,

Therefore, the first step is always the price action, immediately following a move away from the price congestion zone, and this is very similar to the way we identified our congestion entrance using the pivot high and the pivot low, to give us our levels. This gave us our bearings. The previous price action (whatever it may have been) has now paused and is taking a rest. Our pivots have alerted us to this pause, which may be an extended one, in which case the levels will be further reinforced with further pivots to the upper and lower levels, or it may be a temporary one, with few pivot points. It may be a reversal, in which case we can expect to see some extensive VPA action, or a continuation of the previous trend. All this will be revealed as the price action in this area unfolds into our traditional congestion area, with our ceilings and floors in place. However, at some point, the market will break away, and this is where the pivots come into play once again, only this time to help us define the trend as it develops. Furthermore, it allows us to take advantage as soon as possible and NOT have to wait for the higher highs and higher lows (or lower highs and lower lows) to develop before entering a position.

Let's take an example which shows a break out to the up side in Fig 8.11

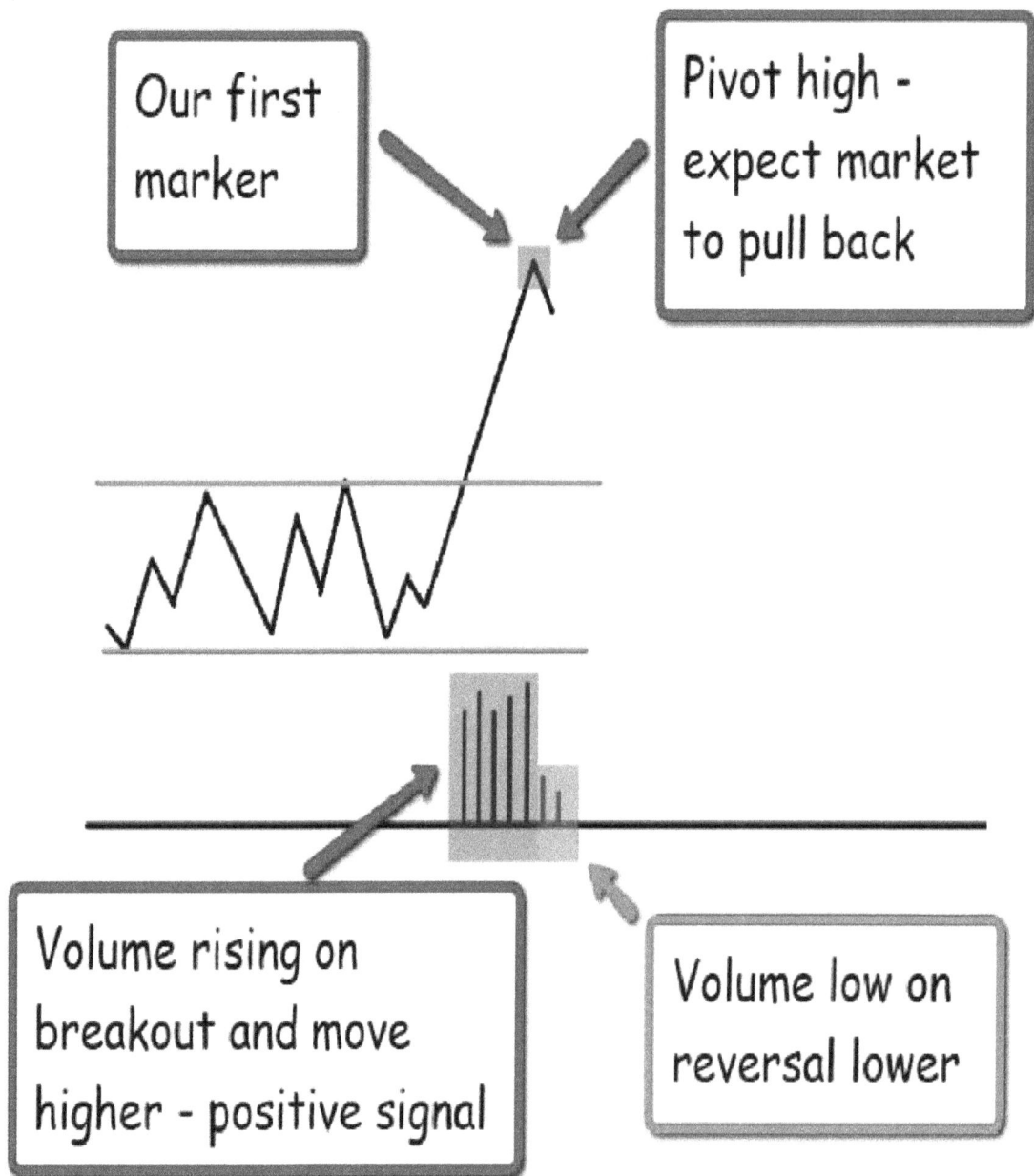

Fig 8.11 First Marker – Pivot High

As we can see in Fig 8.11 the market has been in a consolidation phase and has broken out on robust volume. Our analysis signals that this is a valid move, and we are now looking for signs that a trend is likely to develop. The first signal we have is of a market that is rising on solid and generally rising volumes, and we take a position.

What we are waiting for now is our first marker, which just as in the case of our congestion entrance in the previous chapter, is a pivot, and as we are in a bullish phase we are looking for a pivot high.

As we know markets never go up or down in straight lines and this is the first sign of a reversal, which in turn may also define the upper region of our trend as we break away. Remember the pivot high and the pivot low are combinations of three candles as shown below in Fig 8.12

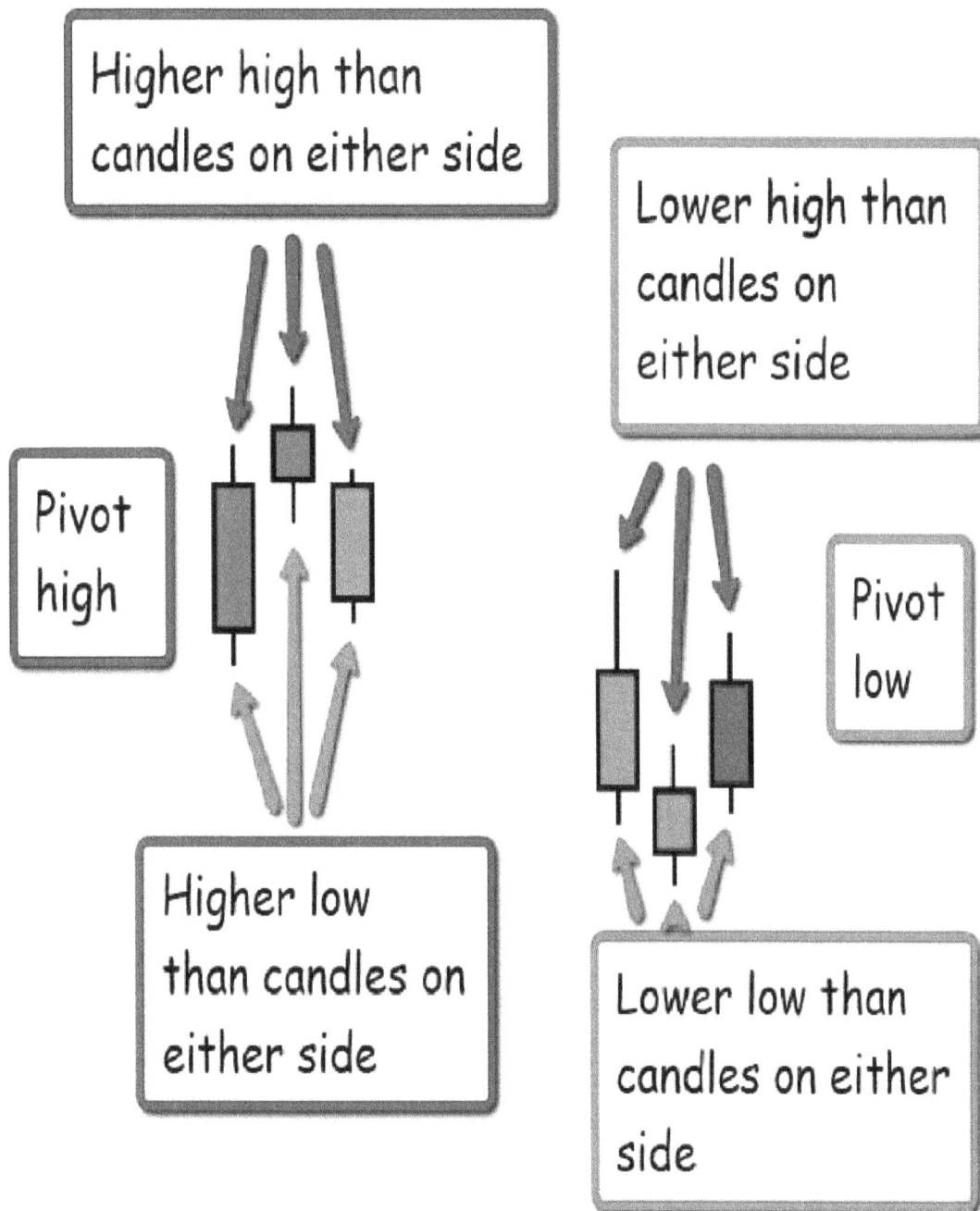

Higher high than candles on either side

Pivot high

Higher low than candles on either side

Lower high than candles on either side

Pivot low

Lower low than candles on either side

Fig 8.12 Pivot Creation

We now have our first point of reference in the price move higher, and since we have a pivot high, we know that the market is going to reverse lower. This could be a major reversal, which is unlikely given the volume profile and the recent price congestion, but at this stage we are never sure and must be patient. The volume is falling, which a good sign, and in due course, the market stops, and reverses higher, posting a pivot low. We now have the second marker in our journey higher, as we can see in Fig 8.13.

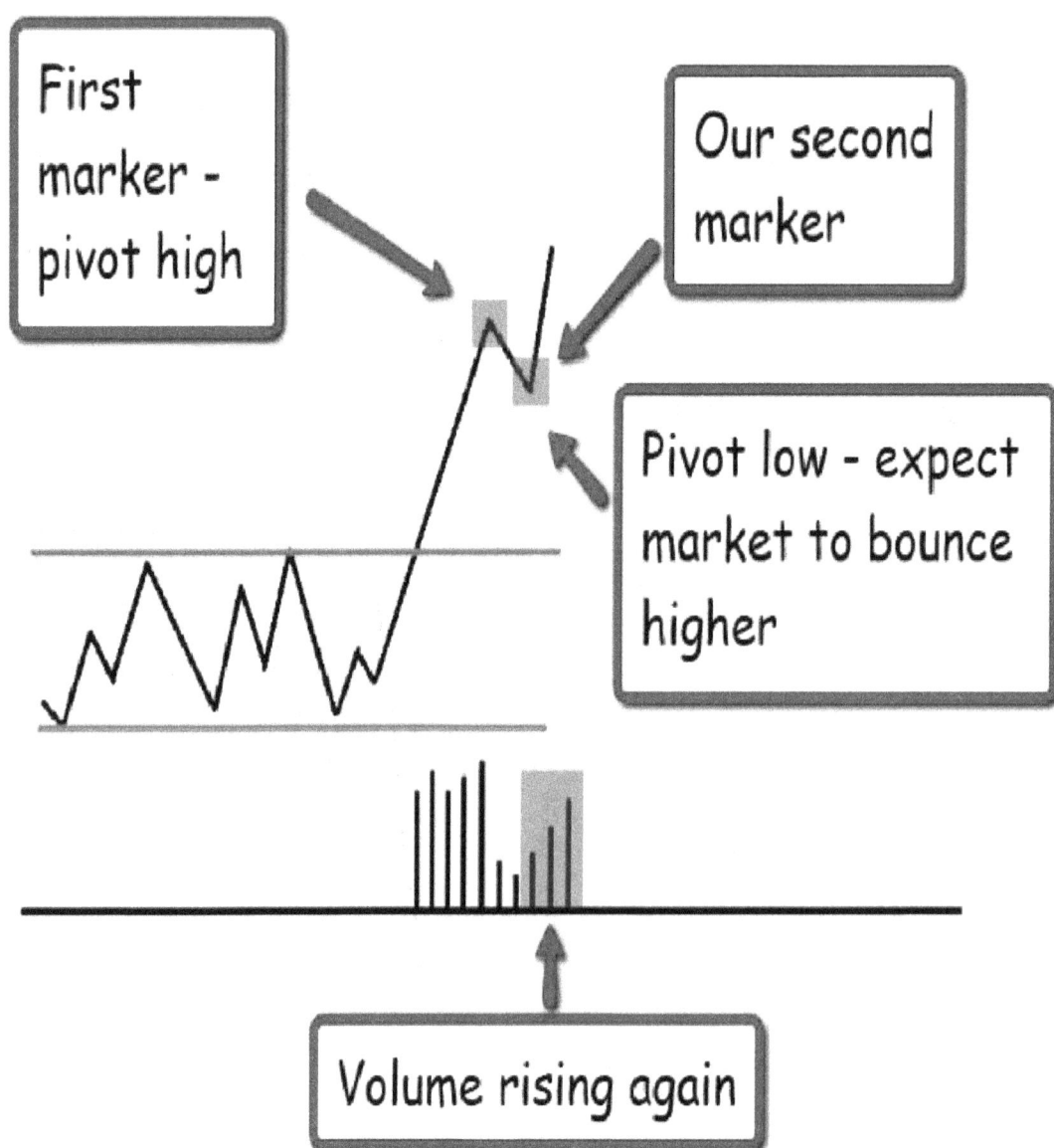

Fig 8.13 Second Marker – Pivot Low

Now we are starting to build a picture of the price action. Remember we have a position in the market, and provided volume continues to confirm price, then all is well with the move higher.

The pivot points which are now forming, are our markers to highlight the journey and define the boundaries of the trend. Unlike the trend lines which most people draw AFTER the event, these are dynamic and created during the price action, and provided they build in a series of higher and lower levels, then we know that the trend is developing and we stay in our position, provided the volume supports our analysis.

Let me scroll forward now and add two more levels to the chart, and based on exactly the same principle. From our current position, we are now looking for the market to push higher, off the pivot low, and the next target for us is a second pivot high, and PROVIDED this is above the previous pivot high, then we are in an upwards trend. Once this second pivot high has formed we are then expecting the market to pullback, but hopefully only in a minor way at this stage, and on low volume, at which point we are now looking for our second pivot low.

This is duly posted, and provided it is higher that the previous pivot low, we stay in our position, as we are now expecting the market to push off this pivot low and develop the trend further.

The market continues higher as expected, and now we are looking for our third pivot high, higher than the previous one, which will then define the upper region of our trend. If this is posted as expected then once again, and I'm sure you are getting the picture now, the market pulls back off this pivot high and moves lower, to post, another isolated pivot low. If this is higher than the previous pivot low, then we continue to hold and now have our third pivot low to define the lower region of the trend.

This is how we build trend lines dynamically, whilst simultaneously holding a position in the market based on Volume Price Analysis and the fundamental principles of VPA breakouts from sideways congestion, as we can see in Fig 8.14.

Whilst the end result is the same, the journey in creating these trend lines is very different and allows you, as a trader to join the trend at the best point, which is the start, and not the end!! This is shown in Fig 8.14 below.

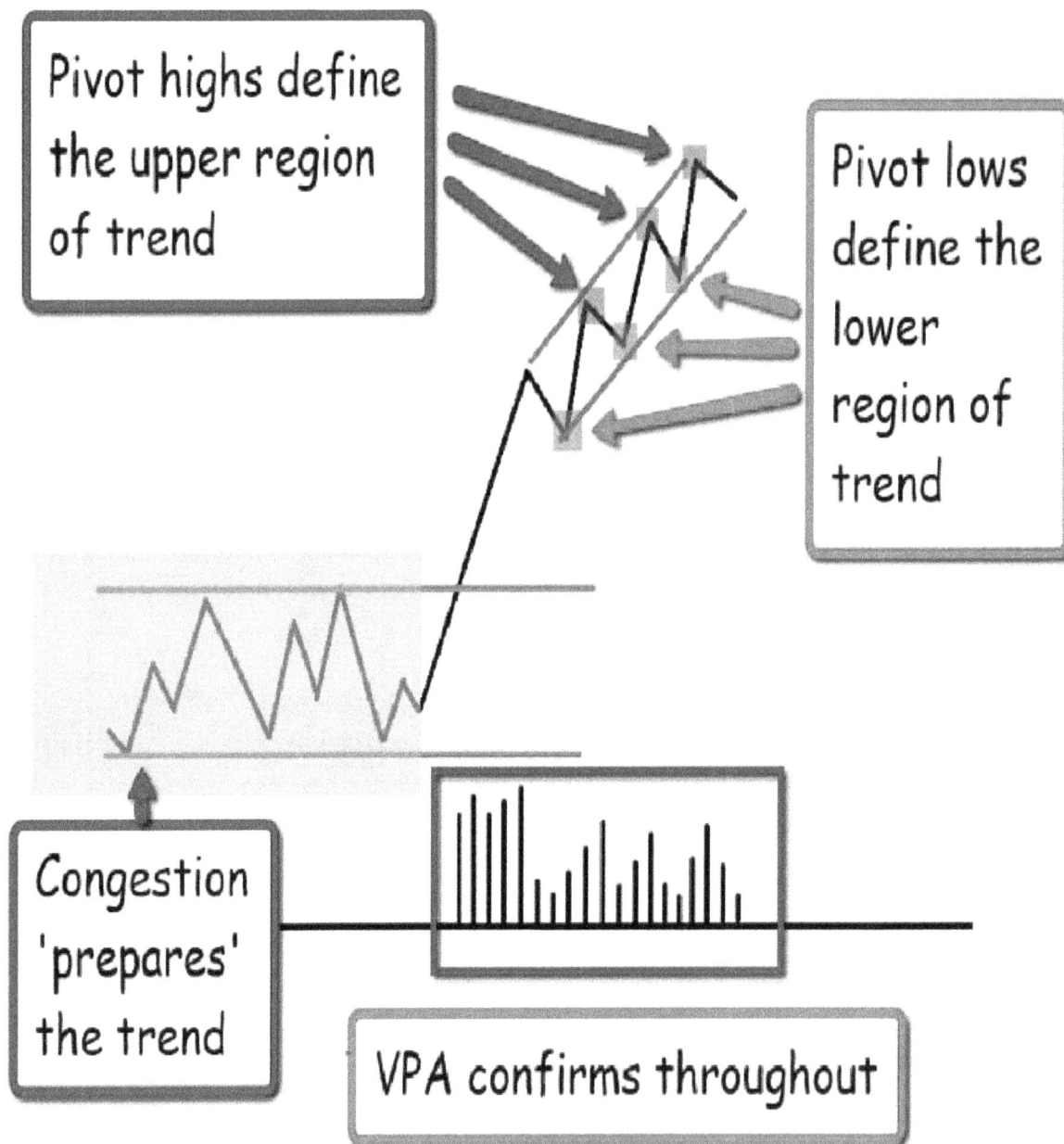

Fig 8.14 Dynamic Trend Lines – Bullish Trend

We can imagine this whole process almost as one of 'scene setting'. The congestion phase sets the scene for the price action, which is then delivered and supported by the volume. The pivots highlight the journey – they are like the lights at the side of the road, giving us a clear view of where we are, whilst also giving us the confidence to hold our position in the market.

Finally, at some point, we see a pivot high posted that is lower or perhaps at the same level as a previous pivot, and it is at this point that we are looking at a market that is perhaps moving into a secondary congestion phase, with a pivot low to follow. If this is at a similar level to a previous pivot low then we are in a second congestion phase and our analysis continues. Now we are looking for confirming signals with further pivots and finally a break out. Again, is this a trend reversal, or merely a trend pause? If we break to the downside then it is a trend reversal, and we exit our position, but if it is a trend pause, and the trend continues on a break higher, then we hold our position, and start the process of building our dynamic trend lines once again.

Naturally, the above is a text book example of what we want to see on every breakout from a congestion phase, but trading life is rarely text book. Sometimes these pivots do not appear. For example on a break higher, the pivot high may not appear, but the pivot low may do so in due course.

At this point we have to make a decision based on our VPA analysis, and judge whether the trend is developing as expected. However, this may be the first early warning signal that this is not a trend which has any sustained momentum. In general, we would expect to see the move away from congestion as having some momentum, supported by volume. As markets move quickly, so buyers and sellers move equally quickly, either to get in, or to get out creating the pivot points on the chart.

If these are missing, for whatever reason, then this alone suggests a market which is potentially lacking in momentum which will always be evident from our volume analysis. If the market is moving higher, but the volume is average or below average then this is a trend lacking momentum. Buyers and sellers are simply not participating in the move higher, and the trend will therefore simply not develop. There is no energy, no activity, and this is reflected in the volume and associated price action.

Therefore, don't expect to see the perfect scenario on each breakout. Every one will be different, characterised by varying degrees of momentum and duration. What we have to do is to look for the clues using VPA, and then wait for the pivots to appear as the price action unfolds. If they do not follow a logical pattern in the trend, then the market is potentially weak, and may simply revert back into a period of congestion at a slightly higher level.

The price action and associated pivots for a move lower away from a congestion phase are created in just the same way, but this time we are looking for a pivot low to form initially, followed by a pivot high, as we can see in Fig 8.15.

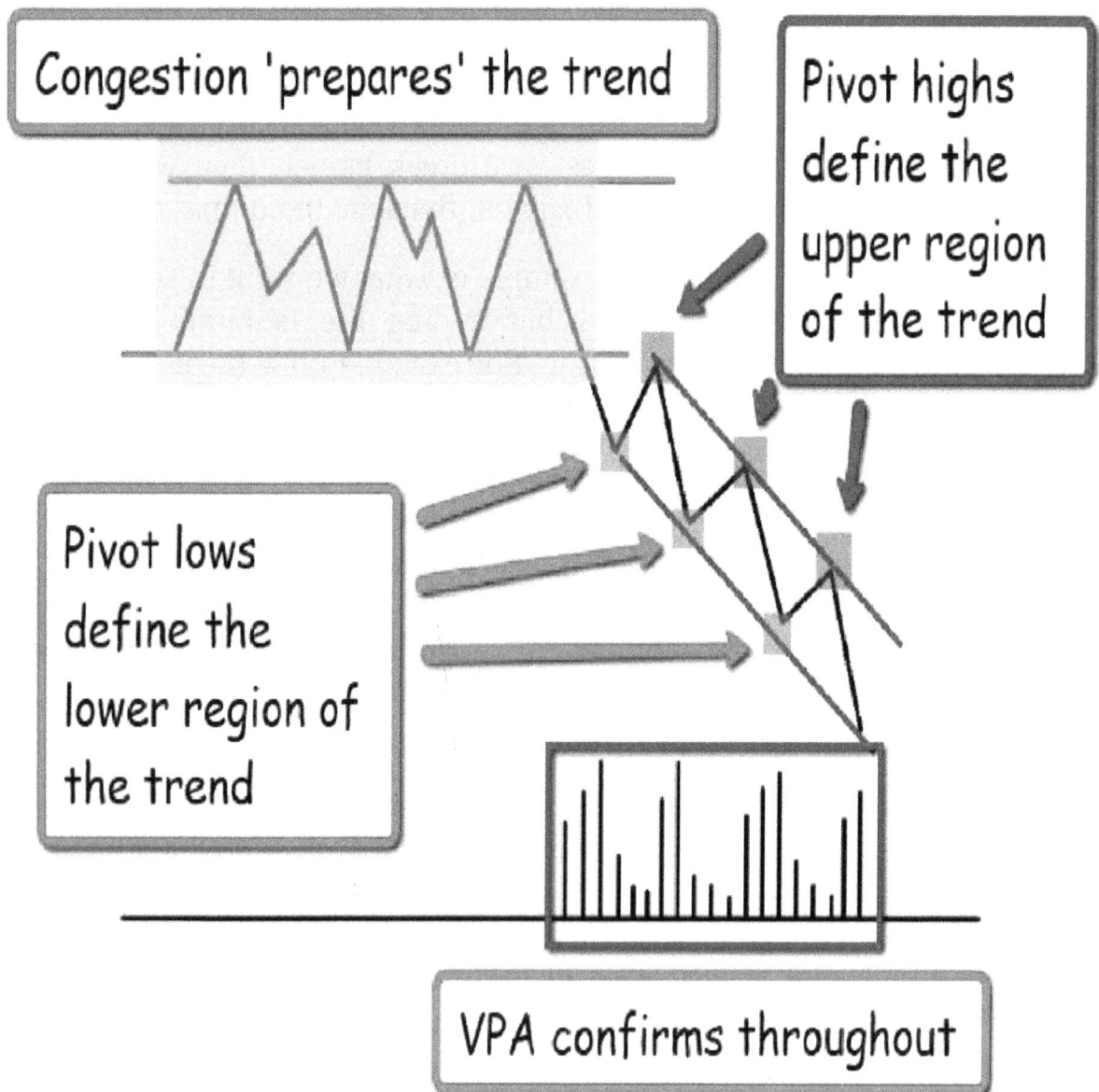

Fig 8.15 Dynamic Trend Lines – Bearish Trend

In summary, and to put all of this into context. There is nothing wrong with drawing what I call 'static' trend lines on a price chart, and in many ways this is what we have done here. The difference however, is that the trend lines in this chapter have been created by the dynamic price action of the market. Obviously this is hard to present in a book, and is best seen live in action as the market unfolds. Nevertheless, what I have tried to describe here is the process of analysis and price action which describes where we are in our trading journey, or perhaps more importantly where the market is in its trading journey.

The pivots are formed dynamically, and as they are created, so the trend is built which we can then define using these points as our 'way points' on the journey. Nothing is ever perfect, but at least using VPA, and your understanding of the importance of price congestion, should put you into a strong position, allowing you to identify a trend BEFORE it starts, and not after. This is what I have tried to explain in the last two chapters, and I hope that in reading them you will at least have a better understanding of how markets behave and the importance of price congestion.

As I have said before, many traders become frustrated when markets move into a congestion phase, which I find hard to understand. This is where the market is preparing the next trend. These areas are the breeding grounds for trends, and in many ways far more important than any existing trend, since this is a new trend, from which we can take advantage, early. It really is that simple. It may be a selling climax or a buying climax, it may be a pause in a longer term trend. Whatever the reason, and whatever the timeframe, you can be sure of one thing. The market is preparing for a move away from this region, it is just building up strength and preparing to breakout, one way or the other. All we have to do is be patient, wait, and then apply VPA to the consequent price action, coupled with our pivots which highlight the journey.

Chapter Nine

Volume At Price (VAP)

In a bull market it is better to always work on the bull side; in a bear market, on the bear side.

Charles Dow (1851-1902)

At the start of this book I made the statement that there is nothing new in trading, and that volume has been around for over a century. It was the iconic traders of the past with their tape reading skills who laid the foundations for today's VPA traders.

Well that statement is not entirely true, as in this chapter I want to introduce you to one of the latest developments in volume studies, which takes volume and Volume Price Analysis to the next level. This is called volume at price, or VAP for short. Now we have VPA and VAP – very neat really!

So what is volume at price and how does this differ from our studies so far using Volume Price Analysis or VPA. But first, let me introduce a simple concept which I hope will help to explainVAP, and once again we return to our wholesaler of goods, who has a warehouse with one product to sell. As a wholesaler, (and indeed anyone selling anything) he or she is always looking to maximise profits from each sale, and one of the easiest ways to do this is to 'test the market'.

This is something companies do all the time. A product will be marketed at one price, and the volume of sales recorded. The price will then be raised or lowered and the resulting sales recorded and monitored. Obviously, if the wholesaler can sell at a higher price and still maintain the same sales volume, then this will increase profits automatically, with no fall in volume.

At some point, the price will reach a point at which volumes do fall, as buyers now perceive the product as over priced, and simply stop buying. The wholesaler then simply drops the price lower, and sales volumes should pick up again.

On a simple bar chart, this price action and volume would be reported on a chart which would look similar to that in Fig 9.10 below.

Sales volume vs price

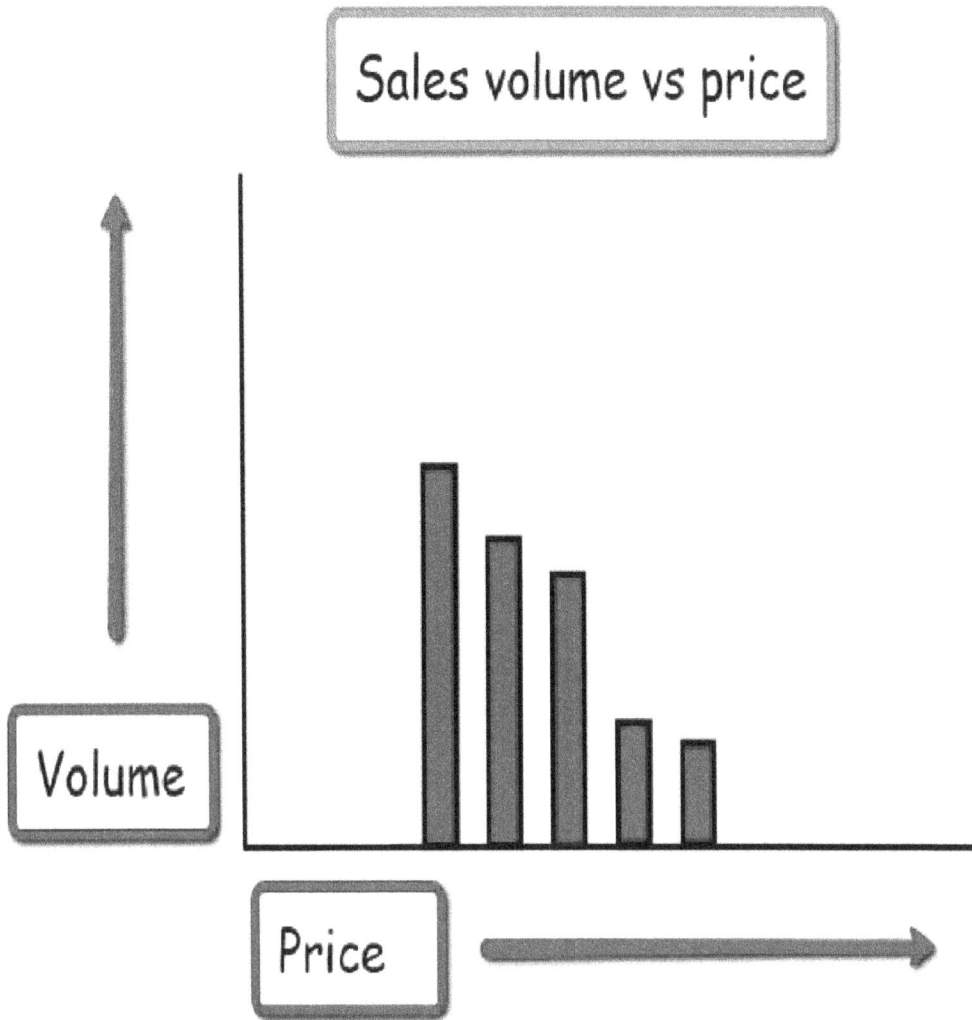

Fig 9.10 Sales Volume vs Price

Here we have a chart of volume and price, with price on the X axis and volume on the Y axis. As you would expect, as the price increases, then the volume of products sold falls. This is not always the case, but generally so in most markets. The point here is that we now have a 'map' of volume against price. In other words, we can now see visually how the volume has changed as the price changes, and this is what Volume at Price is all about. In a normal volume bar, all we see is one bar, but within the price action there are many different levels of price. All we are seeing in our single volume bar, is the total volume associated with the price spread of the bar. What this volume bar does NOT reveal, is the levels of buying associated with the different price points, exactly as in our simple example above. If we swing this chart through 90 degrees, then we have a perfect representation of VAP as it would appear on our chart, as we can see in Fig 9.11

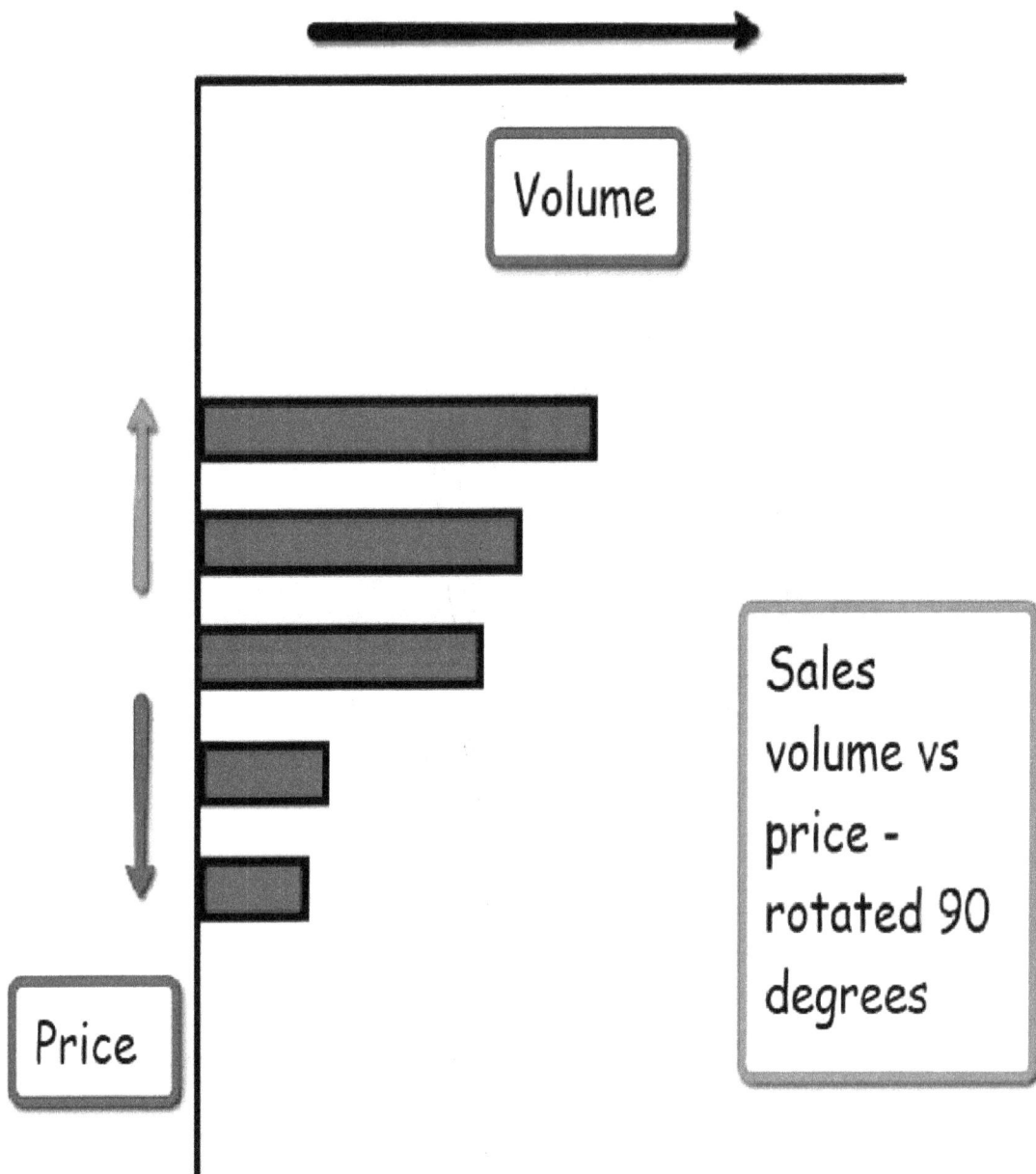

Fig 9.11 Sales Volume vs Price – Rotated

Now perhaps you can begin to see how the principle of volume at price really works, and in many ways the term itself describes the methodology. What we are looking at here, is the volume at the price. In other words, we can see the volumes associated with each price level as the market moves higher and lower. What we have is a volume histogram of the buying and selling volumes associated with each price point. We can imagine this as a dissection of the single volume bar that we use in Volume Price Analysis (VPA). Here the volume bar records all the volume of activity associated within the period of the bar and the spread of the price action.

With VAP, what we are doing is taking that volume bar, and cutting it open to reveal where the concentration of volumes actually occurred. After all, if the concentration of volume was at the bottom, then this is more likely to be buying volume rather than selling volume. Conversely, if the concentration of volume took place at the top of the bar rather than at the bottom of the bar, then this is more likely to be selling volume. Volume at price gives us a different perspective on the more traditional volume bar, revealing as it does, the concentration of buying and selling, at the various price levels, which in turn gives us an alternative perspective, not only in terms of momentum, but also in terms of support and resistance.

And, as far as I am concerned, this is the KEY point.

The way to use this methodology is as an enhancement to the classic VPA approach, and NOT to replace it in any way. As you will discover shortly, volume at price gives us a very different perspective, as it provides an insight into the concentrations of buying and selling areas, which to me means support and resistance. As we have already discovered how to identify these areas using price, and price action, VAP then gives us an additional tool to use, which gives us a visual representation of these areas on the chart. If you remember back to the previous chapter, I referred to support and resistance as invisible barriers, natural barriers if you like – well now, with volume at price, these barriers are actually revealed on our charts.

However, we must remember, VAP is a supporting technique to VPA, NOT the other way round. Whilst VAP is powerful and gives us a three dimensional view of the volume and price action, it does NOT replace traditional VPA, and never will in my view. So please use VAP as a tool with which to identify price congestion along with support and resistance zones, which you can then confirm with traditional analysis using VPA.

Let's look at some examples and the good news is that this indicator, is generally available free on most good charting packages. All the examples in the remainder of this chapter are taken from my NinjaTrader trading platform.

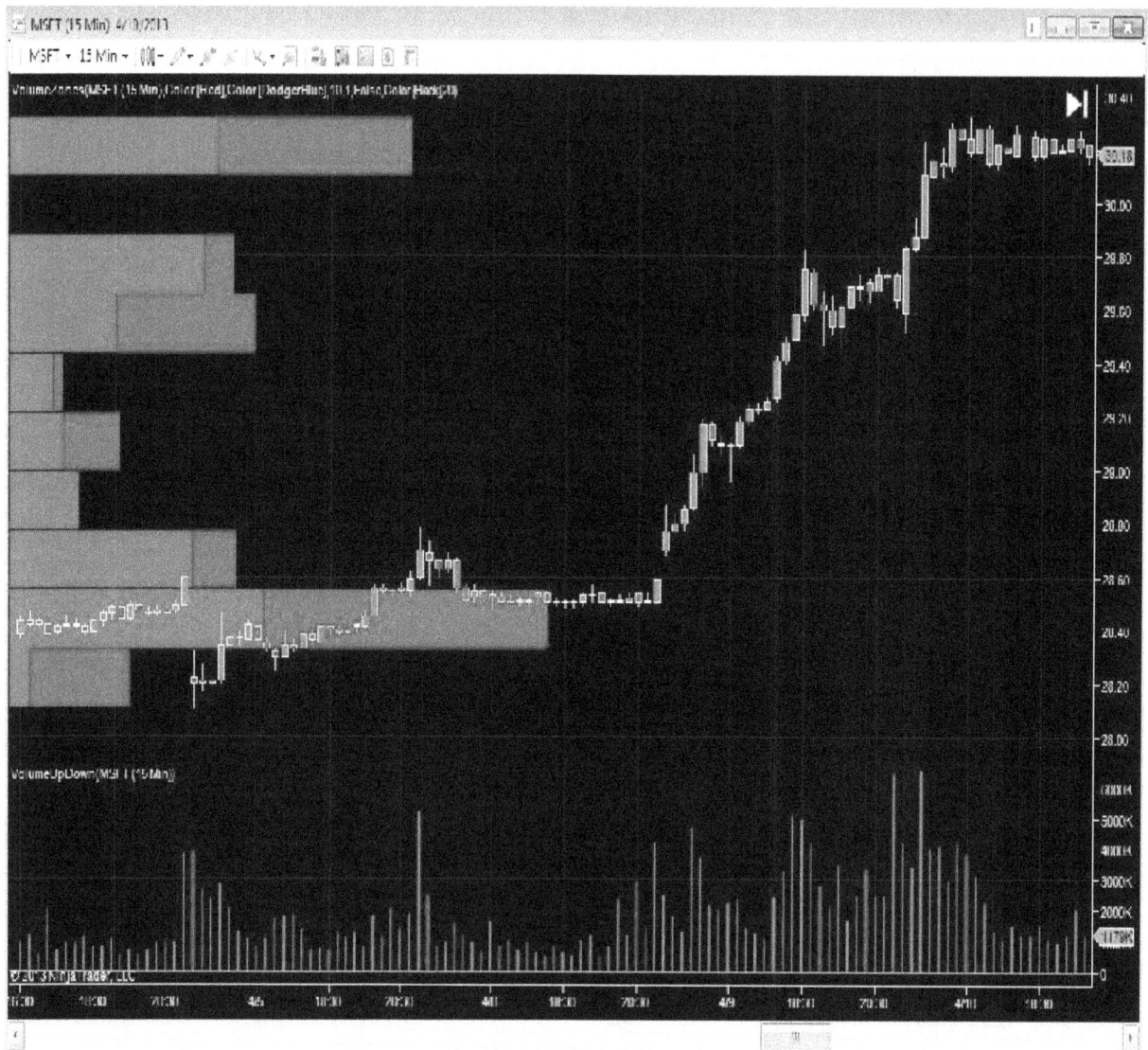

Fig 9.12 Microsoft (MSFT) – 15 Minute Chart

The chart in Fig 9.12 is a 15 minute chart for Microsoft, and as you can see, traditional volume bars are presented at the bottom of the screen, whilst the volume at price indicator presents the volume distribution on the Y axis vertically, as I explained in my first example.

Now throughout this book I have tried to explain and reinforce the concept of support and resistance. It is the breeding ground for trends, it is where they are created and fostered and from which they ultimately break free, and the beauty of volume at price, is that these areas of price congestion are now painted on the chart visually for us. Therefore, let me explain this chart in broad terms, and highlight what is perhaps obvious, and more importantly, what is not so obvious, at first glance.

And before moving to this example, let me just explain the significance of the colours in the VAP bar. Just as with a conventional volume bar, we have red and blue on the chart which reflect whether the associated candle was up or down. In a VAP bar we have the same, and what each bar represents, with the two colours, is the number of up or down candles associated with that phase of price action. If there had been more up candles than down then the fulcrum of the bar would be more blue than red. Conversely, if there had been more down candles than up, then the fulcrum would be weighted more red than blue. This in itself gives us a perspective on the balance of 'buying' or 'selling' at this price range.

Moving to our example, in simple terms, there are four phases of price congestion here, one at the bottom of the chart which continued for an extended period, two in the middle, which were both relatively short and one at the top in the current trading range. The chart covers a 5 day period approximately. What does VAP reveal? First, it defines these regions for us on the chart. Each area of price congestion is marked by the volume histogram which then gives us a sense of the importance of each region. As we would expect, the most dense area of volume is in the first area of price congestion, with two volume bars denoting the significance of this area, one above average and one extreme.

The area of congestion above this level is modest by comparison, with only two volume bars of any significance, both of which are well below average. A very minor area of price congestion indeed.

Next we move to the third level and here we see more sustained volumes at this level with two above average volume bars denoting an area of price congestion which is significant. Finally, we move to the current price area, where we can see one extreme volume bar. What can we deduce from this analysis?

First we can see immediately which of those areas are likely to be significant in the future in terms of resistance and support. When these areas are revisited during future price action, then these levels will become our invisible barriers, and from visual volumes we can judge the likely level of support or resistance. Obviously, time also plays a part here. The longer a market is in a congestion phase, then the higher the concentration of volumes we expect to see within the price range. It goes without saying that if the market pauses for days or weeks, then all this volume is contained in a relatively narrow price range, which in turn will be reflected in the VAP histogram on the left hand side of the chart.

However, whilst this is perhaps an obvious statement to make, what is more revealing as always, is when we bring in the time aspect of the volume and price relationship. Let's take a look and see what VAP is telling us here.

The chart is over a five day period, and the first phase of price congestion lasted for three days. What we see here is what we expect, some high volume bars confirming a dense region of price congestion. All we can say about this price region is that it is significant, and had we been trading, then on the breakout we would have been very comfortable with the volume histogram, confirming a strong platform of support below with the market breaking higher. Equally in the future, if the market reverses to test this region, once again we can say with confidence that there is a strong platform of support, which will take some extreme volumes to penetrate and break.

Moving to the next area of price congestion, which in this case only lasted for a handful of bars, a few hours at most, before the market broke higher once again, and moved on. This is a secondary area of congestion, and instantly recognisable as such with our VAP volumes. These are below average, and only two are of any significance, so if this region were tested in the future, it would not take much effort to penetrate this level, either from below or above.

Finally, we come to the third and fourth levels of price congestion on the chart which are the most revealing. The first of these lasted 14 price candles (approximately 4 hours) whilst the second lasted the entire session of a day. However, look at the associated volume bars and compare these to the price congestion that lasted for 3 days. The most recent price congestion phase at the top of the chart, which lasted a day, has almost the same concentration of volume as in the first area of price congestion, which lasted for three times as long – 3 days.

What is the volume telling us about this congestion phase of price? And once again, as with all volume analysis it is in comparing one with another that the anomalies are revealed giving us the validation we are always searching for in any analysis of price using volume, and in this respect VAP is no different. In this example in Fig 9.12 we have an intraday chart, with the congestion phase at the bottom of the chart giving us our benchmark against which to measure other areas of price congestion and their significance.

Whilst the second phase of congestion is, as we would expect, with below average volume bars in a short phase of sideways price action, the next level above, our third level, is already starting to ring the alarm bells. And the reason is this.

Because here we see a price congestion phase, over a short period of time, but with above average volume bars and spread over a deep area of price. So an alarm signal is sounded. From a trading perspective if we were holding a position, this would give us the confidence on the break out higher, that this was a significant area of price support and we could therefore continue to hold the position with confidence.

Then we arrive at the fourth level on our chart at the top of the price action, with the congestion phase marked with ultra high volume on our VAP, and additional high volume bars in a very narrow trading range on our traditional volume bars. Clearly the market is weak at this level and the volumes are heavy, and likely to be selling in this region. After all, on volume of this strength we would expect to see the market move higher but it hasn't, instead it has remained range bound.

In case you think this was a chart deliberately 'hand picked' to reveal the power of VAP, nothing could be further from the truth. It was the first one I happened to select when writing this chapter, and indeed, you may find this hard to believe, but as I was writing, the market opened, and the Microsoft stock price fell like a stone, down $1.40 on the open.

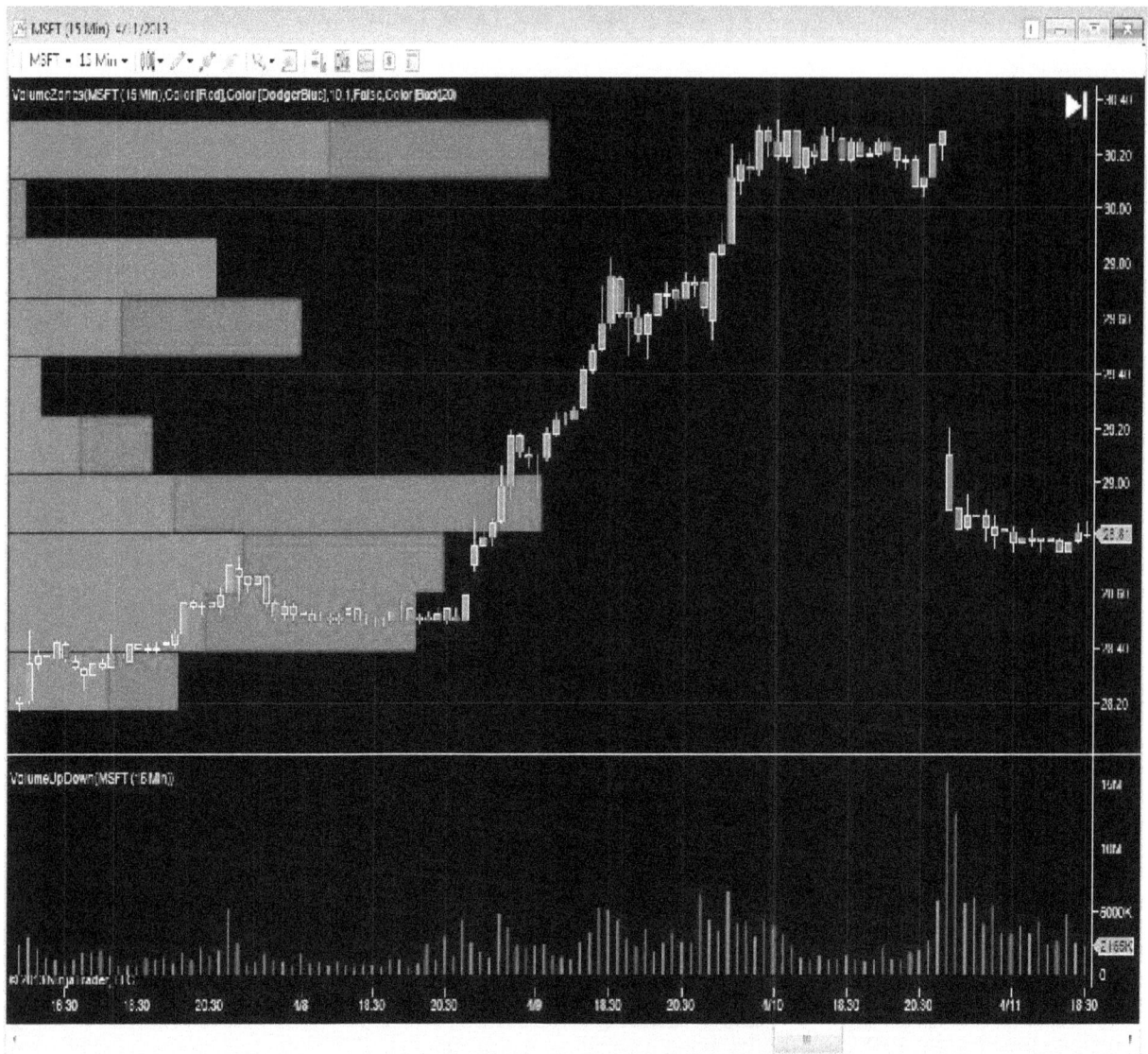

Fig 9.13 Microsoft (MSFT) 15 Minute Chart – After Open

And here it is! As you would expect the volume at price profiles have now changed, as we are seeing heavy volumes coming into the market, as evidenced on both the VAP and also on our traditional volume bars at the bottom of the chart. This once again demonstrates the power of volume at price analysis. Not only are we seeing a potential support region being built visually, we are also seeing this validated in our volume bars at the bottom of the chart, and when we begin to analyse this with our price spread, a complete story of price action backed by volume is created. It still defeats me as to how anyone can ever trade without using volume, and I hope fervently that by now I have convinced you to at least consider it as one of, if not the only one of, your analytical techniques. I sincerely hope so.

Just to round off this chapter, let's take a look at some other examples of VAP.

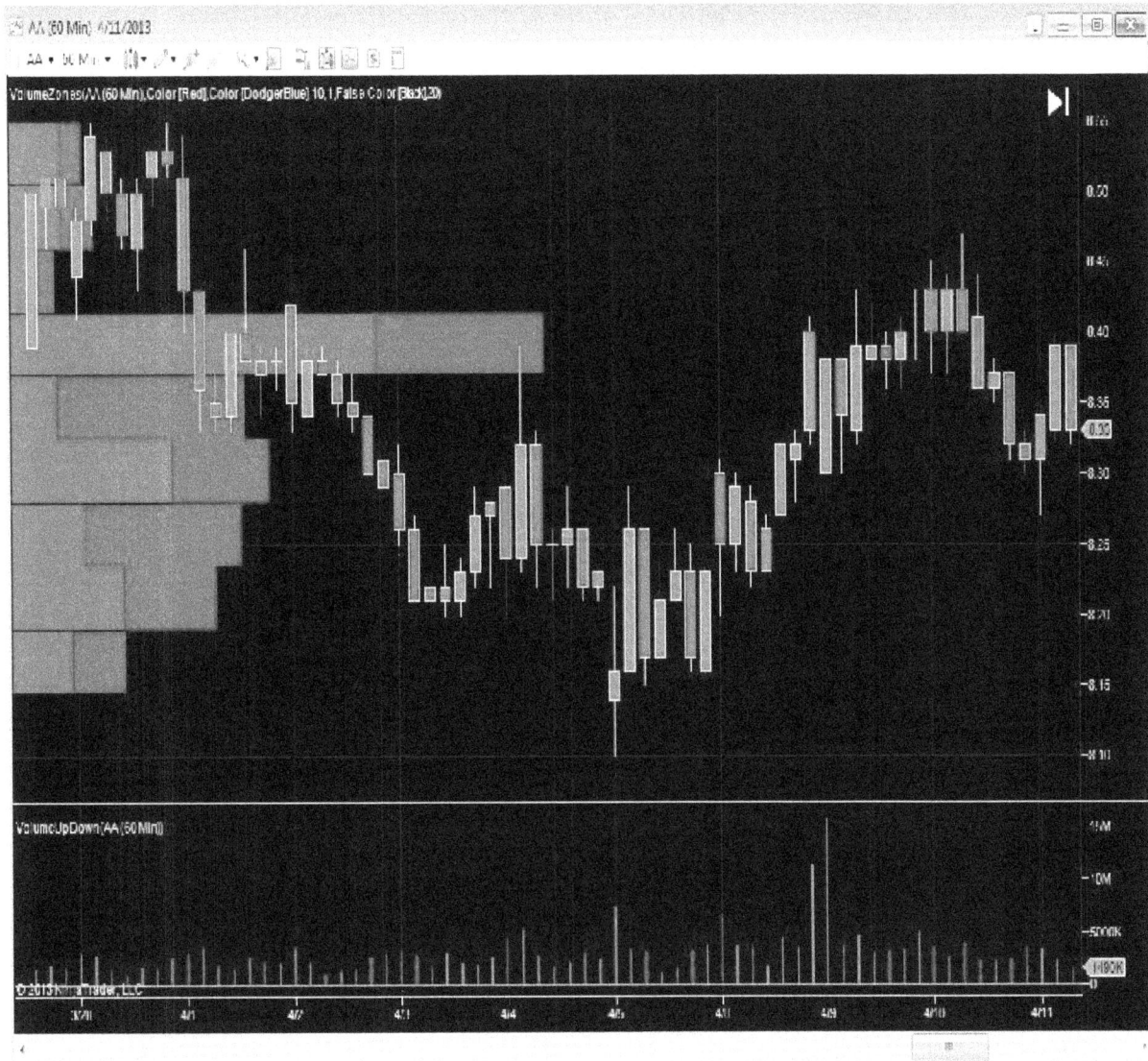

Fig 9.14 Alcoa (AA) – Hourly Chart

Fig 9.14 is a really interesting chart. It's an hourly chart this time for Alcoa, but look at the huge volume spike in the centre of the volume at price histogram. It is enormous, and more importantly is right in line with the current price action which is in congestion. The market has traded in this range before, and clearly this represents a very significant area of price consolidation as evidenced by the VAP. As you can see, in the past few hours the market has rallied and attempted to breach this level, but failed. And no wonder, given the volume profile on the left of the chart in the VAP histogram. At this point we would be moving to our traditional Volume Price Analysis to look for anomalies and validation, which may well confirm this view, and suggest that any break out is likely to be to the down side.

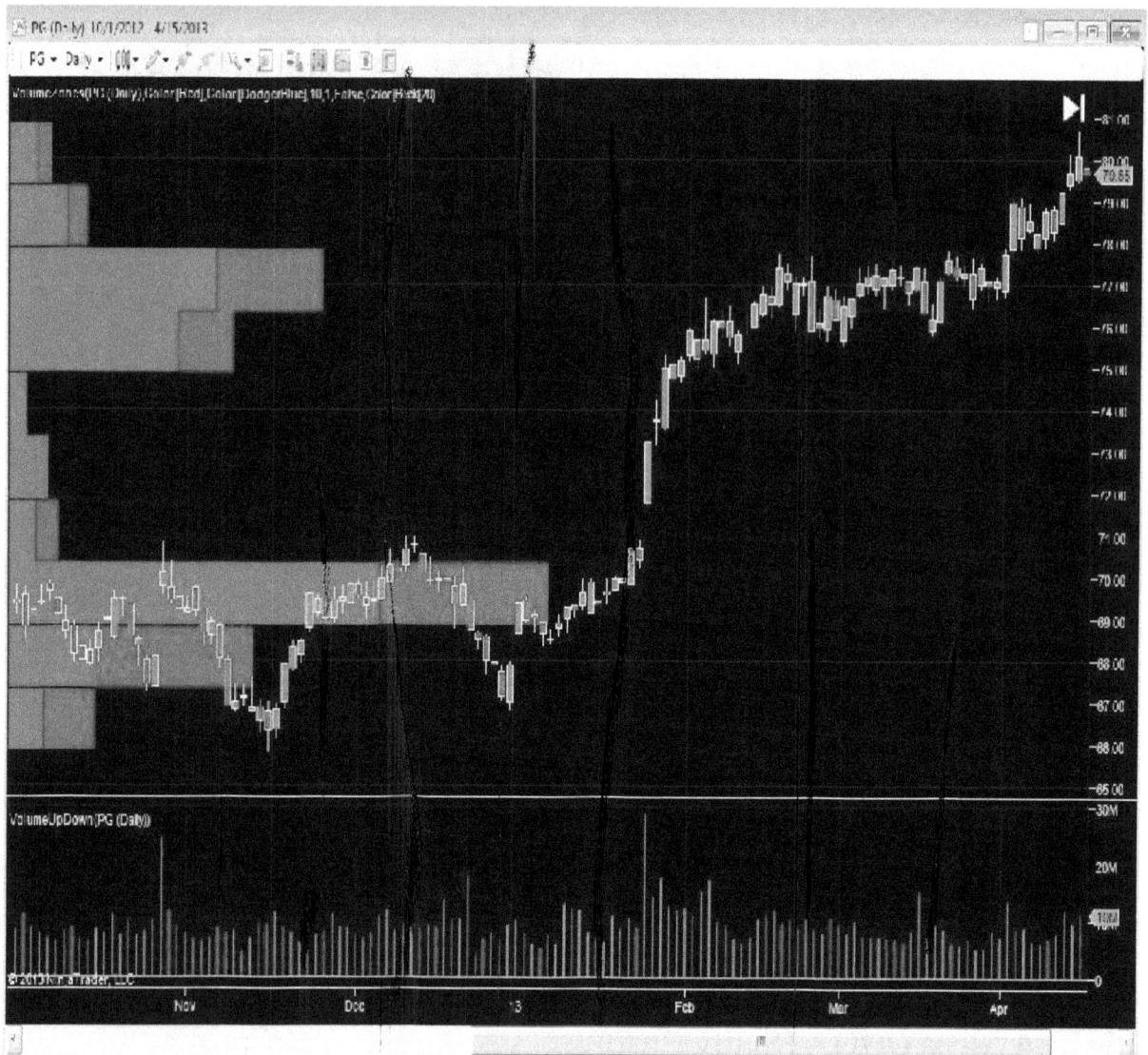

Fig 9.15 Proctor & Gamble (PG) – Daily Chart

Now this looks a really nice stock in Fig 9.15 to be trading right now and the reason is that, as an investor, you would almost certainly have been looking at this as a longer term buy and hold. It is a daily chart and the chart period covers around 6 months in total. And, as we can see for the first three months, this stock was in congestion. However, look at the volumes in the VAP. One extreme volume bar with another of average volume. Whilst the congestion phase was long, looking higher up the chart, we see a further phase of congestion, which lasted for two months, but the volume bars here are only moderate and above average. This gives us our benchmark as clearly the support platform at the lower level is a substantial one, so in the event of any reversal lower, there is an extremely strong, natural barrier in place.

More importantly, when the breakout from this region occurred, it moved higher on a gap up, which is always a strong signal, and then validated by our Volume Price Analysis. From there this stock has risen strongly, and following the second phase of congestion, has moved higher once more. However, the key thing about the second congestion phase is that the volumes, relatively speaking, are lower, and therefore this price region may not offer the same degree of support in the event of a reversal lower. This helps when placing our stop orders in the market, which are always governed by our risk and money management rules.

Nevertheless, the point is this. These visual regions created using the VAP approach, give us vital clues and signals which help us in many different ways. They help to validate the current price action. They reveal the 'depth' of support and resistance in key congestion areas, and they give us confidence on breakouts, when the platform of support or resistance is there for us to see. If it is strong, then we have additional confidence to take a position, if it is weak, we may hold back and wait for other signals. Finally VAP reveals the strength of support and resistance for future price action, which again helps us to visualise and analyse risk.

Now in the next chapter we are going to examine some further examples using Volume Price Analysis (VPA). However I would urge you to discover more about VAP for yourself. The examples I have used here have all been using stocks, but it is a technique that applies equally well to many other markets and instruments.

The CME themselves used to provide a facility called Chart -EX which produced a similar picture for traders in futures, but I believe this is no longer available. However, as I said earlier, most good charting platforms will have this indicator in one form or another.

Chapter Ten

Volume Price Analysis Examples

Two… key factors: correct action and patience. These you must supply yourself.
Charles Brandes (1943-)

I hope by now I have managed to convince you of the merits and power of Volume Price Analysis in all its various forms. My purpose in writing this book has been twofold. First to guide you in the direction that I was fortunate to take, when I first began trading all those years ago. Albert was a rogue, and even though he has attracted many detractors over the years, I for one will always be grateful for the day I happened to stumble across his article in the newspaper. Volume to me just makes sense, it is logical, and is the only way I believe that you can truly see INSIDE market behaviour, manipulated or otherwise. All the charts used here are taken from either my NinjaTrader platform, or my MT4 brokerage account.

My second reason for the book is to explain this methodology in a straightforward way. The markets may be complex, but they are not complicated or difficult to understand, and if you are prepared to learn and study the charts yourself, you too can become an expert in VPA in no time. There are no short cuts, but just like riding a bicycle, once learnt, you will never forget. As I have said before, I do not believe any software program can do the analysis for you. Trading is an art, not a science and the subtleties and nuances of the market are simply beyond the capabilities of machine code, no matter how sophisticated the program. And the principle reason why trading is an art, is because markets are driven by people and their money and underpinned by fear and greed.

Therefore, as we near the end of this book, I'd like to to through some examples from various markets, and from different platforms. All have volume. Some is actual volume, as in the cash markets and the futures markets, others are from the spot forex market. But all of them have one thing in common. The application of VPA is identical in each case, and where we have VAP data, I have added this as well to complete the picture.

And I would like to start with some examples from the US stock markets and the first chart is the daily chart for Honeywell (HON) which if Fig 10.10.

This is a nice example which teaches us several lessons on this one chart. Whilst this is a daily stock chart, our VPA principles still apply, regardless of market or instrument.

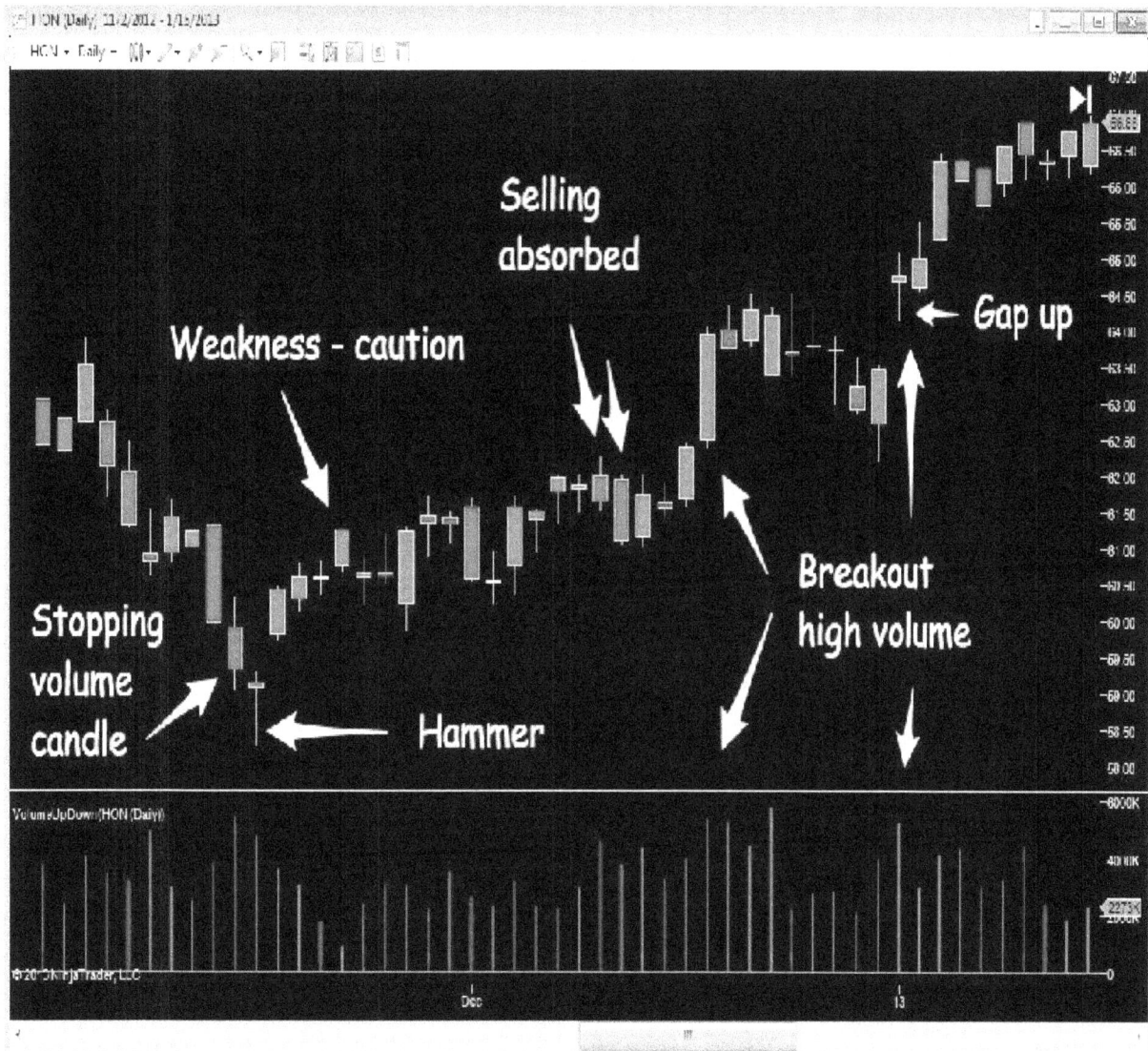

Fig 10.10 Honeywell (HON) Daily Chart

The stock sells off, moving lower, and initial weakness is signalled by the small shooting star candle, which is then confirmed with rising volume and a wide spread down candle. So no anomaly here. This is then followed by a narrow spread down candle with higher volume than on the previous bar. This is an anomaly, and could be stopping volume. The following day, the market closes with a hammer candle, and high volume again. We are now looking for this stock to pause at this level, perhaps move into a congestion phase, or perhaps see more accumulation before a breakout and move higher.

In this case, Honeywell moves higher immediately on the following day with a gapped up open, but the volume is only average. The following day the price spread is narrow, and although higher on the day, the volume is falling away. This is not a good sign and suggests weakness. The stock is possibly not going to move too far, and does move into a congestion phase. However, towards the end of this phase we start to see daily selling pressure absorbed with a narrow spread down candle and high volume, again an anomaly. After all, if this was selling, then we would expect to see a wide spread candle, and we haven't. We have a narrow spread candle, followed by another, three candles later.

The selling is being absorbed, and we are now waiting for a potential break out from this region, which duly arrives. Rising volume with wide spread up candles. A positive signal that the market is bullish. We also have a nice platform of support below. The market then moves sideways again at the higher level for two weeks, sliding lower, but note the down candles. The selling volumes are falling all the time at this level, not a sign of a bearish market. If the stock were truly bearish then we would expect to see falling prices and RISING volume. We have falling volume. Remember, it takes effort to rise AND fall.

Therefore, we are expecting to see buyers come into the market soon, which is precisely what happens next, and with attitude! The buyers come in with above average volume, and note the tail on this candle which is the last in the current congestion phase. This looks positive.

The following day we get the breakout, with high volume. This is NOT a trap up move, but a genuine move higher. And we know it is genuine because VOLUME reveals everything. Not only have we seen a breakout, but this has been accompanied by a gapped up open as well. All signs of a bullish market, PROVIDED this is validated with volume. Three months later the stock was trading at $76.08.

The next US stock is a particular favourite of mine. David (my husband) and I first starting trading Duke Energy back in the days when it was $17! Now it's over $70. In those days we held this stock and wrote covered calls which is a great options strategy, and the topic for another book.

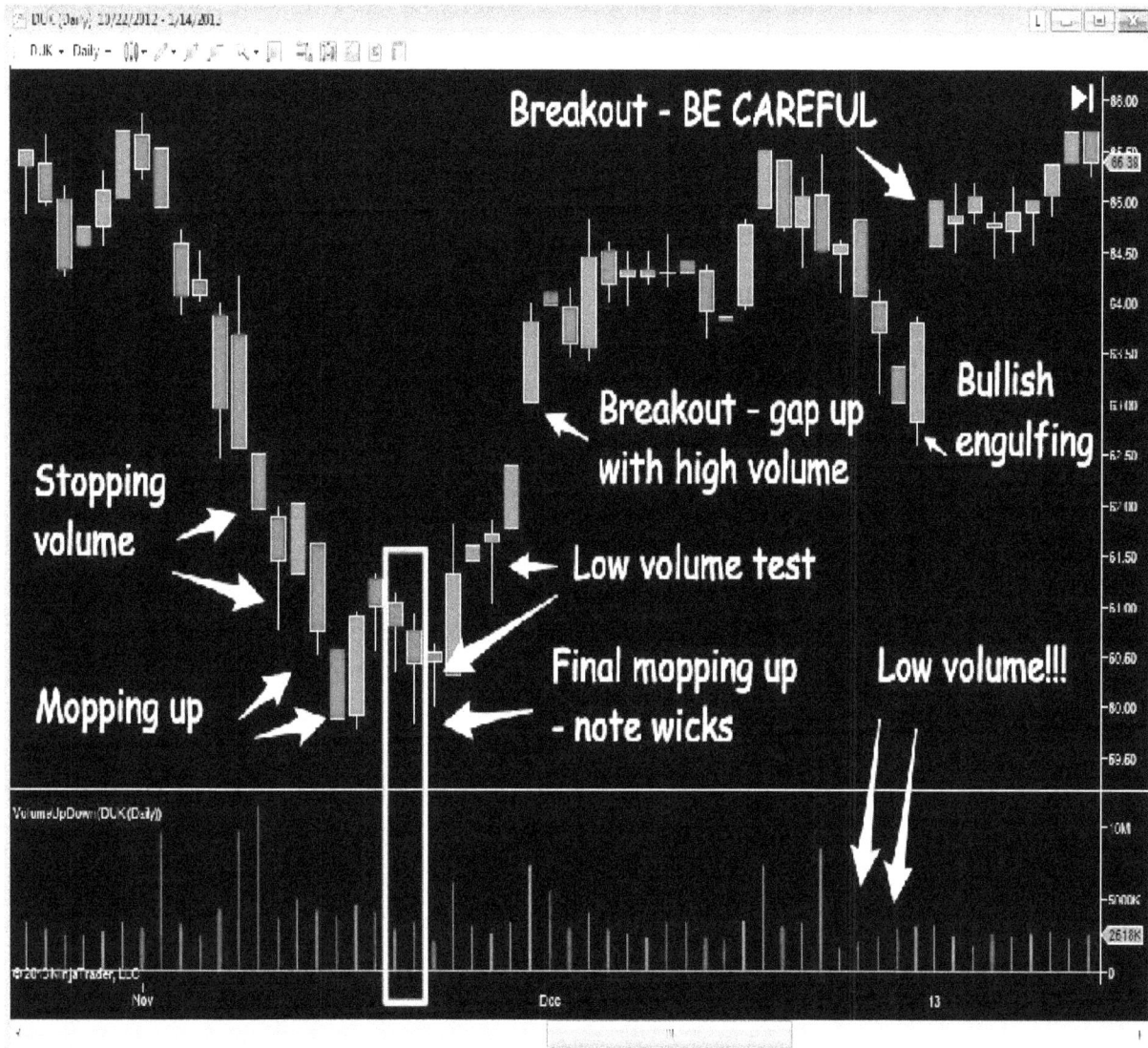

Fig 10.11 Duke Energy (DUK) Daily Chart

Once again, there are several lessons to be learnt here, and the most valuable one is patience. If you recall what I said at the start of the book. When I first started trading using VPA I used to get very excited as soon as I saw a hammer candle, or stopping volume and would immediately take a position in the market. However, remember the oil tanker. It takes time to stop. Therefore, what can we learn from Duke Energy.

First, at the extreme left of the chart we can see that the stock has been rising on relatively low volume. The volume on the last bull candle, a wide spread up candle, is only marginally higher than on the previous candle, which was half the price spread. Clearly there is an early sign of weakness ahead, which duly arrives two candles later. The stock attempts to rally before entering a price waterfall with falling prices and rising volumes, with stopping volume initially putting the brakes. At this point Duke Energy attempts to move higher, but with a wick to the upper body of the candle, this is not a strong response, and the stock price falls further, but on average volumes.

In fact the spreads on both of these candles is wide, and when compared to the equivalent spreads in the waterfall, the volumes should be MUCH higher, so clearly selling is being absorbed at this level. Duke Energy attempts to rally, this time with a bullish engulfing candle, but the volume is average once again, and clearly this is not a sign of strength just yet.

The market then pulls back with two small hammers on low volume. Is this the final phase of mopping up the selling pressure? The answer is delivered on the next candle with a LOW VOLUME test. The insiders are preparing the ground. The selling has been absorbed, the market has been tested for further selling, and the low volume test signals success, Duke Energy is now primed and ready to move.

The stock moves higher on good volume and is subsequently followed by a gap up day, supported with strong volume, not a trap up move but a genuine move higher. The insiders are joining in! Then we move into a congestion phase, followed by a further gap up and breakout on high volume, and from this move, the stock price then declines slowly lower, BUT note the volume. It is low! An anomaly! We can be pretty sure that the stock price is not going to fall far. After all, if it were, we would see high volume and this is certainly not the case with below average volumes.

The final candle in this group was then followed by a bullish engulfing candle, and the following day, with a gapped up move higher. HOWEVER – note the volume on the gap up, it's LOW. Is this a trap up move by the insiders? It certainly looks weak, and the volumes following the move higher are well below average. But note where we are in the overall price action. We are back where we started in terms of price, and this is therefore an area of potential price resistance given the earlier failure at this level. So we should be DOUBLY on guard. A gap up move on low volume, and resistance ahead !!

So what happened next?

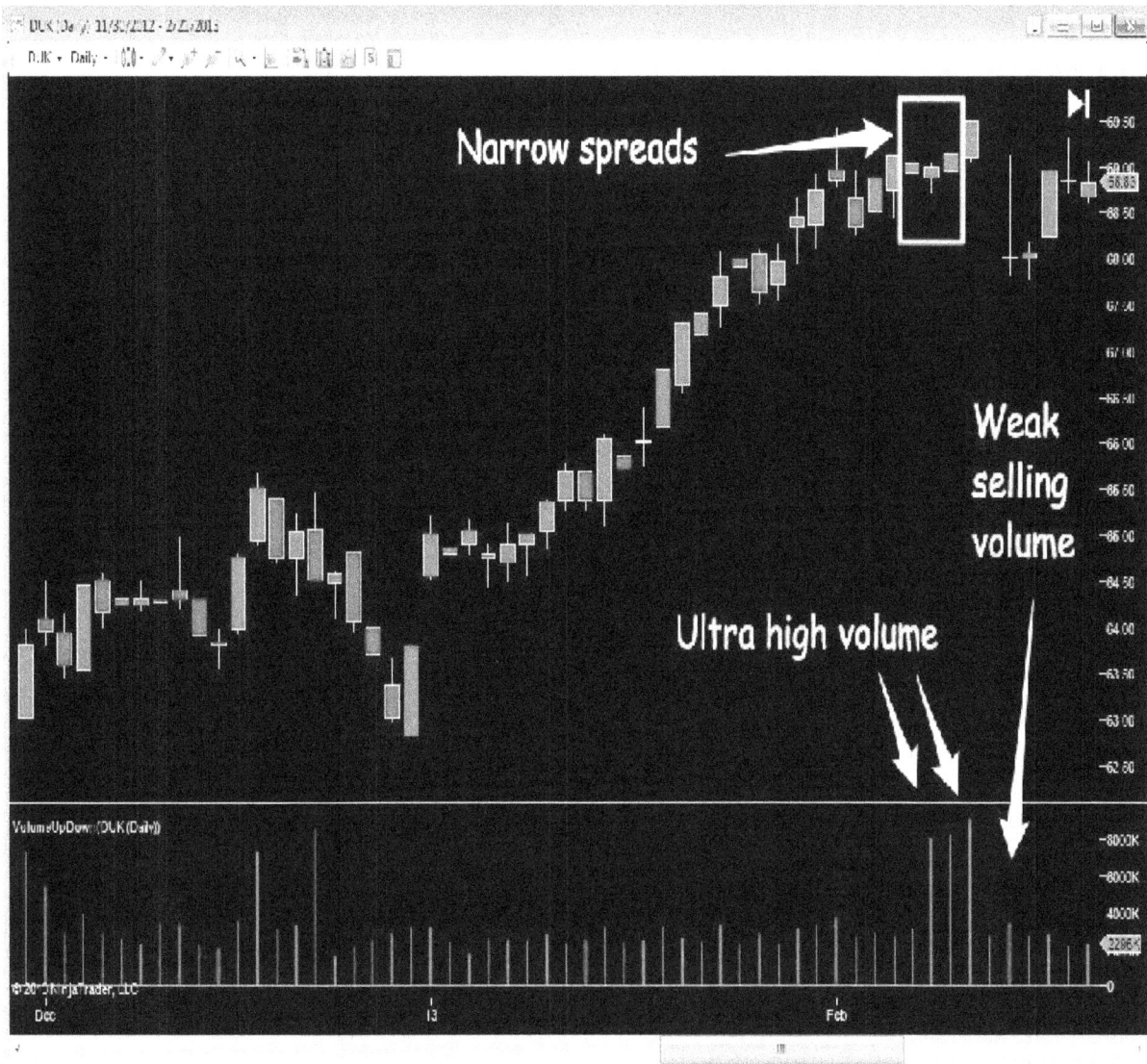

Fig 10.12 Duke Energy (DUK) Daily Chart - Moving Forward

Duke Energy stayed at this price level price of $65.75 for several days, before finally breaking above the resistance area, and then moved steadily higher on steady volumes. Finally, the move runs out of steam, and volume as always tells the story. Right at the end of this trend we have three ultra high volume bars, beneath narrow spread candles. Is the market strong or weak? And the answer of course is weak, and we see the price fall sharply. But once again, the selling volumes are average, so clearly not a major turning point for Duke Energy which continued higher and remains bullish, for the time being. At time of writing Duke Energy is trading at $74.41.

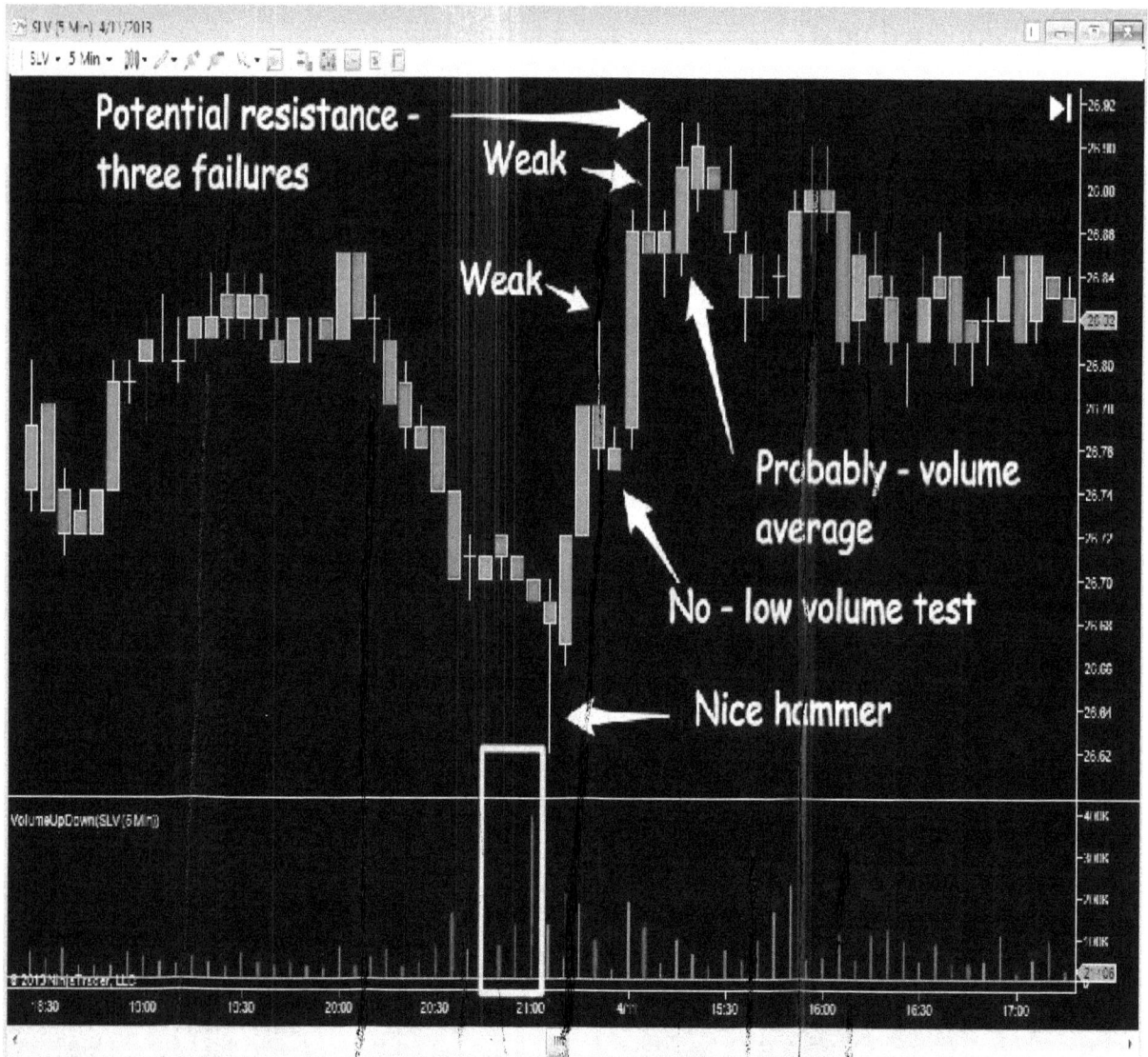

Fig 10.13 SLV - ETF 5 Min Chart

I now want to consider different markets and time frames and the first example is the SLV which is an ETF (Exchange Traded Fund) for silver. ETFs are a very popular way for many traders to enter the commodity markets, and the SLV is certainly one of the most popular. It is a straightforward ETF, un-leveraged and is backed by the physical metal. Here we have the 5 min chart, so perfect for an intra day, scalping strategy.

As we can see from the chart, starting at the far left the SLV had been moving sideways, albeit with a bullish tone before starting to fall, breaking below the interim platform of support with 5 consecutive down candles, on rising volume. A signal that the price action was being validated by volume, which at this point is above average.

The SLV then drifts sideways for a few bars before we see two narrow spread down candles, the first with above average volume, an anomaly, and the second with extremely high volume. This must be stopping volume and therefore buying, otherwise the candle would be wide. Instead it is narrow. This is followed by the hammer candle, on high volume, signalling more buying in the market. The response is muted with the up candle, which moves higher on low volume, not a sign of strength, but is followed on the next candle with rising volume and a wide spread candle, so an encouraging signal. The insiders then test on low volume, and move higher on solid volume, before weakness starts to appear with a wide spread up candle and a subsequent failure at the same level.

What happened next was that SLV then drifted along at this level for some time, before selling off again the following day.

It would be very easy for me to show you hundreds of examples where VPA gives us great trends and great trading opportunities. It does. But what it also does, is give us sound common sense logic on which to base our trading decisions, and more importantly to quantify the risk on the trade itself, which is what trading is all about.

In this example we are looking at this opportunity as a scalping trader. However, if you were an aggressive trader, then you may well have taken a position based on the hammer alone. After all, this looks like a strong signal. However, the following candle suggests weakness at this level. The volume is well below average, and at this point we would be wondering if this was a wise decision. Any stop loss by the way would be below the wick of the hammer, with the market setting this level for us. Assuming we continue to hold, the next candle is much more encouraging, a wide spread up candle with high volume, so a good sign. No reason to exit just yet.

The next candle suggests weakness, a shooting star (although not at the top of a trend, weakness nevertheless with the deep upper wick) and above average volume. We are expecting a reversal on the next bar, when in fact we see a positive signal – a low volume test which is followed by a wide spread up candle with above average volume once more, with a further pause before the final leg to the top of the move.

At this point a more cautious trader would have seen the initial response to the hammer, and taken this as a sign of weakness, which it is, and decided, based on this signal to stay out of the market for the time being, and perhaps waited for the second candle, which IS a sign of strength, before entering a position. If so, in this case, this would probably have ended as a small profit, a small loss, or perhaps break even. But my point is this.

The examples I have chosen here are designed to teach, to educate and also to show you VPA applied in a variety of time frames and markets, and perhaps more importantly, that all trends and trading opportunities are relative. Here we might have taken a position as a scalping trader and netted perhaps 20 or 30 cents on the contract.

In the earlier examples with stocks, market positions there may have been in place for days, weeks or even months and netted hundreds, if not thousands of dollars. It is all relative. The beauty of VPA is that your trading decisions are based on logic. The logic of volume and price. From there, it is down to your skill as a trader to balance your money management with your own risk tolerance and trade accordingly. VPA will give you the trading opportunities, but you will have to judge the risk on the trade, and how much capital you are prepared to risk based on your assessment.

And remember, your assessment of risk will also be based on your analysis using multiple time frames, and in the example above, a slower time frame may well have been signalling a warning that this was a weak move and therefore the risk on the trade was high. This may even have been against the dominant trend. In fact it was, as the general trend for silver at the time was bearish, so by definition, the trade was a higher risk trade anyway.

Fig 10.14 GLD - ETF 15 Min Chart

This next example is another extremely popular commodity for traders, gold, and the ETF is the GLD fund. Once again I've taken a faster time frame here to use as an example, and in this case my commentary is on a candle by candle basis with no annotation. The reason is that the chart would simply be too cluttered!

Before starting, let me put the gold market into context for you. At the time of this chart, gold had been weak for some time, and in a low inflation environment with higher returns in risk markets, money flow in general at this point was away from safe havens. The longer term trend for gold was therefore bearish. This is the context against which to view this intra day price action.

The market opens gapped down on extremely high volume, a clear signal of weakness. We are starting with weakness which has been validated by volume. The next candle forms, a small hammer, again with ultra high volume. Is this stopping volume – perhaps, and we wait for the next candle to form, a small candle with an upper wick, suggestive of further weakness, and coupled with high volume.

Clearly not a positive response to the 'stopping' volume. The next two down candles suggest a modicum of buying on each, with the lower wicks showing some support, but the market continues lower on rising volume with the penultimate candle suggesting stopping volume once again. Finally the last down candle in this price waterfall closes on average volume, followed by the first up candle of the session. A weak response if ever there was one, with a deep upper wick and narrow spread with above average volume. This is hardly a market that is preparing to reverse at this point. The next candle is perfectly valid, a narrow spread up candle with average volume – this looks fine.

Then we see a repeat of the first candle in this sequence of up candles, but this time, look at the volume – it is extremely high. This is sending a LOUD signal that the market is VERY WEAK. If this were buying volume then the market would be rising fast – it isn't, so it must be selling volume. Everyone is selling and trying to get out of the market before it collapses, with every attempt to rise knocked back by the pressure of selling. The next candle is even worse, sending an even stronger signal, if any were needed, that everyone is selling and the market is now incredibly weak.

Here we have ultra high volume and a market that is going nowhere. The price spread is narrow, and if the volume were buying, then the market would have risen. The insiders are propping the market up, selling stock accumulated in the price waterfall, before taking it lower.

The next two candles give no clues, narrow spreads with low volume, then the market sells off sharply, as expected, and validated with ultra high volume, as it lurches lower once again. The next candle hints at stopping volume once again with a narrow spread and deep wick on very high volume. The buyers are moving in at this level, and this is repeated on the next candle with high volume again on a narrow spread. Now we should see the market recover, but look at the next candle. The market attempts to rise, but falls back to close near the open on above average volume. Not a strong signal. A small hammer follows, on ultra high volume so perhaps there are more buyers in the market, and based on the volume of the last few bars, perhaps a reversal is now in prospect?

Three bullish candles then follow, each with a narrow spread, but the volume is flat, so we have a market rising on flat volume, and therefore unlikely to go very far. The market reverses from this level, and as it falls volumes are increasing signalling selling pressure once again. The final candle in this sequence is a very narrow spread doji candle, with high volume, and again we can assume that this is stopping volume with buyers coming in once more.

This is confirmed with the next candle which is a wide spread up candle with above average volume, but as the market rises on the next two candles, volume is falling away. The insiders are not taking this market far. The market then drifts sideways for an extended period in the session with several attempts to rally all failing, and with volumes generally falling to low levels throughout this phase the market duly closes, looking very weak.

What then happened in the following day's trading session is that the bearish tone of the previous day was taken up in dramatic fashion, as the GLD opened gapped down once again on three times the volume of the previous day's open.

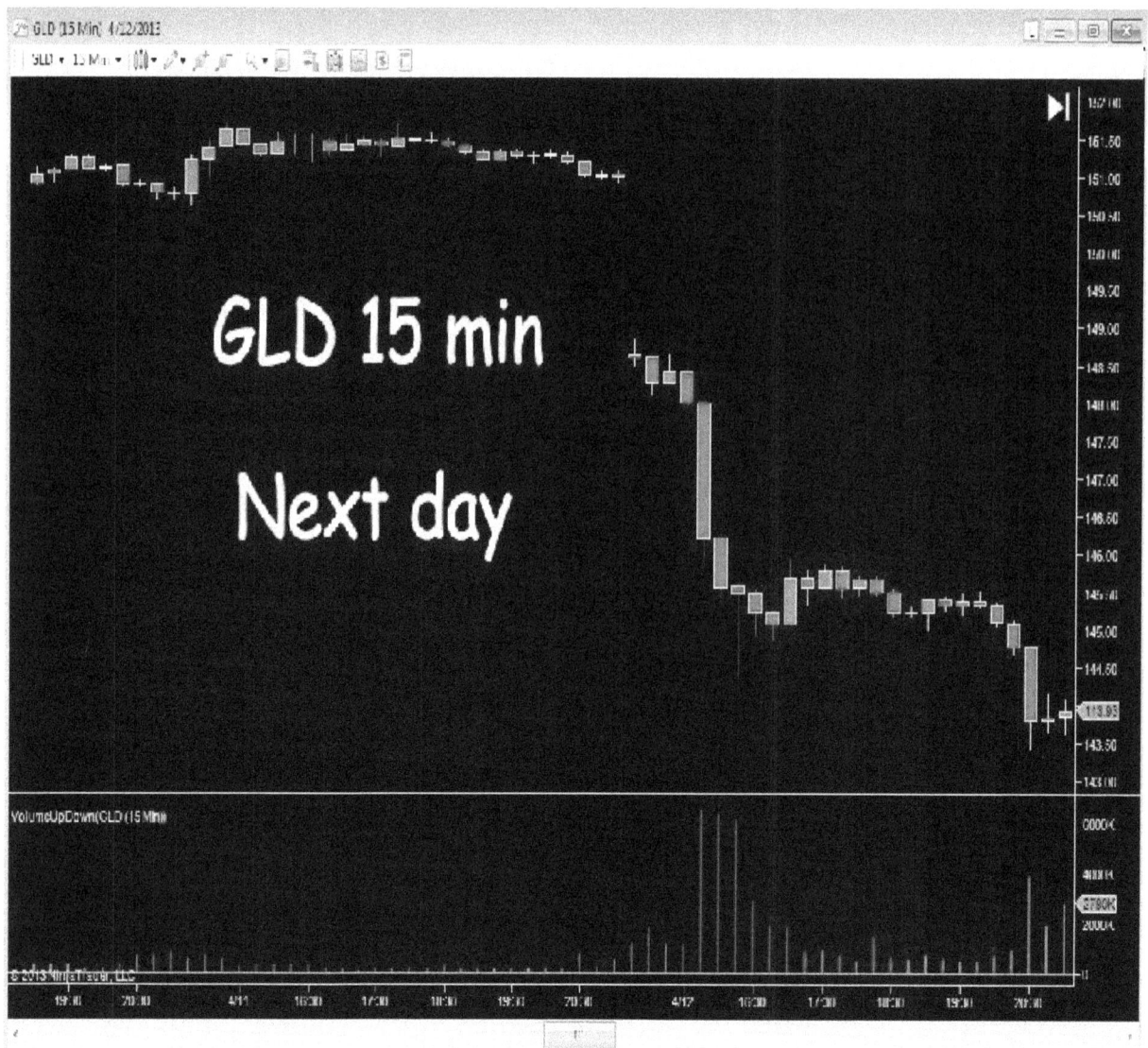

Fig 10.15 GLD - ETF 15 Min Chart - Next Day!

Whilst the open was bad news for those traders bullish on gold, even worse was to follow, and candles five, six and seven were accompanied with volume which can only be described as extreme. Trading volumes on each candle were in excess of 6 million, with average volumes around 500,000. In other words, panic selling.

Even the hammer candle and the associated volume was not sufficient to slow the market momentum and the solitary wide spread up candle on high volume, failed to follow through, with the market moving into a congestion phase before rising volumes on the four down candles at the end of the sequence signalled yet more bearish pressure and heavy selling.

The above market analysis, which I have written here for you in long hand, is really a transcript of the conversation that I would have in my head as this price action appeared on the screen and could be for any chart, any instrument and in any time frame. All I need is volume to give me a view of what is going on inside the market. With this insight I can draw my conclusions from the price behaviour. The above is on gold, but it could be any ETF or other instrument. It makes no difference.

I now want to move to the spot forex market and here the charts are from the MT4 platform. With MT4 we have time charts and tick volume. However, the same principles apply.

The first example is from an actual trade I took on the Aussie Dollar on the 15 minute chart.

The currency pair had been rising nicely for a little while, volumes were average (as marked with the dotted white line) with no anomalies or signs of weakness at this stage. Then suddenly we see the blue candle form, with a wide body but also with an equally deep wick above.

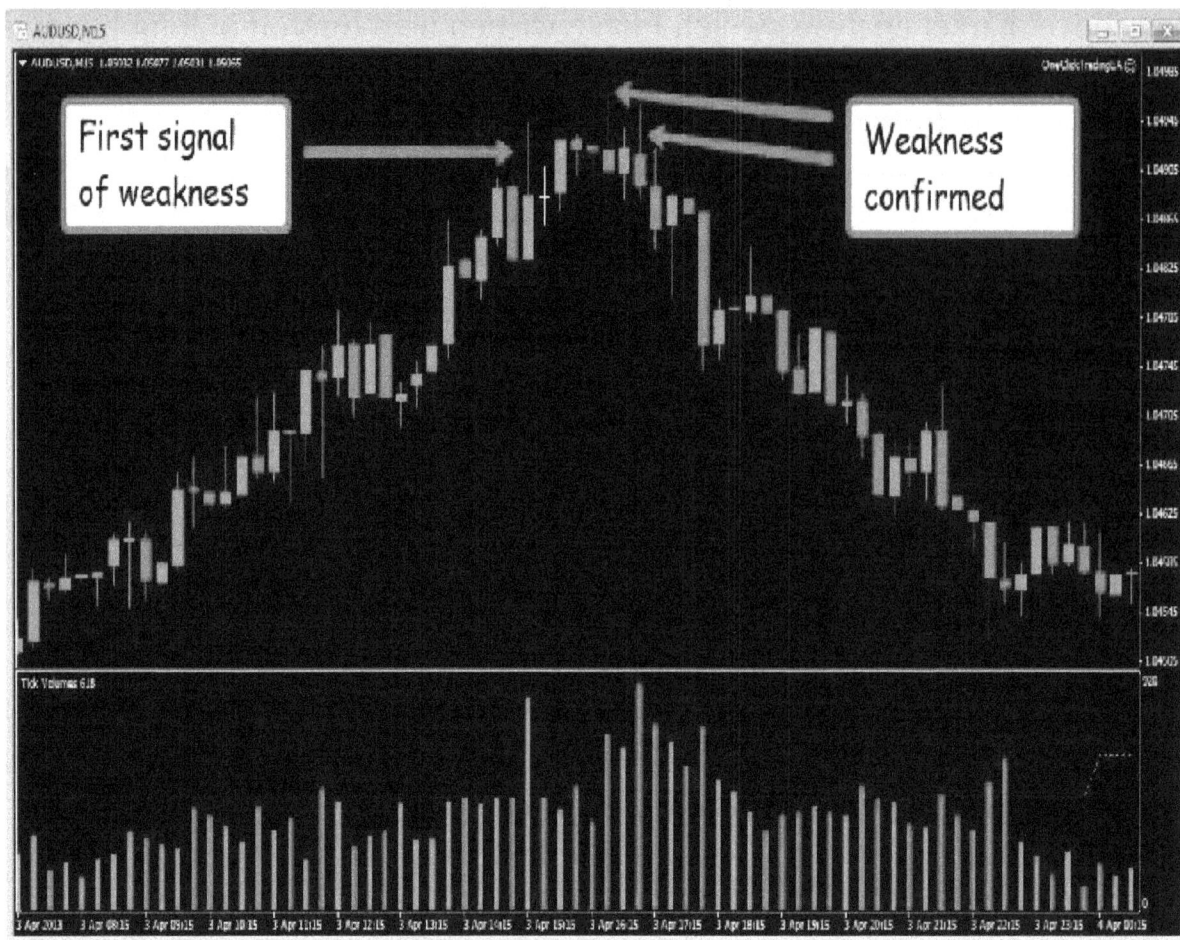

Fig 10.16 AUD/USD - 15 Min Spot Forex Chart

We are now paying attention as with this volume bar, the pair should have risen strongly, and clearly in the volume bar there is a large amount of selling, confirmed by the deep wick to the top of the candle.

The pair manage to move higher for a couple of bars, but the warning has been flagged and sure enough five bars later we see a shooting star candle with high volume. The next candle is also weak, a narrow spread doji candle with high volume. A potential reversal awaits! The next candle confirms the weakness, another shooting star candle this time with higher volume still. And what is also important here, a lower high than the previous candle. This is the time and place to take a short position with a stop loss above the level of the wick of the first candle.

The pair sell off and duly start to move lower, and one aspect that I want to highlight here is how volume helps you to stay in a strong position and hold it in order to maximise your profits from the trend.

As we all know, markets never move in a straight line, they move lower, then pull back a little, before then moving lower again. Here we can see this in action perfectly illustrated, and the point I want to make is this.

Four bars after the second shooting star, we have a wide spread down candle, and we are delighted. Our analysis has been proved correct, and we are now in a strong position. Then the market begins to reverse against us. Is this a trend reversal, or merely a pause in the move lower?

Well, the first candle appears. The spread is relatively narrow and the volume is above average, so this is an encouraging sign. In addition, we have not seen any evidence of stopping volume with narrowing spreads and rising volume, so this looks like a pause point. The next candle confirms this as does the third, and on the completion of this last candle we can see that we have a market attempting to rise on falling volume, and we know what that means!

The next candle is weak, and whilst the volume is below average it is another small shooting star.

The market moves lower in steps and each attempt to rally is seen in the context of falling volume, confirming the weakness further which is my point.

Once you have a position in the market, you must keep revisiting your VPA techniques as they will give you the confidence to hold and stay in the trend. If you are short the market and it pulls back against you, but the volume on the upwards moves is falling, then you KNOW that this is simply a temporary pullback and not a change in trend. Equally, if any pullback has not been pre-ceded with signs of stopping volume, then the buyers are not in the market at that level and any reversal will not last long, so you can continue too hold.

Equally, if you are long the market the same applies. In an up trend the market will pull back against you. If the volume is falling on these pull backs then you KNOW this is simply a minor reversal lower and not a change in trend, particularly if you have seen no topping out volume.

Finally as we can see on the right hand side of the chart, stopping volume finally appeared, with the market moving into a congestion phase with the selling pressure dropping away to below average. The pair completed this phase of its journey and we exit.

Our entry, our management, and exit of this position have all been executed using one simple tool. VPA. Nothing else. Why more traders, speculators and investors don't pay attention to volume is beyond me, but there we are.

Here are some further examples from the world of spot forex.

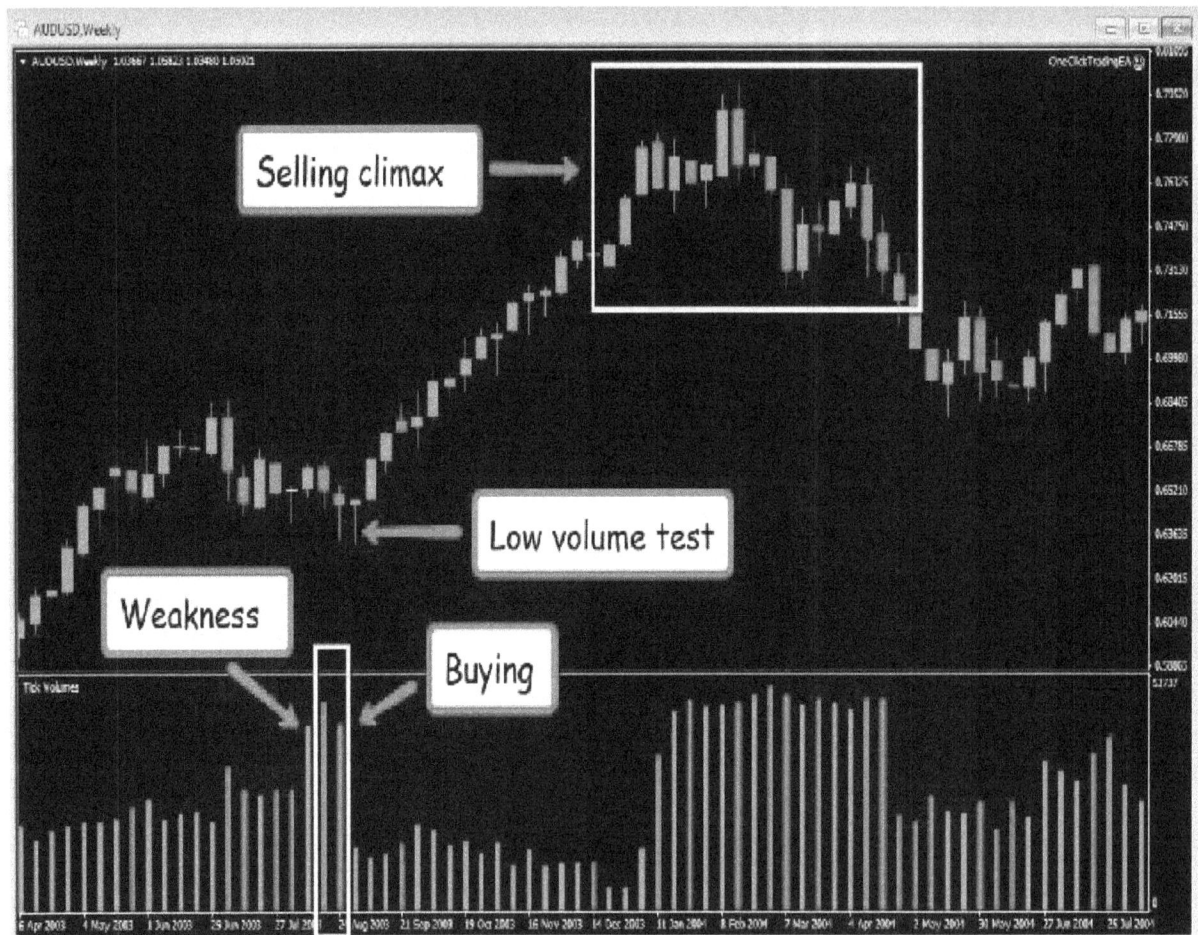

Fig 10.17 AUD/USD – Weekly Spot Forex Chart : Selling Climax

The reason I've chosen the weekly chart for the AUD/USD is that not only is it a good example of a selling climax, it also gives us a perspective on how long this may last. As I have said several times in this book, we have to be patient. Major changes in trend take time to come into effect, and this is an example. It also shows that VPA works in all time frames.

Remember, here we are looking at a period of around 18 months, so long term trends with big profits to be made if you are patient, and believe in the power of VPA of course!

As we can see from the chart the AUD/USD pair has been bullish, before moving into a congestion phase on average volume. Then we see our first anomaly. A narrow spread up candle with very high volume. The pair are struggling at this price point and the market is not responding. The next weekly candle arrives with ultra high volume, and if this pair were going to sell off sharply, then we would expect this to be a wide spread down candle – it isn't. It's a narrow spread. The buyers must be supporting the market at this level. The next candle arrives, a hammer with a deep wick, and this confirms the previous candle. This is buying, and now we wait for any further signals, which arrive on the next candle, a low volume test on a smaller hammer candle. The high volume selling that we were seeing in the previous candle, which was absorbed by the buyers, has now dissipated and the forex market makers are ready to take this pair higher. And off it goes at a nice steady pace, marching higher on nice steady volume.

The move higher extends over several months, but the point to note here, is the slow steady fall in volume over this period. It's not dramatic, just a steady fall, and then as we enter the yellow box on the chart – what do we see? Two wide bars, one after the other, but look at the volume. It has fallen away to almost nothing. This is a HUGE warning signal that this pair is becoming exhausted, and either running out of steam, or there is some alternative explanation. What is clear, is that the market makers are moving prices higher with NO volume, and have withdrawn from the market.

Traders who have missed this long trend higher, are now jumping in on fear and greed. They fear missing out on a golden opportunity. After all, they have watched this market go up and up, and have finally caved in and bought, just when the market makers are leaving by the side door.

Then the selling climax begins. The market makers are selling in huge volumes at this level, before finally after several weeks the pair break lower, and attempts to rally giving us signs of further weakness, before breaking lower again.

Note the attempt to rally at the right hand edge of the chart. Here we see narrow spread up candles on very high volume, and falling, another very strong signal of further weakness to come, which duly arrives.

One point I do want to cover here in a little more detail is the whole issue of rising and falling volumes when associated with trends, because we do have to apply some flexibility to any analysis and interpretation here. After all, if the market moved higher for ten consecutive bars, and you wanted to apply the volume principle to the letter of the law, then you would have to see 10 volume bars each higher than the last. Clearly this would place a limit on how far any trend could go, since it is unreasonable to expect volumes to go up and up and up for ever!

The above example is a case in point. The first few candles on the up move are supported by good volume, which is up and down, but above, or just around, average. This is fine. After all, there are always going to be variations particularly when you begin to look at the longer term timescales. There may be seasonal effects, days when the markets are thinly traded during holidays, and of course days when the markets actually close. This rarely happens in forex, but it does happen in other markets and affects the forex markets accordingly.

Please be a little flexible in your approach when judging volume in trends, and allow a little bit of latitude in your analysis. Here we were waiting for an anomaly, and until the two low volume candles arrived, there was nothing to signal that any change in trend was imminent.

I now want to consider the opposite, namely a buying climax and once again we have a nice example on the AUD/USD weekly chart in Fig 10.18 below.

On this chart, we are looking at an eighteen month period approximately, and we can see that the pair has topped out and rolled over into a nice price waterfall, all confirmed with nicely rising selling volumes, validating the move lower.

Then a hammer candle arrives and we need to assess whether there is sufficient stopping volume? The next candle gives us the answer with a small shooting star on high volume.

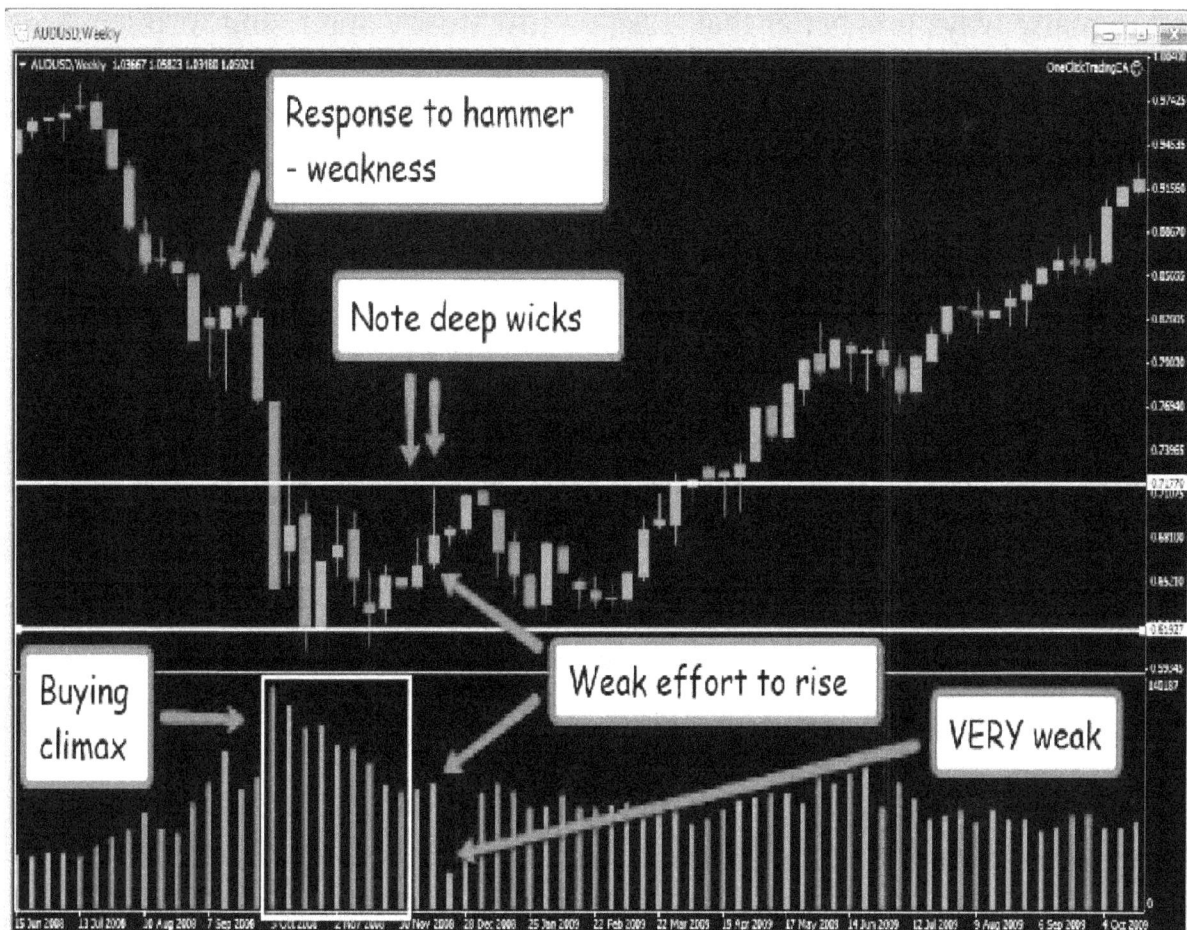

Fig 10.18 AUD/USD - Weekly Spot Forex Chart : Buying Climax

Clearly the market is NOT ready to rise just yet and the selling pressure continues as we finally enter the buying climax phase. However, as the pair attempt to rally the first candle we see is a narrow spread up candle with a deep upper wick, hardly a sign of strength, on high volume. The pair are not ready to rise just yet, and the following two candles confirm this, with very low volume. The second of these is particularly significant with a wide spread and ultra low volume.

The AUD/USD pair then roll over again and back down into the congestion area, which I have marked on the chart with the two yellow lines, and this is the ceiling of resistance that we would now be monitoring, along with the floor of support below.

Any break above through this resistance area would now need to be supported with good rising volume. It doesn't have to be 'explosive' volume, and in many ways it is better that it isn't – just steady and rising. If this were a gap up breakout, as we saw in earlier examples, then we do expect to see volumes well above average, and even ultra high if the move is dramatic. But for normal breakouts through an area of resistance, then above average is fine.

The pair then develop a nice even trend higher, with some pauses along the way. This trend lasted for over nine months before finally running out of steam with a selling climax developing.

I now want to move into the world of futures and back to my NinjaTrader platform. The first chart is the 5 minute on the YM E-mini futures contract, an extremely popular index futures contract for scalping, and derived from the Dow Jones Industrial Average in the cash market.

There are two versions of the index, the 'small' Dow and the 'big' Dow. This is the small Dow with each index point worth $5, whilst the big Dow is $25. I ALWAYS recommend new traders to any market to start with the smallest instrument, so if you are new to index trading or indeed the futures market in general, start with the mini Dow.

The reason I wanted to show this example is really to focus on the open of the market. As I explained earlier, these contracts now trade virtually 24 hours a day, and therefore the open of the physical market is not the surprise that it once was, as this will generally follow the trend of the electronic contract, which will have been trading overnight following the close of the exchange.

Fig 10.19 YM E-mini 5 Min Chart

What do we see here? First, we have a gapped up open, so the electronic contract must have ticked up from the physical close of the day before, which you can see here. Volume is high and a nice wide spread up candle closes the first five minutes of trading. The big operators are joining the move. The next two candles are down, but the volume is falling, so we do not expect the market to move far, and indeed the lower wick on the second of these candles, is a clue that this is simply some early profit taking on the gap up open, and that the buyers are in control.

From there, the market moves steadily higher. There are no signals of a reversal, just a steady rise, with minor pull backs, but each time we see a little wave lower, then this is balanced by a wave higher in the volume trend, which is what I was trying to describe earlier. You do have to be a little flexible in how you view volume in a rising (or falling) trend. What is interesting here is if we compare the first 'wave' with the second 'wave' in terms of the buying volumes. Volumes on the second wave in the up move, are slightly lower than volumes in the first wave, so we may begin to think that perhaps this move was running out of steam, and possibly time to exit the trend. However, there is nothing particularly frightening in any of the subsequent price action, and indeed as we can see on the right of the chart, the down candles have very low volumes. But interest appears to be waning and we need to be vigilant.

One further point on this chart, before we move on to look at another.

The move higher after the first few candles of the open would also have given us confidence as the index broke above the initial resistance area created at the open. This is only a secondary resistance level, but nevertheless another 'confidence builder' for us in taking a position in this market. The same applies at the right hand side of the chart as the market moves into a congestion phase, and coupled with the general decline in volumes, this may prompt us to exit at this stage.

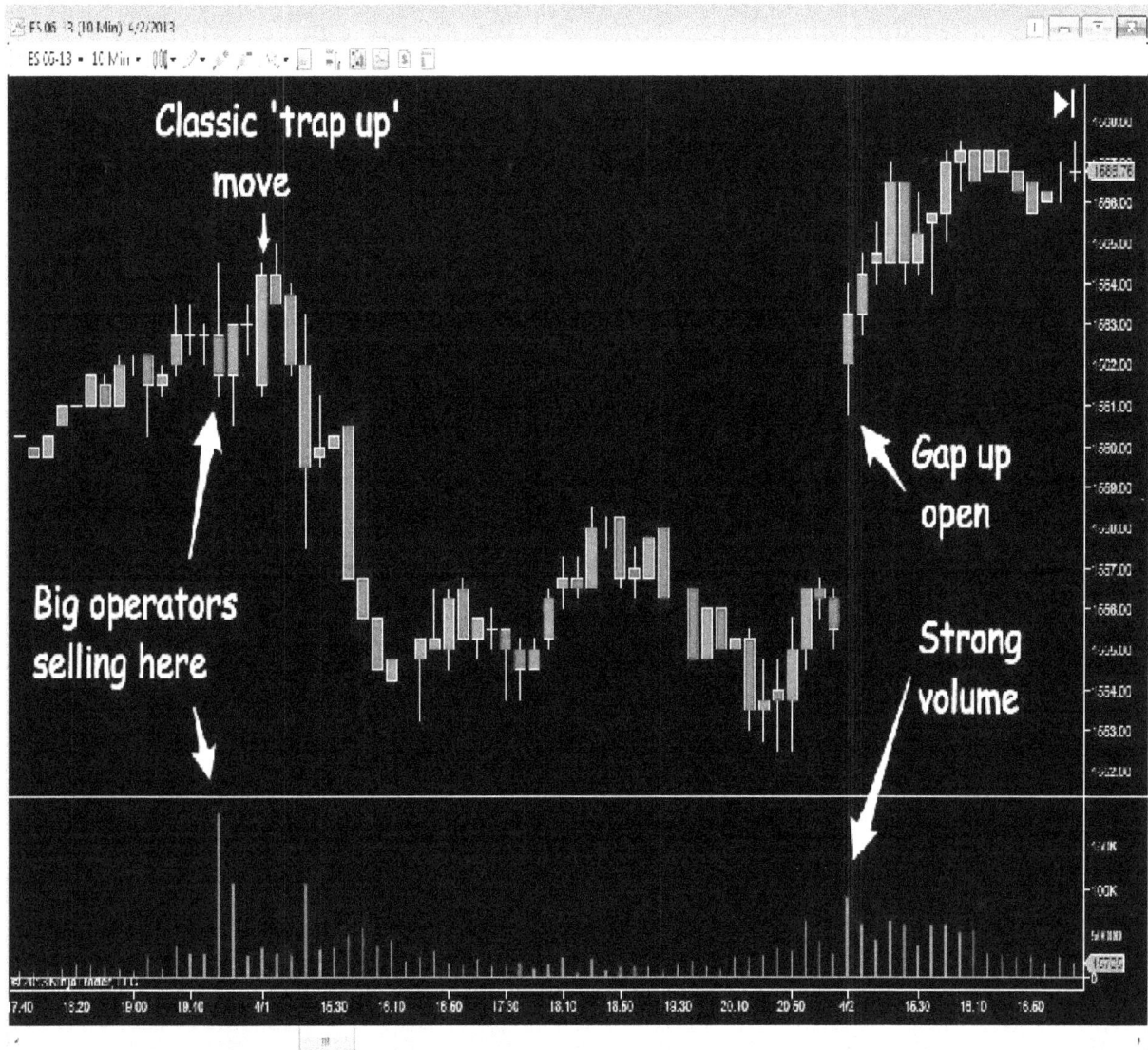

Fig 10.20 ES E-mini 10 Min Chart

Fig 10.20 is another very popular futures index for scalping traders, the ES E-mini which is a derivative of the S&P 500. However, it is extremely volatile and of all the indices, is the most manipulated by the big operators, which is what I wanted to show here. In this example we are looking at a 10 minute chart, and here we have a complete daily session, sandwiched between a day either side.

Working from left to right, as the trading session comes to an end we can see the extremely high volume bar in red, standing like a telegraph pole above all the others. The big operators are clearing out of the market preparing for the following day. This ultra high volume is associated with a shooting star candle, a sure sign of selling, followed by an up candle with very high volume, which goes nowhere. The big operators are selling into the market and struggling to hold it at this level. Finally, the session ends with a small doji on average volume.

The following day, the market opens at much the same level as the close of the night before, with a classic trap up move by the big operators, a wide spread up candle on low to average volume. Compare this volume with that of the up candle of the night before following the shooting star candle. The price spread is much the same, but the volume is substantially lower.

This is a TRAP up move, and one that was prepared the night before. It is a classic move that happens all the time, particularly at the open of a session, and you will see this time and time again in the futures markets and the cash markets. The insiders, whether they are the operators or the market makers, love to trap traders into weak positions, and this is the easiest time to do it, when traders are waiting for the market to open, eager with anticipation, and jump in making emotional trading decisions, frightened to miss out on a nice move higher or lower. Then the selling starts, and down it goes! Easy really, and given the chance we would do the same! It goes without saying that volume is the ONLY way to see these tricks in action – watch out for them and you will see them ALL the time, in every market, and in every time frame.

Finally, and just to prove the point, on the third day on our chart the market opens gapped up, but look at the volume – it's high, and well above the volume of the previous day, so this is a genuine move, and the big operators are buying into the bullish trend higher.

Moving to yet another platform, a different market and a different type of chart. So far, all the charts we have considered in our volume analysis have been based on time, but many traders, myself included like to trade tick charts for some markets. If you have never used such charts to trade, then I would urge you to consider these as part of your trading education, for one simple reason.

When we trade on a time based chart, for example a 15 minute chart, every bar or candle on the chart is created in 15 minutes. By contrast when we trade on an 80 tick chart, each candle will be created according to the time it takes to complete. In other words, the time taken to build each candle will depend on the energy and activity in the market. It is, yet another way to consider volume or market activity. A tick on a futures chart essentially records an order, but that order could be for one contract or a hundred contracts. However, the point with a tick chart is this. If the market is very active and there is a great deal of buying and selling, let's say after a news announcement, then each 80 tick candle will form very quickly, perhaps in just a few seconds, as there are hundreds of orders flowing through the market in a very short space of time, each of which is recorded as a tick.

Therefore if we were watching a tick chart following the release of the NFP data, then the candles would form as though being fired from a machine gun – they would literally print on the chart at high speed, but each tick candle would take a different length of time to form. So in seeing the speed of creation of the tick candles, we are also, in a sense, seeing inside the market and the 'volume' or activity that is associated with this buying and selling frenzy.

This is something you will NEVER see on a time based chart, since each candle is defined by the time frame of the chart. On a tick chart it is not, and this is a key difference and why many full time traders and professional traders only use tick charts.

To put this into context for you, imagine a tick chart in the following scenarios.

First in the example above, the open of the New York trading session and an NFP data release. Each 80 tick candle would form in seconds and perhaps in milliseconds. Now imagine the same chart overnight in Asia, where perhaps we are overlapping the close of one market and the opening of another. Then the time taken for each candle on the chart might be 30 seconds, perhaps even a few minutes.

And the point is this. With a tick chart, you see the activity visually with the speed the candles are created. With a time chart, you never see the activity, just a price moving higher or lower as the candle forms. This is the difference between tick and time based charts and is why many traders prefer to trade on tick charts. With a tick chart, we are seeing 'inside the market' and it is reinforcing our volume analysis. After all, volume is really nothing more than 'activity' which is what we see visually with a tick chart.

One important point about tick charts is if the volume is also represented as ticks, all we would see would be a series of 'soldiers' of equal height, with each one representing 80 ticks or 80 transactions. In order to overcome this problem, most platforms will provide the option of selecting either tick volume or trade volume when setting up a chart, and this is certainly the case with another of my trading accounts. Here we simply select trade volume when setting up the chart, rather than tick volume, and we then have volume reported in trade size, which gives us our variable volume bars.

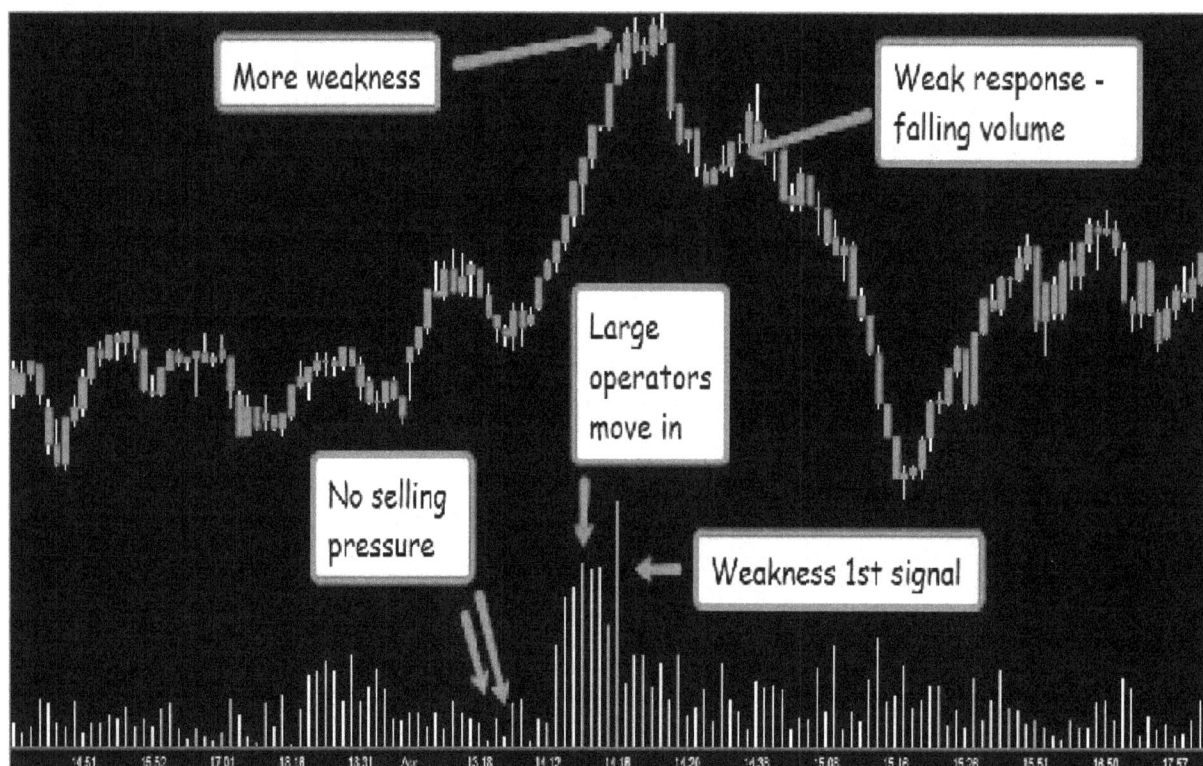

Fig 10.21 Coffee Futures - 80 Tick Chart

The session for the Coffee contract as shown in Fig 10.21 opened with a weak move higher before rolling over and sliding lower, but as you can see, with very little selling pressure at this stage.

The market is moving lower, but the volume is falling so this is not a market that is going far.

Then we see the large operators moving into the market. Volume spikes higher and continues to rise with the market which marches North in nice, even wide spread candles. However, on the 9th volume bar, we see our first sign of weakness, ultra high volume and no price action to match. The candle spread is wide, but judged against the candles and price action that has just pre-ceded it, the reaction from the market should have been much stronger. This signals weakness and the large operators are starting to struggle, although there is only a small upper wick on the candle at this point.

The market then goes into consolidation with above average volume and narrow spread up candles with wicks to the upper body, confirming the initial weakness first seen in the trend higher. The market then rolls over and sells off on high volume, and the attempt to recover, is marked with rising prices and falling volumes, a further sign of weakness. This is duly confirmed again with the price action at this level marked with a shooting star candle, the catalyst for the price waterfall which followed.

It is interesting to note, even though I did not add this example for this particular reason, but the recovery from the price waterfall appears to have occurred with little evidence of buying volume or stopping volume. This in itself is suspicious. After all, this is a significant fall, and despite being a fast intraday chart, we would still expect to see high volumes at the bottom. Therefore could this action be a further extended trap up move higher on low volume? Not quite and this is where we always have to be careful.

The volumes in the move up were so extreme they tended to distort the volumes elsewhere during the session, and in fact scrolling forward, the volumes at the bottom of the price waterfall were well above average, but distorted by the volumes in the bullish trend. Nevertheless, this coffee future did sell off the following day and never moved higher during this session. Therefore, this is always a point worth remembering. Whatever the instrument we are trading, we must try to have an idea of what is considered to be high, low and average volume. So that when these extremes of volume do appear, they do not distort our view of what follows in the remainder of the trading session.

Finally, to round off this chapter I would like to examine one of the most widely followed indices around the world, and that is the Dow Jones Industrial Average. The Dow 30 is considered to be, by the media, who know very little if anything about the financial markets, a leading benchmark of the US economy. It is not, but never mind, and it simply gives me a topic for another book!

I wanted to end this chapter with this index, as it really makes the powerful point, that VPA works in all time frames for all instruments and for all markets. Here in Fig 10.22 we have the weekly chart for the DJIA and really for those investors amongst you reading this book, this is precisely the sort of time horizon you would be considering for longer term investing in stocks, of which the primary indices will be key.

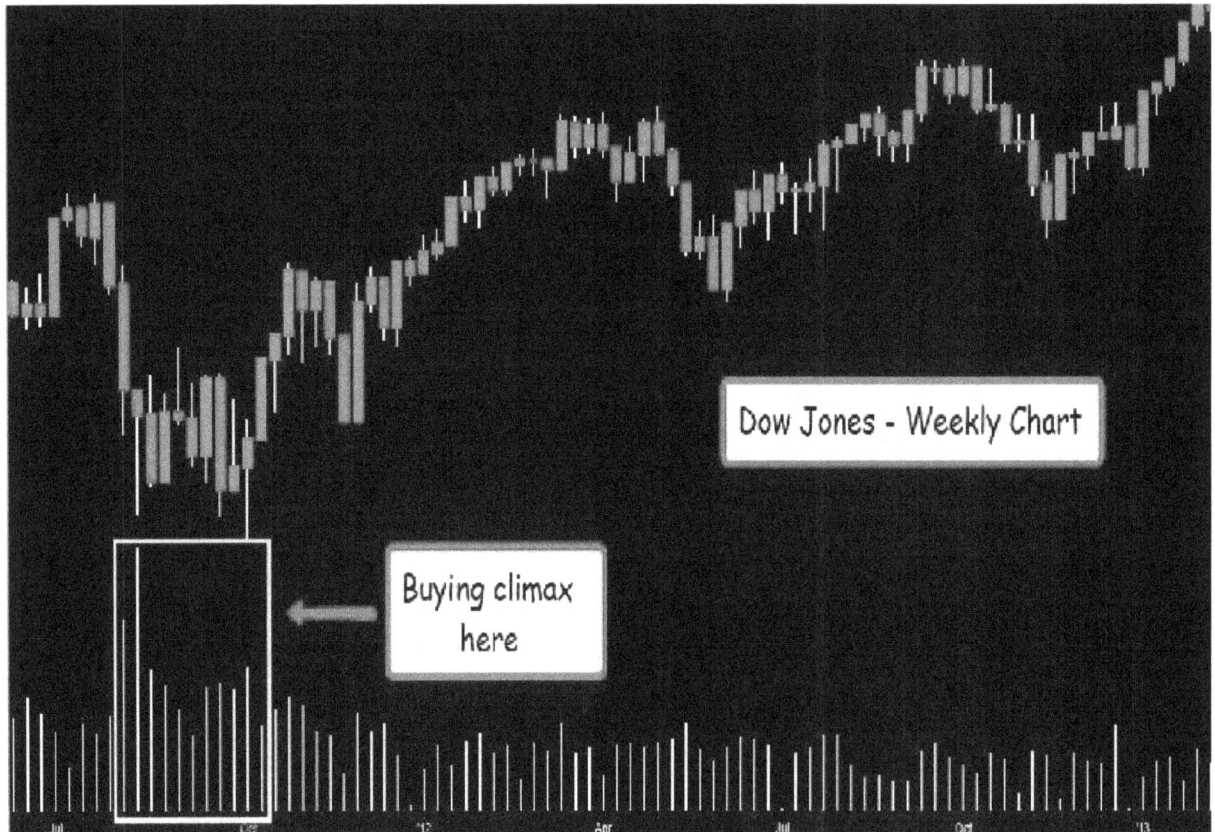

Fig 10.22 DJ30 - Weekly Chart

Even just a quick cursory glance at this chart tells us where the major buying occurred. It is so obvious, and proves the point about VPA. Your eye should be drawn instantly to those anomalies, of either extreme highs, extreme lows, or concentration of volumes in certain areas. From there, you then dig deeper and take a more forensic view at the macro level. This is a classic chart with the market rising, then rolling over a little, before rising further, then rolling over again with the classic rounded tops.

The market makers came into the market strongly over an eleven week period (the yellow box), and then continued to stock up over the next six to eight weeks at this level, so the market was consolidating in this region for 4 - 5 months. This is the length of time that accumulation may take, and no move will be made until they are ready.

The question everyone is now asking, is how much further can this market go, and the answer is to look at the volume. Since the accumulation phase, the index has climbed steadily on average volume with no particular extremes one way or the other. For a major reversal to occur, we need to see signs of a selling climax in this time frame, and this is certainly NOT the case at the moment.

If and when this does appear, then as VPA traders we will see it instantly, whether on the monthly, weekly or daily chart. Volume CANNOT be hidden from view, and no matter how hard the market makers try, and they do have tricks to hide large block orders, most of the daily trading volumes are free for all to see. They may be clever, but have yet to work out a way to hide volume from view!

Now in the next chapter I want to highlight some of the price patterns, that I believe help to give us additional pointers and guidance in our analysis of price action and the associated volume.

Chapter Eleven

Putting It All Together

The market does not run on chance or luck. Like the battlefield, it runs on probabilities and odds.
David Dreman (1936-)

As we come towards the end of this book on volume and price, I wanted to pass on some thoughts, observations, advice and comments based on my sixteen years of experience, using volume as my predominant indicator. As I have said before, I was lucky to start my trading education and journey with volume. It saved me a huge amount of wasted time and has made me substantial sums over the years from both trading and investing. Many aspiring traders spend years trying systems and methods which never work, and result in them losing confidence, to say nothing of their financial losses. Most then simply give up.

Eventually some of these traders and investors stumble upon volume. Some buy into the methodology instantly, just as I did. Others do not, and if you are in this latter group, I hope that I have at least made the case for VPA in this book. However, if you decide VPA is not for you, then you have lost nothing, other than the few dollars this book has cost you. If you do decide that VPA is logical and makes perfect sense, then I am delighted, as a lifetime of trading and investing success awaits. Provided you follow the principles I have explained here.

Now, let me introduce some further analytical techniques that I use in my own trading, which when combined with the basics of VPA, will help to develop your trading skills, with volume as the foundation.

The first technique I would like to explain is price pattern recognition, which we covered when we considered the importance of price congestion. However, I want to revisit it here, and look at some actual market examples. At the same time I would also like to include other key patterns that play an important role in breakouts and reversals, all of which ties into Volume Price Analysis.

The reason for revisiting price pattern recognition is that in the previous chapter I was very conscious of keeping the focus on the volume price relationship, and less so on the broader price behaviour on the chart. My rationale throughout the book has been to explain VPA in stages, and this is another layer that we can now add to our knowledge of VPA.

The market chart examples in this chapter will focus entirely on market congestion and subsequent reversals and breakouts, which I hope will cement this aspect of price behaviour firmly in your mind.

The first is a lovely example from the forex market and is from the 15 minute chart for cable (GBP\USD).

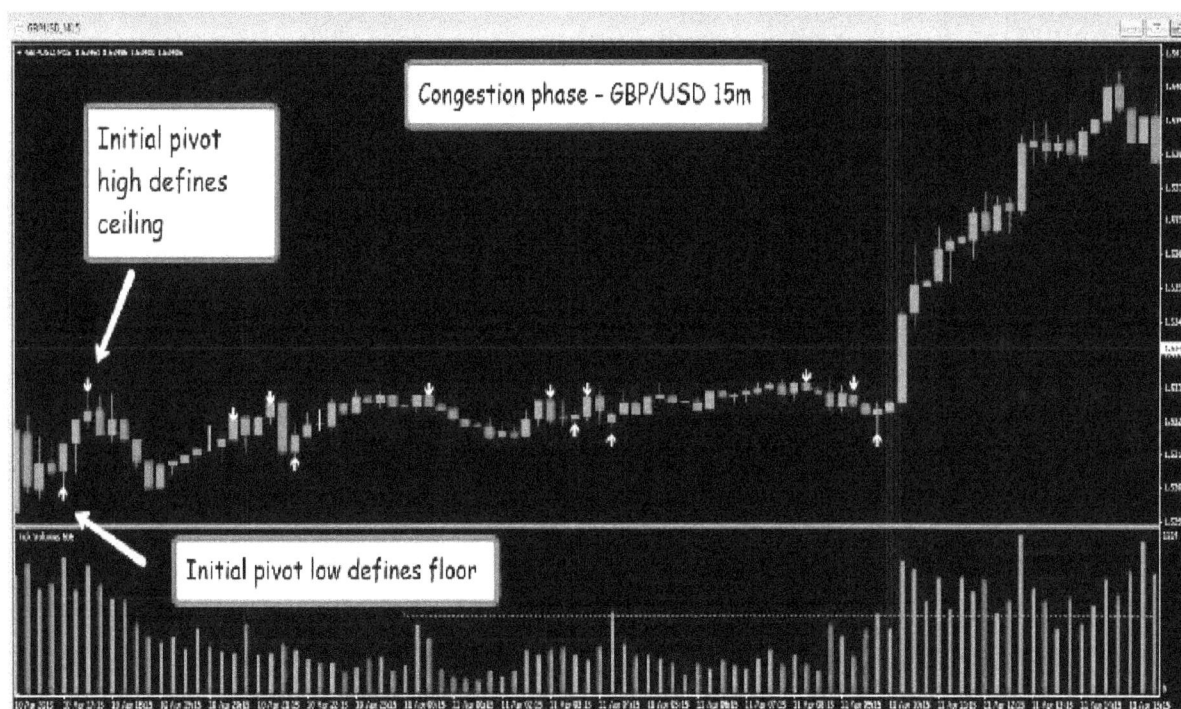

Fig 11.10 GBP/USD – 15m Chart

The chart in Fig 11.10 really explains all we need to know about price congestion and how it relates to the volume breakout when it arrives. As we can see the chart covers an extensive period with 70 candles in this phase.

The initial entry into the congestion phase is marked by a pivot low which gives us the floor of our price congestion, and two bars later a pivot high is posted with above average volume. The GBP/USD is weak and not ready to move higher with the pair then falling on declining volume, so weakness, but not a trend that will be sustained. And the reason should now be obvious - falling prices and falling volumes. Volumes then decline in general moving between buying and selling, and as the market moves sideways in the congestion phase, we see two further pivot highs posted, followed by a pivot low.

These are followed by a whole series of pivots, both at the ceiling and the floor of the congestion, and as I explained earlier when we were examining this concept, you do have to think of these levels as rubber bands and not as rods of steel.

We can see in this example that the pivot points (the little yellow arrows), are not all in a straight line. The market is not linear and technical analysis is an art and NOT a science, which is why volume software that attempts to predict changes in trend can be unreliable. This analysis has to be done manually.

At this stage, as the price continues to trade within the congestion, we are waiting for the catalyst, which will be the signal for any breakout. And on this occasion was provided by an item of economic data in the UK. From memory I believe it was the RPI release. However, the actual release is unimportant. What is important is the reaction on the price chart.

First, we have a breakout which moves firmly through our ceiling of resistance, which has now become...... support. And if you remember what I said in the chapter on breakouts – we MUST wait for a clear close well above the congestion phase, and the first candle here delivered this for us. A nice wide spread up candle. Second, we have to check that this is a valid move, and the good news is the breakout has been validated by the volume.

As this has been an extensive area of price congestion, any break away will require substantial effort which is what we have here with buyers taking the market firmly higher. Can we join the move here? This is what we have been waiting for. We have a market that has been in congestion, waiting, and gathering itself, when finally the catalyst arrives and the market moves on high volume.

Furthermore, we now have a deep area of natural price protection in place below, and our stop loss would be below the level of the last pivot low. Time has also played its part here, with cause and effect coming into play.

Remember, this is a 15 minute chart, so an extended phase of consolidation and congestion, and therefore any consequent effect should reflect the time taken in building the cause. In other words, the trend, when it breaks, should last for some time. We just have to be patient, and wait!

Finally, there is one further aspect to the breakout, which again I mentioned in an earlier chapter and it is this – the volume has validated the news. The market makers have confirmed that the data is good news for the UK pound, and the market has responded. Volumes pick up once again as the market moves higher and away from the congestion phase, and to return to my salmon analogy, another trend has been spawned.

This is the power of the congestion phase – it is the spawning ground of trends and reversals. In this case the ceiling was breached, but it could equally have been the floor. The direction is irrelevant. All we wait for is confirmation of the breakout, validated with volume, and then trade accordingly.

The second example in Fig 11.11 is once again taken from the GBP/USD. This time we are looking at the hourly chart over a period of approximately 4 days in total.

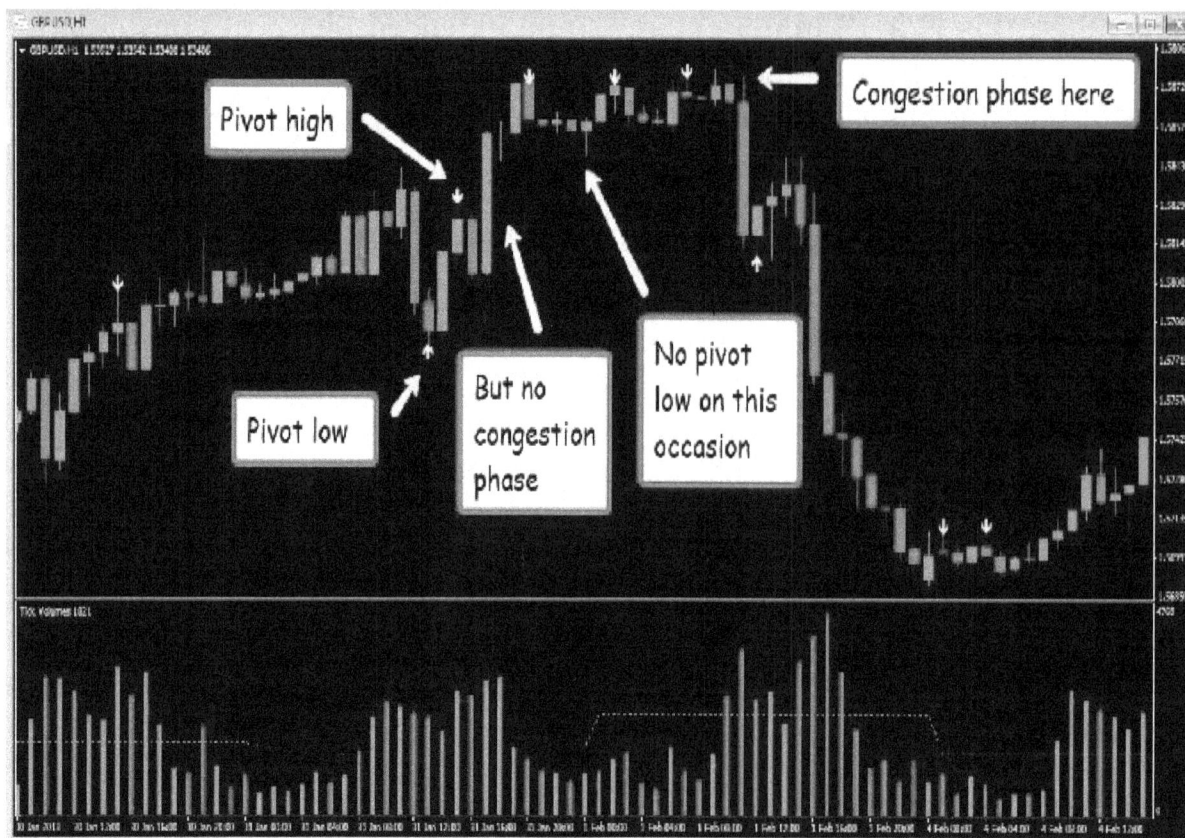

Fig 11.11 GBP/USD – 1 Hour Chart

Once again here let me explain the highlights and key points. As we can see the pair has been rising, but the market moves lower as shown by a wide spread down candle. This is followed by a narrow spread down candle with above average volume, and signalling possible buying on this reversal lower. The market pushes higher on the next candle, a wide spread up bar, and posts a pivot low as shown with the small yellow arrow. We are now looking for a possible pivot high which will start to define a potential period of congestion.

This duly arrives two bars later, and the pivot high is now in place. Now we are watching for a potential congestion phase, and further pivots to define the trading range. However, on this occasion, the next candle breaks higher and moves firmly away from this area. The potential congestion phase we were expecting has not materialised, so we know this was simply a minor pause in the trend higher, as the pair move up on good volume.

Two candles later, another pivot high is formed, and once again we are now looking for our pivot low to form and define our levels of any congestion phase. In this example the pair do indeed move into congestion, with low volume, and on each rally a pivot high is posted which gives us a nicely defined ceiling. However, there are no pivots defining the floor. Does this matter?

And this is the reason I wanted to highlight this example to make the point, that in fact it doesn't.

A pivot is a unique combination of three candles which then create the pivot, and this helps to define the region for us visually. Pivots also help to give us our 'roadmap' signals of where we are in the price journey. But, sometimes one or other does not arrive, and we have to rely on our eyes to define these levels. After all, a pivot is simply an indicator to make it easier for us to see these signals. In this case the pivot high forms, but there is no corresponding pivot low, so we are looking for a 'floor' to form.

After four candles, the market moves higher again and posts a second pivot high, so we have our ceiling well defined, and this is now resistance. The next phase lower made up of three candles then stops at the same price level, before reversing higher again. We know this pair is not going to fall far anyway, as we have a falling market and falling volume. Our floor of support is now well defined by the price action, and it is clear from the associated volume, that we are in a congestion phase at this level. And, my point is this.

When using any analytical method in technical analysis, we always have to apply a degree of leeway and common sense. Whenever a market moves into a region of price congestion, it will not always develop the perfect combinations of pivot highs and pivot lows, and we then have to apply common sense as here, bolstered, of course, by our volume. At the start of this congestion phase, we have a very good idea that we are entering a congestion phase, simply from an assessment of the volume. The volume is all well below average (the white dotted line) therefore we already know that we are in a congestion phase, and the pivots are merely aids, to help define the price region for us.

Therefore whilst pivots are very important it is the volume which will also help to define the start of a congestion phase, and the pivot highs and lows are there to help to define the floors and ceilings of the trading range. If one or other is missing, then we simply revert to using our eyes and common sense.

The analogy I use here is when sailing. When we are sailing our boat, we have two forms of navigation. A GPS plotter which does all the work for us which is nice and easy, and the old fashioned way using a map, compass, time, tides and way points. In order to pass the exams and charter a yacht, you have to learn both. And the reason for this is very simple. If there is a loss of power on board, then you have to be able to navigate using a paper based chart. The same principle applies here.

We can define where we are by using volume and price visually from the price action on the chart. The pivots are simply there as a quick visual guide, to help identify these price combinations quickly and easily.

Returning to our example in Fig 11.11, we now have the floor defined by our price action and the ceiling defined by our pivot highs. We are now waiting for a signal, and it duly arrives in the form of a hanging man, one of the candles we have not seen in earlier examples, and suddenly the volume has jumped higher and is well above average. The market breaks lower and through the floor of our congestion phase with a wide spread down candle. We now know that, on this occasion, the price congestion phase has been developing into a trend reversal, and is not a continuation of the existing trend.

It is here that we would be looking to take a short position. The market pauses and reverses higher but the volume is falling, and in addition we see a second hanging man candle, suggesting more weakness in the market. We also have the comfort of knowing that above us we have one of our invisible barriers of price congestion.

What was the floor of support, has now become the ceiling of price resistance as the market attempts to recover, and this is why congestion zones are so significant to us as traders. Not only do they spawn the trend reversals and breakouts, but they also give us our natural barriers of protection which have been created by the market. Where better to place any stop loss than on the opposite side of a congestion region.

The resistance region holds, and the market sells off sharply with a beautiful price waterfall. However, as the bearish trend develops, so the volumes are falling away, and we know as VPA traders that this trend is not going too far. And sure enough, after seven hours of downwards movement, it bottoms out and moves into…........another congestion phase at a different price level.

Ironically, here too, we have a phase which is once again marked by pivot highs, but no pivot lows. However, the volume and price action tell us exactly where we are in the price journey. We simply wait for the next phase to start, which it does, several hours later. Again, how do we know? Volume gives us the answer. The breakout has been associated with above average volume, which is what we expect to see, and off we go again.

I hope that from this example, which spans a period of four days or so, you can begin to see how everything comes together. I did not particularly select this example, but it does highlight several key points that I hope will reinforce and cement the concepts outlined in earlier chapters.

Reading a chart in this way is not difficult. Every market moves in this way. They trend for a little, then consolidate in a congestion phase, then continue the trend or reverse completely. If you understand the power of VPA and combine it with a knowledge of price congestion, then you are 90% of the way there. The rest is practice, practice and more practice, and it will come.

Furthermore, you will then realise the power this gives you in your own trading and how it can deliver financial independence to you and your family. It does takes a little effort, but the rewards are high, and if you are prepared to study and learn, then you will enjoy the thrill of being able to forecast market price action, before it happens, and profit accordingly.

I would now like to revisit a very important concept, that I touched on earlier in the book. It is a cornerstone of my approach to trading. Again, it is not unique and can be applied to any market and any instrument. Neither is it unique to VPA. What this concept does do, is give you that three dimensional view of price behaviour, as opposed to the more conventional one dimensional approach that most traders take. The principle advantage of this concept is that it allows us to assess and quantify the risk on a trade.

This concept involves using multiple time frames to analyse price and volume. It allows us to qualify and quantify the risk of any trade, and assess the relative strength or weakness of any trade, and so its likely duration. In other words, multiple time frames will reveal the dominant trend and primary bias of the instrument under consideration.

Fig 11.12 represents our three time frames. Despite its size we can see both price and volume and this method of analysis is something I teach in my online and offline seminars.

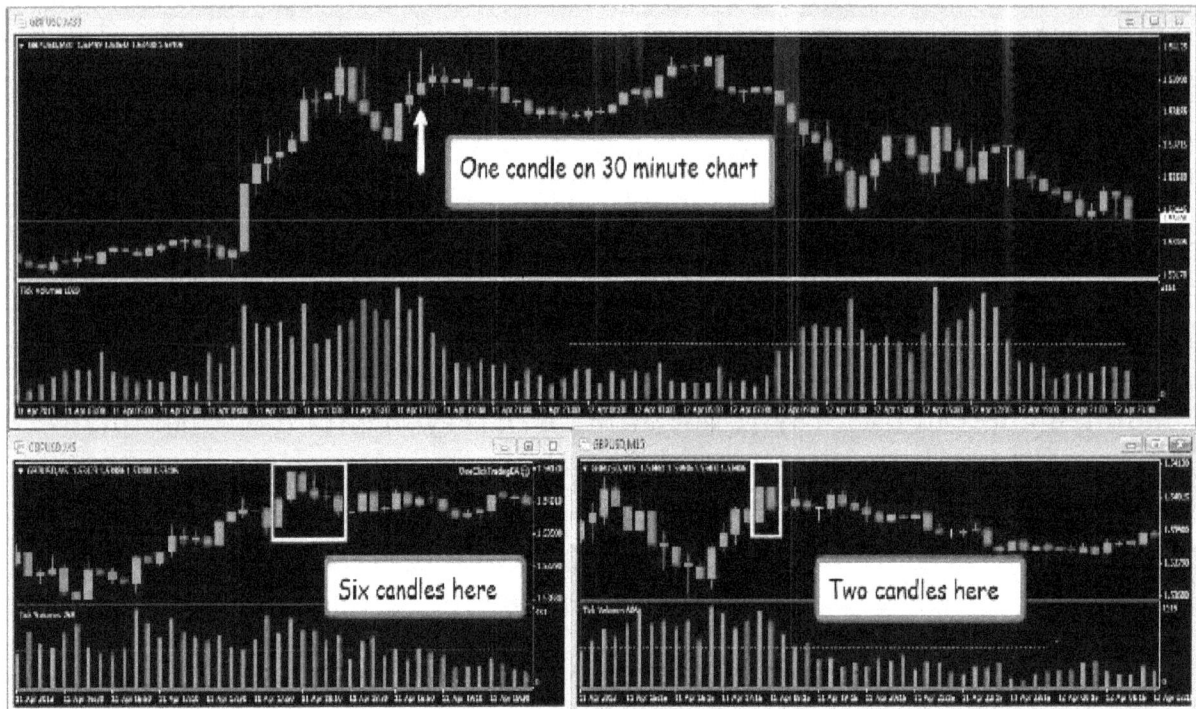

Fig 11.12 GBP/USD – Multiple Time Frames

What we have in Fig 11.12 are three charts for cable (GBP/USD). The chart at the top of the image is the 30 minute and is what I often refer to as our 'benchmark' chart. In this trio it is this chart which gives us our bias, and is the one against which we relate the other two. Bottom right is the 15 minute, and the chart at bottom left is the 5 minute. All the charts are taken from one of my favourite platforms for spot forex, namely MT4.

The candle I have highlighted on the 30 minute chart is a shooting star, with ultra high volume, sending a clear signal of weakness at this level. The shooting star was pre-ceded by a narrow spread candle also with ultra high volume, and which gave us our initial signal. But how does this appear on our faster time frames? On the 15 minute chart the shooting star is two candles, and on our 5 minute chart it is six candles. I have annotated the chart with the yellow box on each to show you the associated price action.

Now the reason I use three charts is very simple. My primary trading chart is the 'middle' time frame of the three. In this example it is the 15 minute chart, but using the MT4 chart settings we might equally have a 30 minute, 60 minute and 240 minute chart. In this trio our primary trading chart would be the 60 minute. However, in this example we are using a 5, 15, 30 minute combination, so the primary or trading chart is our 15 minute.

The 30 minute chart is there as our slower time frame, our dominant or benchmark time frame, which tells us where we are in the slower time frame trend. Imagine we are looking at price action using a telescope. This is where we are viewing from some way off, so we can see all the price action of the last few days.

Then using our telescope we start to zoom in, first onto the 15 minute chart, and then in fine detail to the 5 minute chart. By using the 15 minute chart we are seeing both sides of the price action if you. A slower time frame helps in gaining a perspective on where we are in the longer term journey, and a faster time frame on the other side will give us the fine detail view of the related price action.

What do we see here? First the shooting star sent a clear signal of weakness, and on our 15 minute chart this is reflected in two candles, with high volume on the up candle which is also topped with a deep wick to the upper body. And here the point is this. If we had seen this price action in isolation on the 15 minute chart, it may not have been immediately obvious what we were looking at here.

It takes a mental leap to lay one candle over another and imagine what the result may be. The 30 minute chart does this for us, and in addition, and perhaps more importantly, if we had a position in the market, the 30 minute chart is instantly more recognisable as possible weakness than the 15 minute. So two benefits in one.

If putting two candles together to create one is difficult, putting six candles together is almost impossible, and yet this is the same price action represented on the 5 minute chart. The market then moves into consolidation, which again is much easier to see on the slower time frame chart than the faster ones, and I have deliberately left the pivot points off these charts, so that the charts remain as clear as possible.

The next point is this. In displaying a slower time frame above, this also gives us a perspective on the 'dominant' trend. If the dominant trend is bullish on the 30 minute chart, and we decide to take a position on our 15 minute chart which is bullish, then the risk on the trade is lower, since we are trading with the dominant trend. We are trading with the flow, and not against the flow. Swimming with the tide and not against it.

If we take a position that is against the dominant trend in our slower time frame, then we are counter trend trading, and two conditions then apply. First, the risk on the trade is higher, since we are trading against the dominant trend of our lower time frame, and second, we are unlikely to be holding the position long, since the dominant trend is in the opposite direction.

In other words, what we are trading here is a pull back or a reversal. There is nothing wrong with this, as everything in trading is relative. After all a reversal on a daily chart might last several days. It is all relative to the time frame.

The third reason for using multiple charts is that this also gives us a perspective on changes in trend as they ripple through the market, this time in the opposite direction. The analogy I use here is of the ripples in a pond. When you throw a pebble into the centre of a small pond, as the pebble hits the water, the ripples move out and away before they eventually reach the edge of the pond. This is what happens with market price action.

Any potential change in trend will be signalled on our fast time frame chart. This is where you will see sudden changes in price and volume appear first. If this is a true change, then the effect will then appear on the primary chart, which in this case is the 15 minute chart, before the change ultimately ripples through to our 30 minute chart, at which point this change is now being signalled on the dominant chart.

This is how to trade, as we constantly scan from the slower to the faster and back again, checking and looking for clues and confirming signals between the three time frames, with VPA sitting at the centre of our analysis. Even if you ultimately decide that VPA is not for you, trading using multiple time frames is a powerful approach which will give you a three dimensional view of the market. You can have more than three, but for me three is sufficient, and I hope will work for you as well.

Finally to end this chapter, I would like to include a short section on the candle patterns I have found work, and work consistently. And you will not be surprised to learn, all these patterns work particularly well with price support and resistance, as well as price congestion.

By watching for these candle patterns whenever the market is in a consolidation phase and preparing for a move, coupled with VPA and multiple time frame analysis, this will add a further dimension to your trading. And the patterns I would like to consider here are the falling triangle, the rising triangle, pennants and finally triple tops and bottoms.

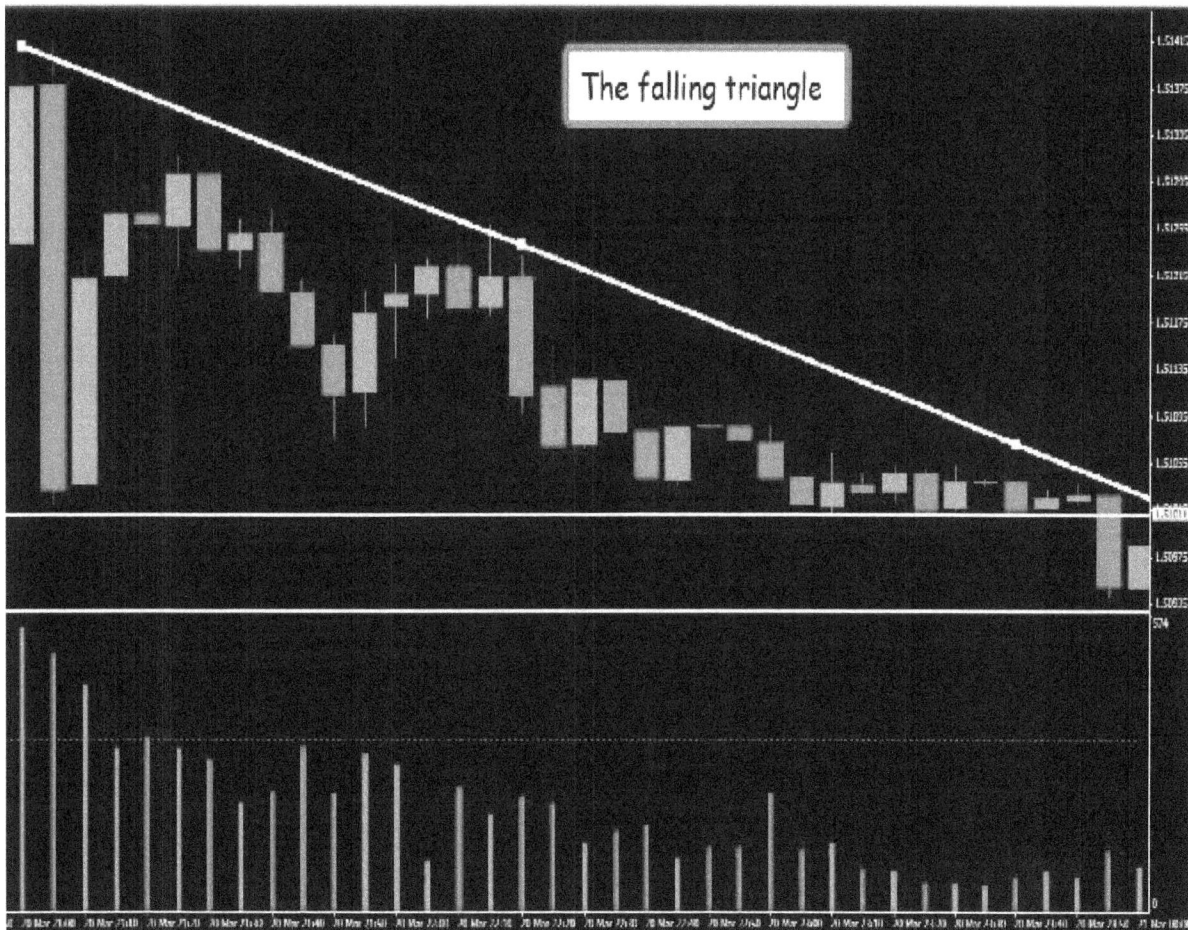

Fig 11.13 Falling triangle – 5 Minute Chart

Let's start with the falling triangle as shown in Fig 11.13 above. As the name suggests, a falling triangle pattern is a sign of weakness. We can see immediately from the volume, that we are in a congestion phase, but in this case the market is also moving lower. Each attempt to rally is seen as a series of lower highs, and is a clear signal of weakness. If this market is going to break anywhere, there is a strong chance that it will be to the downside, since each attempt to rally is becoming weaker and weaker in terms of the high of the candles. The floor of the congestion area is very well defined, and any sustained break below here will be signalled with volume.

As with all price patterns, the falling triangle appears in all time frames and on all charts, and we must always remember Wyckoff's rule of cause and effect. If the cause is large then the effect will be equally large. In this case we are looking at a 5 minute chart, but this type of congestion will often appear on daily and weekly charts and is immensely powerful in generating new trends, or reversals in trend, on the breakout.

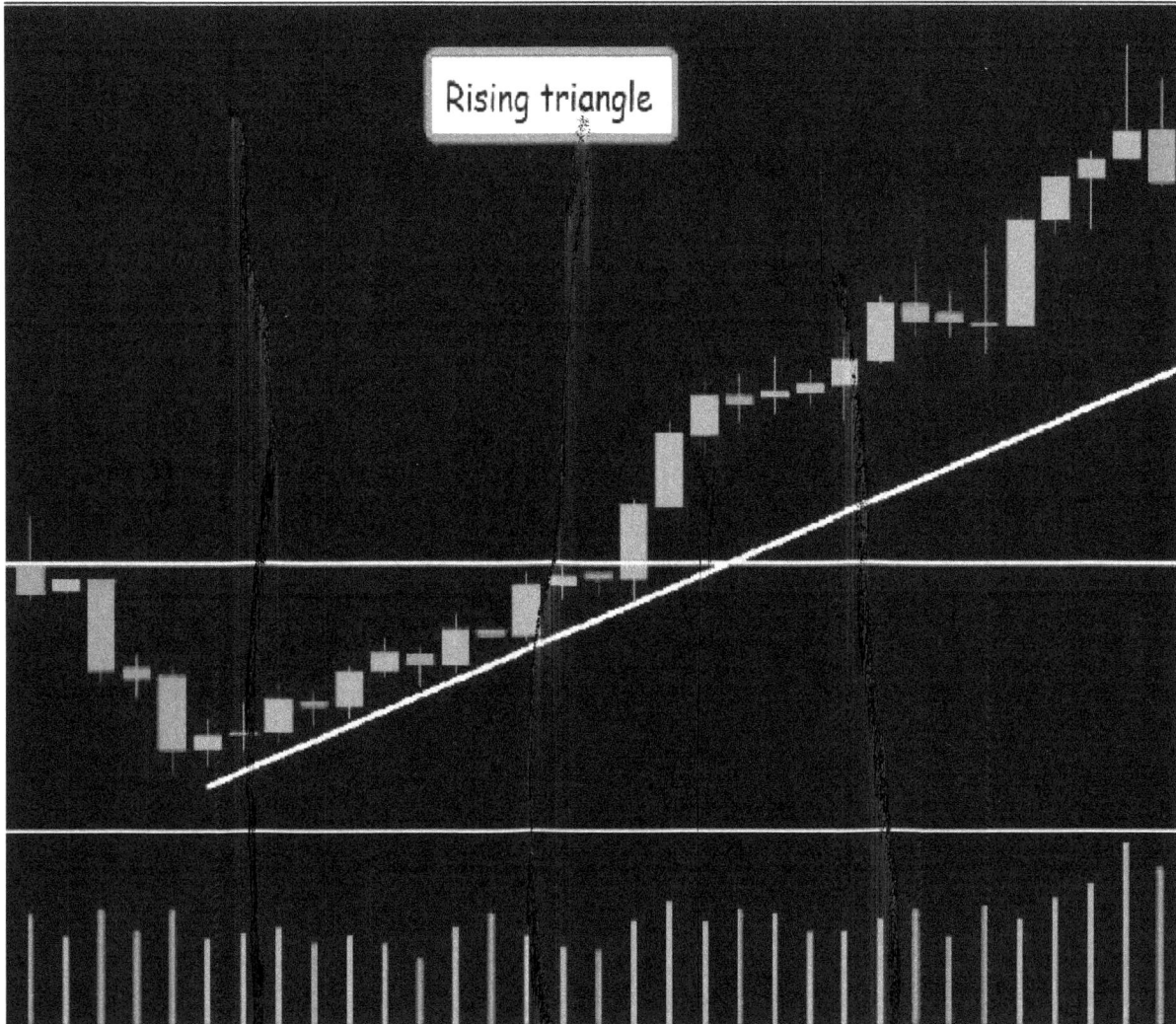

Fig 11.14 Rising triangle – Daily Chart

Fig 11.14 is from the daily chart of the EUR/USD, and as we can see the rising triangle is a bullish pattern. In this example the market is moving higher and testing the same ceiling level, with the low of each candle slowly rising, signalling a market that is bullish. After all, if the market were bearish, then we would see the lows of each candle falling. Instead the lows are rising, suggesting positive sentiment in the market, and as we approach the ceiling (or resistance), then we are prepared for the subsequent breakout, which is confirmed with volume. Once clear of resistance, the ceiling becomes support, and gives us a natural price barrier for positioning stop losses as we take a trade.

The third pattern in this series is the pennant, so called as it resembles a pennant flag on a mast.

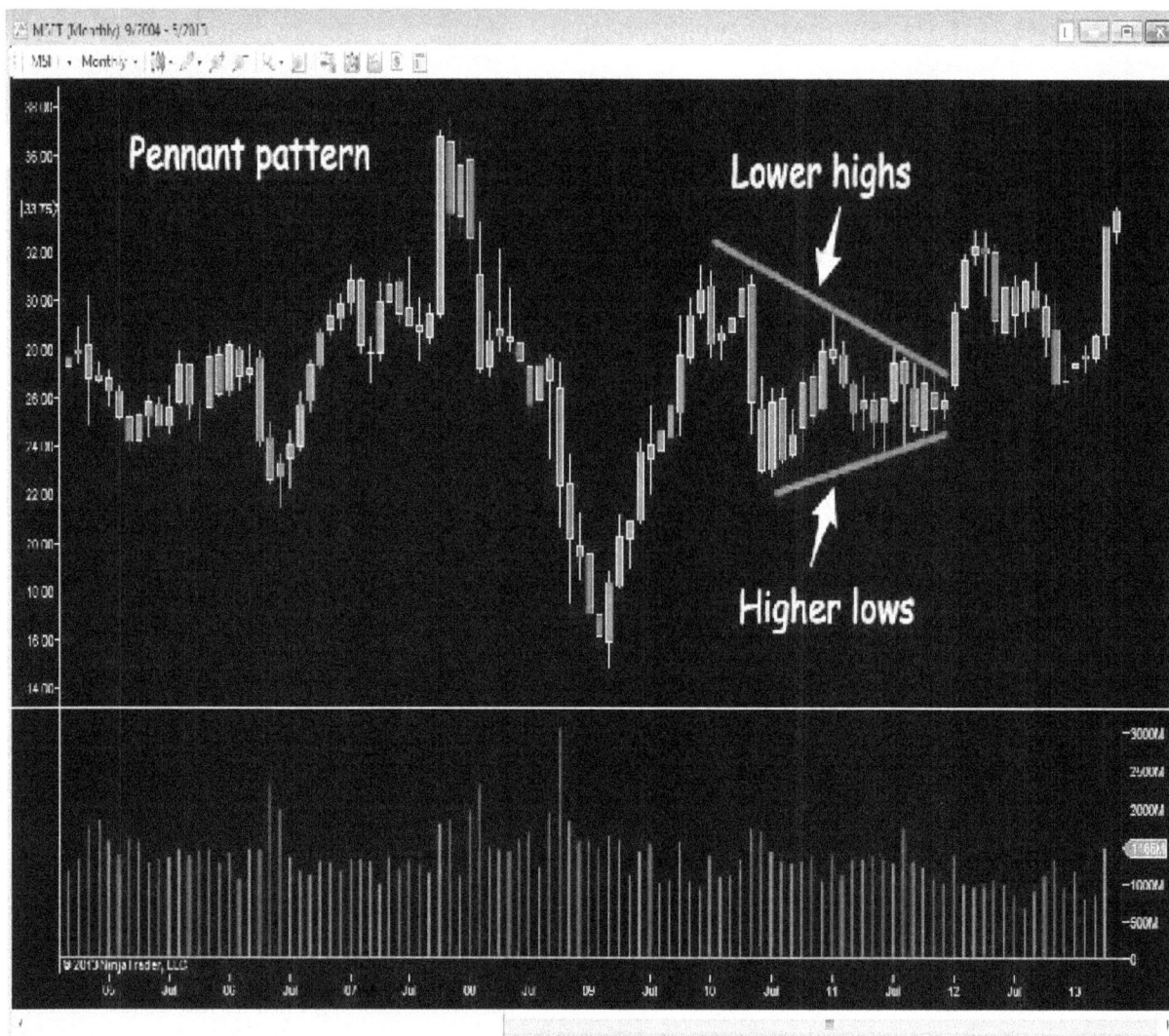

Fig 11.15 Pennant pattern – Monthly Chart

Here in Fig 11.15 is an example of a candle pattern on a much longer time frame and is from the monthly chart for Microsoft and shows an EXTREMELY long congestion phase, but look at the contraction in the price action just prior to the final break out.

The pennant pattern is so called as it resembles a flag on a flagpole. The pattern is created by a series of lower highs above, as the market tries to rally, coupled with higher lows below. As we can see on the Microsoft chart, here we have a stock which is struggling to break higher, yet is not prepared to fall. It is this tension in the price action which creates this unique pattern. Again as with all these formations, the law of cause and effect applies, and in the case of the pennant the longer the tension continues, the more the price action creates what I call a 'coiled spring'.

In other words, the energy stored and built up in the price action is suddenly released in an explosive breakout. The problem is, that with this kind of pattern, unlike the previous two, there is generally no clue as to which way the price is likely to break. Nevertheless, it is a great pattern for trading direction-less strategies with options, but for trend trading, we simply have to be patient and wait for the break out.

The last two patterns in this set are reversal signals and ones I am always looking for. The market has risen or fallen, and is now testing support or resistance. As with the patterns already mentioned, these also occur in all time frames and on all charts and I want to start with some examples of markets which have run into resistance and are struggling to move higher.

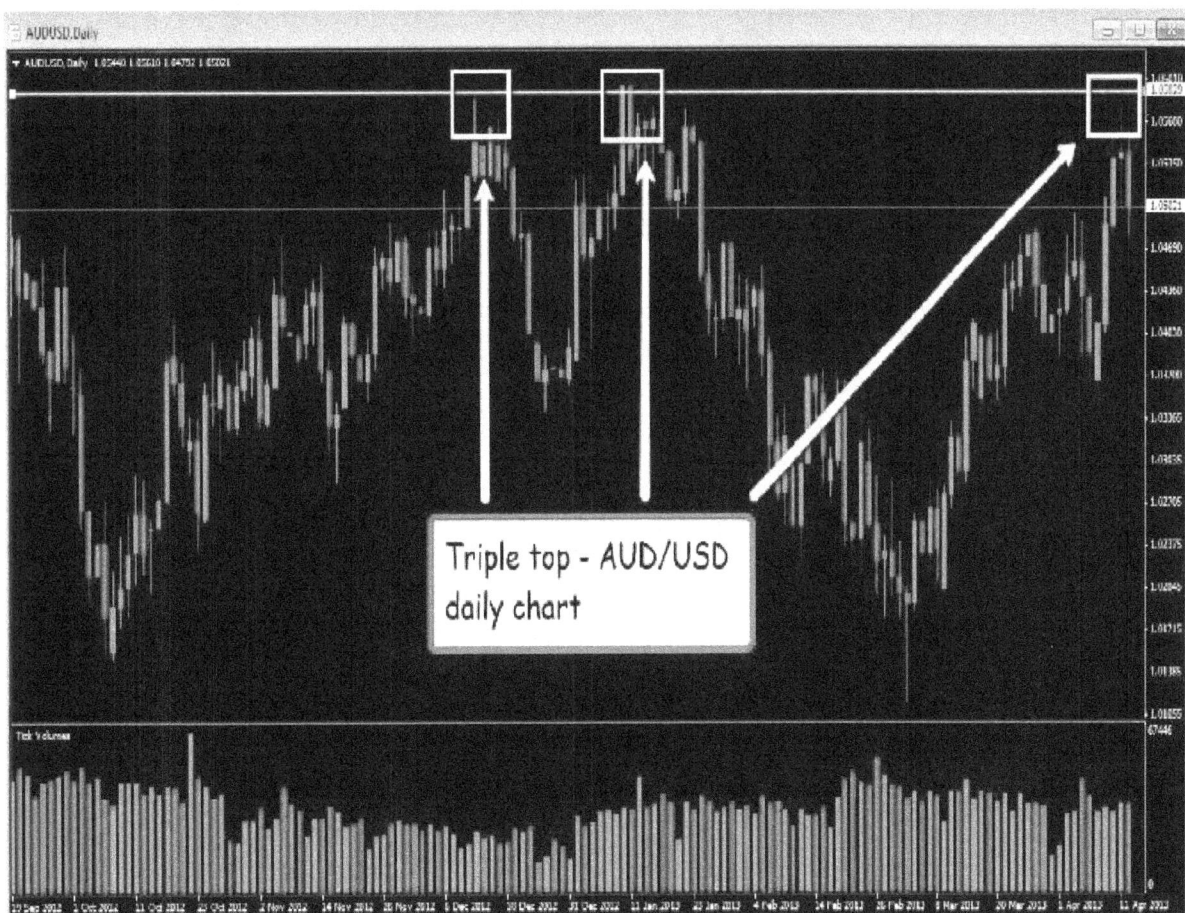

Fig 11.16 Triple Top – Daily Chart AUD/USD

Fig 11.16 is an example of a classic triple top pattern from the daily chart of the AUD/USD, where we can see the pair has tested the 1.0600 level on three separate occasions. This region has been tested several times over the last few years, but in the last year it has been tested three times, failing on each occasion. And here there are two opportunities.

First a position to the short side should our VPA and multiple time frame analysis confirm this view. Second, if the market breaks above this region, then this will build an extremely strong platform of support, if this ceiling is eventually breached.

The opposite of a triple top is a triple bottom.

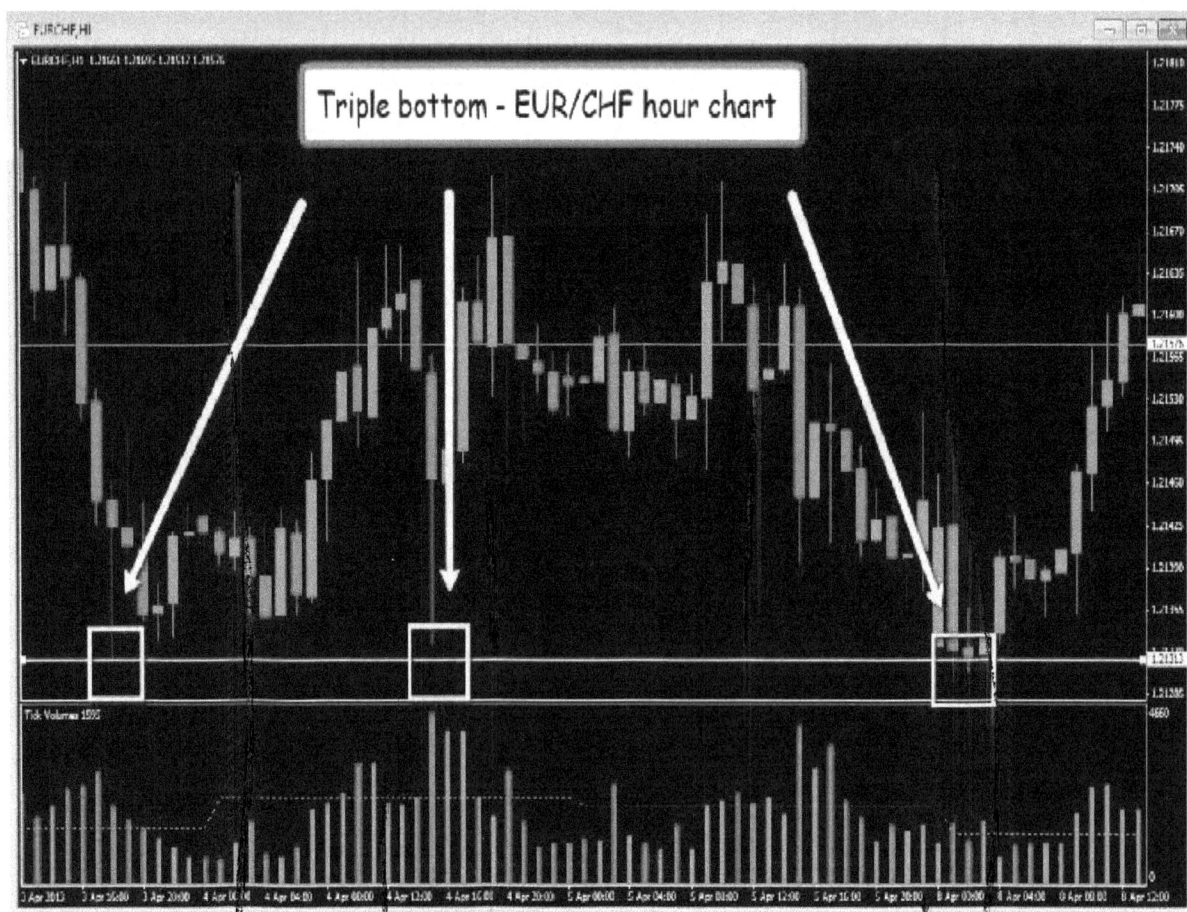

Fig 11.17 Triple Bottom – EUR/CHF Hour Chart

In a triple bottom pattern, the market is testing support, and each time bouncing off. Our example of a triple bottom is taken from the hourly chart for the EUR/CHF (Euro Swiss) currency pair where we can see a classic formation of this pattern.

As with the triple top, there are two trading scenarios. The first is a long position, validated by VPA or wait for a break and hold below the support region, for a short trade. Any follow through to the short side would then provide strong resistance overhead.

The good news is that we see all these patterns in every instrument and market. In bonds, commodities, equities and currencies, and in all time frames.

These patterns all have one thing in common - they are creating trading opportunities for us by signalling two things. First, an area where the market is in congestion, and second, a market that is either building a ceiling of price resistance or a floor of price support. From there will come the inevitable breakout, signalling a trend reversal, or a continuation of trend, and from there, all we need to do is to validate the move using VPA, and of course VAP, which will highlight these areas for us visually on our charts.

Now in the final chapter of the book I would like expand on some of the latest developments in volume based trading techniques. After all, the approach and basic concepts have changed little in the last 100 years, so perhaps it's time for some new developments!

Chapter Twelve

Volume And Price – The Next Generation

My biggest winnings were not in dollars but in the intangibles: I had been right, I had looked ahead and followed a clear cut plan.
Jesse Livermore (1877-1940)

I began this book by stating that there is nothing new in trading, and indeed this is certainly true in terms of volume. Its foundations were laid by the iconic traders of the last century, and since then, little has changed. The methodology remains as valid today, as it was then. The only changes have been in technology and markets. Other than that, we use the same principles as they used, all those years ago.

However, that said, as a devotee of volume, I am constantly looking for developments in this analytical approach to the market, which has formed the cornerstone of my own trading career. I would be foolish to ignore them. After all, candlesticks were virtually unheard of in Western trading before the 1990's - now they are the 'de facto' standard for technical traders.

Therefore in this final chapter, I would like to introduce you to some of the latest developments in volume and price analysis, which are both new and innovative. I have not used these myself, so cannot comment on their validity, but feel it is important to present them here, and as this book is updated in future versions, I can then add further chapters as these techniques develop and perhaps incorporate them into my own trading.

Equivolume Charts

The volume price approach termed 'equivolume' was developed by Richard Arms and first published in his book, Volume Cycles In The Stock Market, written in 1994. The concept is one in which volume is considered to be more important than time, and as such the X axis of the chart is replaced with volume, whilst the Y axis remains as before with price. The principle idea is that in adopting this approach in presenting the price and volume relationship on the chart, this emphasizes the relationship, with volume moving to the chart itself, where it joins price, rather than as an isolated indicator at the bottom of the chart. As a result, and with the change in the X axis from time, to volume, the 'time' element is removed and the focus is then solely on the volume price relationship.

This relationship is then presented in the form of 'boxes'. The vertical element of the box, in other words the height, is simply the high and low of the session in terms of price. The horizontal element is volume, which of course varies, as to whether this is ultra high, high, medium or low, which in turn means that the width of each box varies. On our chart we no longer have candles, but a series of boxes, both narrow and fat, tall and short which then represent the direct relationship between volume and price in a very visual way, but with the time element removed. The time element is still there, but on a separate axis below, otherwise it would be impossible to know where we are on the chart.

As Arms himself said:

'if the market wore a wristwatch, it would be divided into shares, not hours'

and indeed in some ways this sums up the concept of trading on tick based charts which I mentioned in an earlier chapter. After all, time is a man made concept, and something the markets can and do ignore. The beauty of trading on a tick chart is that it is the market dictating the 'speed' of the market. In other words, on a tick chart, we are trading in harmony with the market. When we move to a time based chart, it is we who are dictating to the market our chosen timeframe, a subtle but important difference. On a tick chart we trade at the speed of the market - on a time based chart we don't.

This same philosophy can be applied to equivolume, which attempts to remove the rather 'false' aspect of time from the analysis, to create a purer and more meaningful relationship between the two elements of volume and price.

Let's take a look at how these boxes are created and what they actually tell us about the volume price relationship. Below is a schematic in Fig 12.10

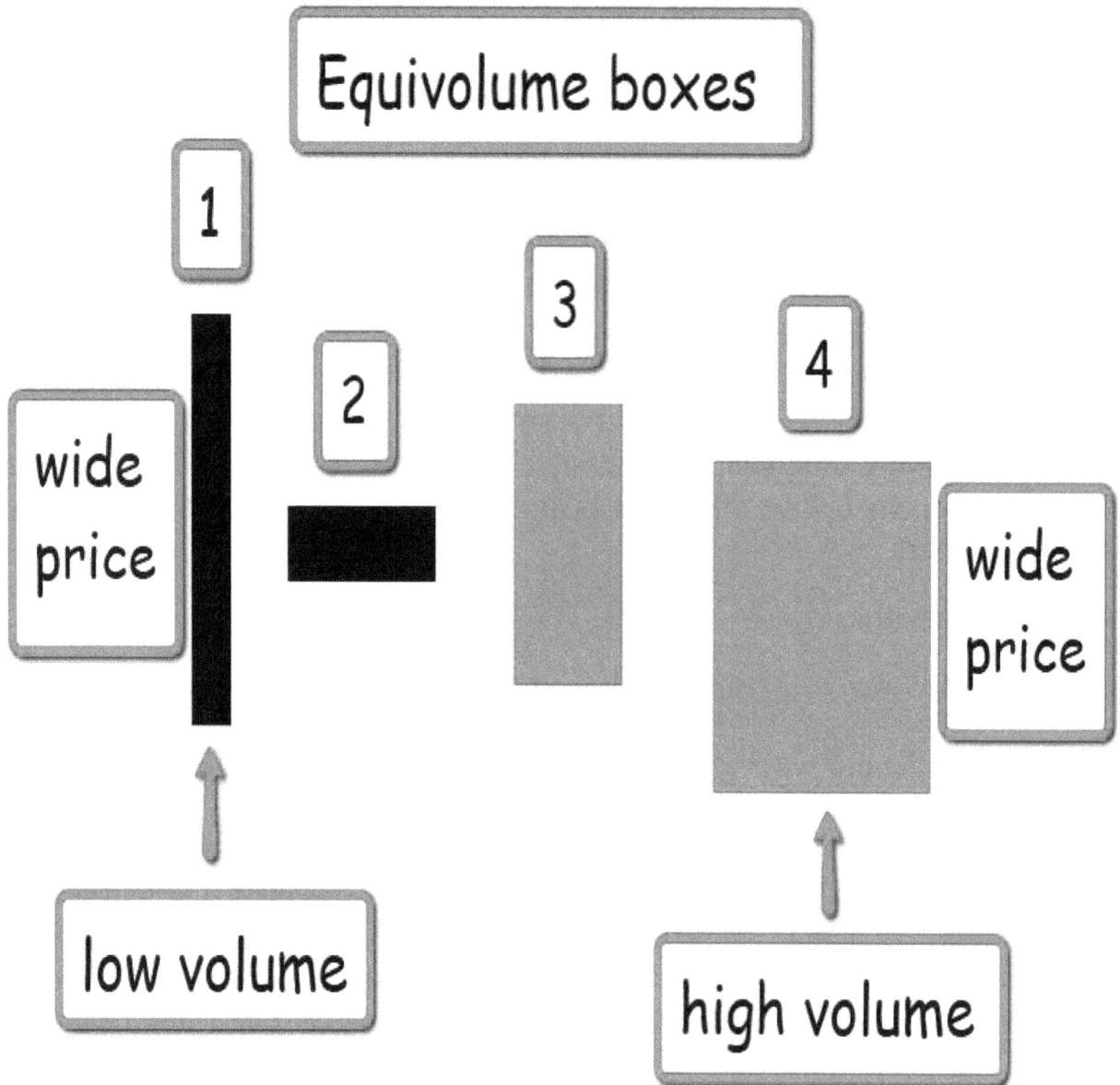

Fig 12.10 Equivolume Boxes

Remember, the X axis for each box is volume and the Y axis is price, so if we look at box 1, here we have a narrow but tall box. In other words, the volume has been low, but the price action has been wide, so this might be equivalent to a wide spread up candle on low volume, so an anomaly.

Next to this in box 2, we have the opposite, where we have a small change in price, and remember we are talking here about the high and the low, and NOT the open and the close, coupled with a large amount of volume. This too might be equivalent to an anomaly where we have above average or high volume and a narrow price spread.

Box 3, might be considered representative of a 'normal' volume and price relationship, with good volume supporting a solid price change. Finally in box 4, we have extremes of both volume and price. The box is wide, so above average volume and the price is wide as well, so clearly effort and result are in agreement here, as they are in box 3.

The color of the boxes is dictated by the close. When the close is above the previous close, then the box is painted black, and when the close is below the previous close, then it is painted red.

In order to maintain aspect ratios and to keep the charts meaningful, the volume is then normalized by dividing the actual volume for that period, by the total of all the volume displayed on the chart. Whilst time has been removed from the boxes themselves, it still appears, to help keep the chart in context for the trading session.

Whilst it is difficult to imagine trading using these boxes and moving away from candlesticks, many of the techniques I have explained in this book will still apply, as they are equally valid. The focus using this approach is on the box, its shape, and location within any trend. Breakouts from congestion are just as important for equivolume trading as with more conventional VPA, and here we might expect to see what is often referred to as a "power box", which is high volume and wide price. In VPA terms, above average volume and a wide spread candle on the breakout from congestion. The principles are much the same, it's the display which is very different.

At this point let me add my own personal thoughts here.

Whilst I like the concept of showing the price and volume together on one 'box' which instantly reveals whether we have a high/low combination, anomalies, or an average/average combination which may be normal, the issue I have is the removal of time. After all, as Wykcoff himself stated, it is the cause and effect which holds the key to the development of the trend. In other words, time is the third element of the volume and price relationship. Remove time, and the approach becomes two dimensional, and not three dimensional, and as I hope I have made clear throughout the book, the longer a market is in a consolidation phase, then the greater will be the consequent trend once the market breaks out. Consolidation phases are where trends are born or pause before moving on, and if you remove the time element, then to me, this removes one of the pillars of Volume Price Analysis which is the judgment of the power of any subsequent trend.

This is just my own personal view, and I would encourage you to explore the idea of equivolume further for yourself. The other issue is that candlestick analysis no longer plays a part, but help is at hand here, with candle volume charts.

Candle Volume Charts

Candle volume charts are exactly as they sound, and are a hybrid version of equivolume and traditional candlestick charts. In other words, the 'box' of equivolume is then laid over a candlestick with the traditional open, high, low and close, to create a unique chart. This charts displays candles of varying width and height due to the volume aspect, but with the upper and lower wicks added. A combination of both approaches which is shown in the schematic below in Fig 12.11

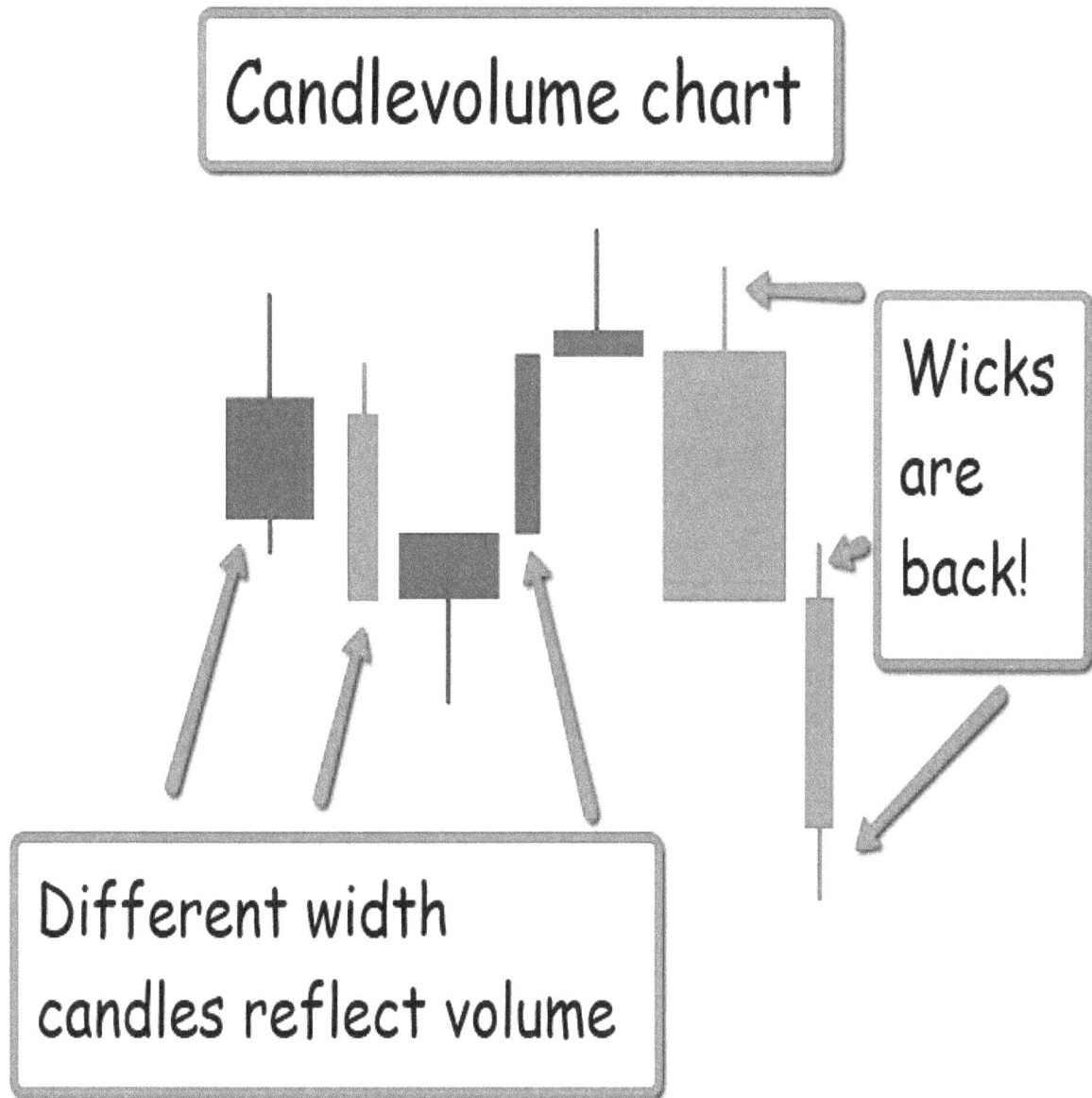

Fig 12.11 Candlevolume Chart

A little more recognizable! On these charts the candles are now all different widths to reflect the volume on each candle, with the price action represented vertically as usual, but with the open, high low and close displayed. On this chart we see our traditional wicks to the top and bottom of each candle. This is not an approach I have studied personally in any great detail, but it may have some advantages, and at least overcomes what I consider to be one of the big drawbacks with equivolume, namely the lack of time, which I believe is fundamental to any VPA approach. However, I always keep an open mind, and if any readers of this book have used candlevolume and have found this system helpful, please do drop me a line and send me your thoughts and comments. You can never stop learning in trading!

Delta Volume

Finally just to round of this chapter on the 'future' for Volume Price Analysis, there are two further approaches to analyzing volume which are gaining some traction, and these are delta volume and cumulative delta volume.

In simple terms delta volume refers to the difference in volumes between those contracts that trade at the 'ask' and those that trade at the 'bid'. In other words, orders that are sell orders and those that are buy orders, with the net difference between the two then displayed as 'delta'. For example, if the software calculates on one bar, that there have been 500 contracts sold at the bid and only 200 contracts bought at the ask, then this would represent a net difference of 300 contracts sold. Any indicator measuring delta volume would then display this as a negative volume bar of -300 and generally these appear as shown in the schematic below in Fig 12.12

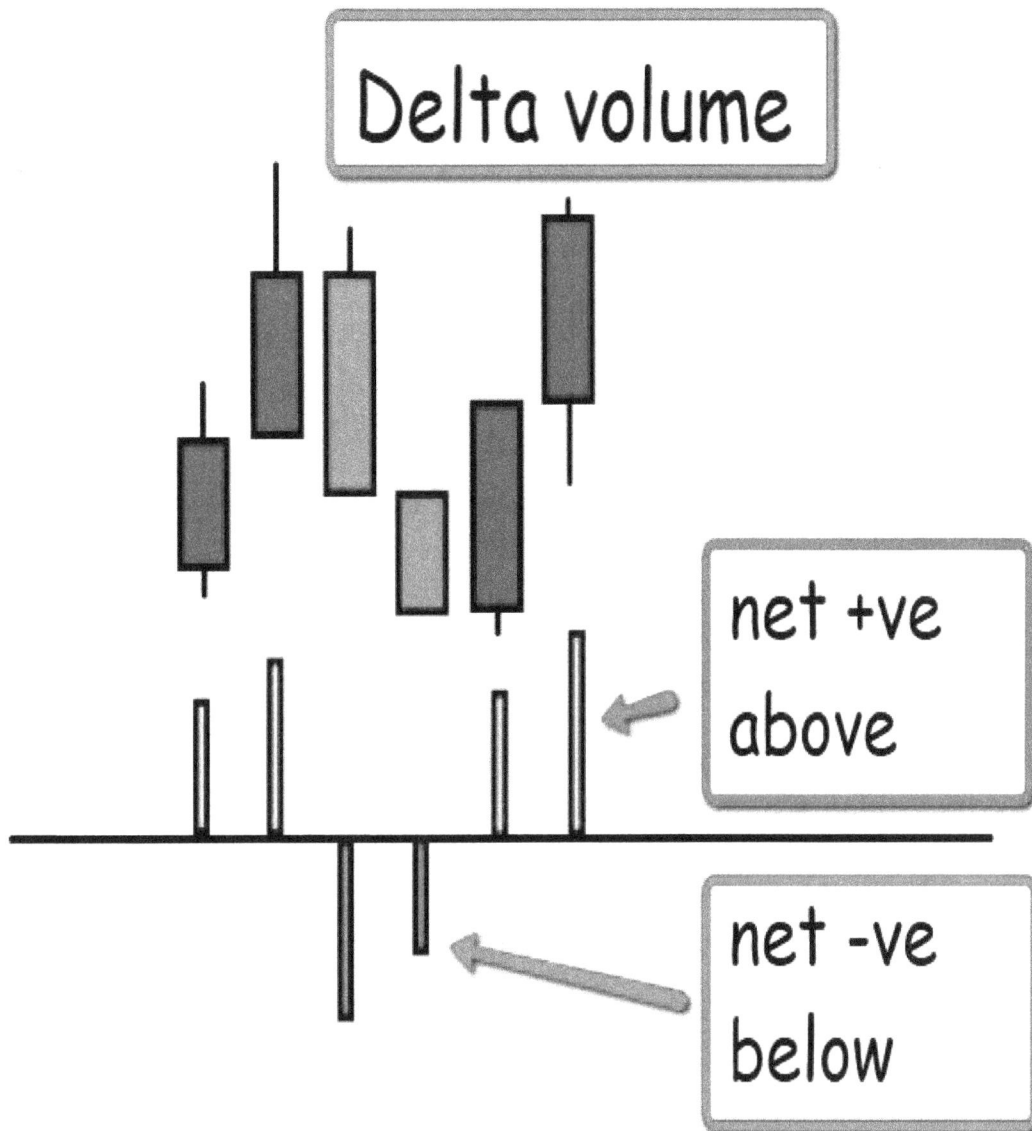

Fig 12.12 Delta Volume

From this schematic the delta volume gives an indication of the net difference between the buying and the selling as the market moves higher and lower. In other words, yet another way of interpreting the volume and price relationship. This approach is ideally suited to those markets where there is an open exchange, such as for futures and equities.

Cumulative Delta Volume

Finally cumulative delta volume collects all the delta data and adds each subsequent bar to that of the previous bar - summing the totals in other words, and then presents this as a series of bars, to provide a perspective on the daily or intra day price action. In other words, it attempts to give a perspective on the strength of the buying or selling associated with the price action.

Delta and cumulative delta are relatively new in the world of Volume Price Analysis and as such, neither is generally available free as a standard indicator. This may change in the future, and as we move forward over the next few years, I believe that delta and its derivatives may be increasingly adopted for certain markets. One market that springs to mind in particular is for E mini traders in indices, where it all started for me!

I have now reached the end of the book. It is a book I have wanted to write for many years, and finally found the time to do just that. I have tried to explain everything as carefully as I can, with what I hope are some clear examples, and now it is for you to practise reading the charts and applying these techniques for yourself.

I hope I have managed to convince you of the power of volume and price, and the potential success that awaits if you are prepared to adopt this methodology. It does require a little time to master but, in my opinion, is worth the effort. However, I would urge you again, NOT to spend thousands of dollars on software which suggest that VPA can be done for you. It won't. VPA is a technique that takes time, effort and patience, but once you have grasped the basic concepts then the rest falls into place very quickly.

Volume and price together are the only indicators that truly reveal market sentiment and the activity of the insiders. Without it you are trading blind. With it, everything is revealed. There is no hiding place with VPA.

www.ingramcontent.com/pod-product-compliance
Lightning Source LLC
Chambersburg PA
CBHW081807200326

41597CB00023B/4178